THIRD-WORLD CONFLICT
AND INTERNATIONAL SECURITY

That there will continue to be conflict and instability in the Third World seems certain. Much less certain is how this conflict will affect international security. The tendency to press all conflict in the Third World into an East–West matrix is tempting but is not supported by the evidence. Many of the sources of conflict have had and are likely to have their origins far removed from the East–West competition but experience shows that it is not easy for conflicts to play themselves out without involving powers external to Third-World regions. Resource dependency, political relationships, commercial links and the provision of military facilities for outside powers will all tend to involve the interests of external powers in Third-World conflict. At the same time the control mechanisms are hardly adequate and the prospects for the peaceful resolution of conflicts dim.

These issues were addressed at the 1980 Annual Conference of the International Institute for Strategic Studies in Stresa, Italy. While the conclusions are not optimistic, the background, the linkages, the dependencies and the possible responses are analysed in the papers in this volume. This is a subject of critical importance for the years ahead and these essays are a substantial contribution by a group of prestigious international figures to this very lively debate.

The editor
Christoph Bertram

The other contributors

Barry M. Blechman
Shahram Chubin
Melvin Conant
Shai Feldman
Sir John Hackett
Stanley Hoffman
Anthony Murray
Michael Nacht
Robert Perlman
James R. Schlesinger
Udo Steinbach
Jusuf Wanandi

Third-World Conflict
and International Security

Edited by

CHRISTOPH BERTRAM

Archon Books
Hamden, Connecticut

First published in the U.K. 1982 by
THE MACMILLAN PRESS LTD
and in the U.S.A. as an
ARCHON BOOK
an imprint of
The Shoe String Press, Inc.
995 Sherman Avenue,
Hamden, Connecticut 06514

Printed in Great Britain

ISBN 0-208-01957-X

Library of Congress Cataloging in Publication Data

Main entry under title:

Third-World conflict and international security.

  Based on the papers given at the 1980 annual
conference of the International Institute for
Strategic Studies in Stresa, Italy.
  Includes index.
  1. National security—Addresses, essays, lectures.
2. Underdeveloped areas—Strategic aspects—
Addresses, essays, lectures. I. Bertram, Christoph,
1937–   . II. International Institute for
Strategic Studies.
UA10.5.T47 1982   355′.033′0047   81–19036
ISBN 0-208-01957-X   AACR2

CONTENTS

Introduction

CHRISTOPH BERTRAM

The papers printed here and in Adelphi Paper No 167 were originally presented at the Institute's 1980 Annual Conference in Stresa and have been amended in the light of discussion at the Conference.

Rarely has a Conference of the Institute dealt with a subject as difficult and complex as the one which is explored in the papers which follow. This is not only because, to much of the strategic studies community, the issues of third-world conflict and international security constitute a novel theme; it is primarily because it is by definition a confusing and disturbing one. There are no ready answers to the problems, only tentative ones, and for each of these there are counter-arguments at least as weighty. It is perhaps this inevitable frustration with the subject that makes strategists seek safety in assessing the requirements and implications of military power, of subjecting third-world conflict, with a sigh of relief, to the more familiar parameters of the East–West conflict. But that relief will be short-lived. The 1980s will be marked by more, not less, conflict outside the defined regions of East–West Alliances, because of a combination of factors: internal strains within developing countries themselves and the concomitant decline in the structure of international order. The disagreement over the reasons for this decline persists: for some it is the result of the decline of American power; for others, the deadlock in East–West détente; for yet others, the Soviet search for either global involvement and opportunities for aggrandizement or an excessive definition of Soviet security needs; or it may be the result of the developed world's anxiety about secure raw-material supplies. Yet whatever the view, there is no disagreement over the fact that because of these two factors – internal instability in the Third World combined with external fluidity – our present decade can lay claim to the sobriquet of the 'nasty 1980s'.

The recognition of general insecurity is scarcely sufficient to answer more strategic questions: what matters, to international security, and why? How to distinguish between 'good' and 'bad' development, between benevolent and malign shifts? And where to draw the line that divides tolerable distrubance from dangerous upheaval, tolerable extension of Soviet influence from dangerous encroachment on vital security interests and so on? These questions can perhaps be answered in the context of the extreme, but rarely will the extreme come overnight. Essentially, the issues boil down to distinguishing not between tolerable and intolerable *states* of things but between tolerable and dangerous *dynamics* in a world of, at best, limited predictability.

The Impact of Internal Change

It was this difficulty which confronted the discussion throughout the Conference. In assessing the implications of domestic instability for regional conflict it was one thing to identify categories of instability, as Michael Nacht proposes in his paper, but this does not make prediction significantly easier. Many regimes in the world – and not only in the Third World, as Eastern Europe underlines – are in a general state of brittleness, and yet they muddle on. What is almost impossible to predict, by definition, is the cataclysmic event, the straw that breaks the camel's back. Strategists are professional worriers, but even revolutionary ideologies believe that it is not enough for a situation in a country to be ripe for revolution; an additional push is required to turn potential into reality. Brittleness can perhaps be measured, but collapse is not automatic.

This may provide us with some comfort when it comes to the only country in the developing world where internal upheaval has the potential to threaten the functioning of the Western world immediately: Saudi Arabia. Here predictions of the overthrow of monarchical rule in the near future must be seen for what they are: analyses of the *present* situation and *present* evaluations of the dynamics. As such, their value lies in defining not the future but the policy problems and tasks of the present. Moreover, the more pessimistic forecasts may be the results as much of informed guesses as of our own uncertainty over effective responses.

Resources and Security
Another reason for relating third-world instability to international security is that of resources, but, with the exception of oil, raw-material dependence, as Robert Perlman's and Anthony Murray's paper in Part II shows, does not reduce developed countries to the state of vulnerability that would amount to a serious loss of security: short-term supply disruption, yes; but no general undermining of the industrial structure on which security in the developed world is built. This will not be unchallenged. The general situation may be comforting, but it may look very different for different countries. The key issues are on whom one is dependent, and for what? Moreover, the perception of one's own vulnerability, justified or not, can in itself become a security problem. Resource issues inevitably have a profound effect on political attitudes, which in turn influence strategic and defence planning. In addition, the security of the developed world could be affected by resource vulnerabilities in the poorer countries, where resource shortages could cause major upheavals with much wider repercussions. Yet the raw-material issue is, perhaps, a case for the de-escalation of concerns and the correction of perceptions.

This leaves oil as the major and special resource problem. Melvin Conant's paper counter-balances the heightened anxieties of the political analyst with the caution and moderation of the economist: conflict within the Third World is not a cause for particular concern about adequate and continuous oil supply. While there remains controversy over Soviet need for oil imports in the future, this need is unlikely to lead to open conflict. But perhaps – and again the difficulty is one of distinguishing the dynamics – this depends on too strict definitions of third-world conflict and of Soviet interference. Conant himself makes the obvious

and important exception of the Arab–Israeli dispute. The issue of oil has become so sensitive that it must now be taken into account in any assessment of contingencies provoked by Soviet–American conflict. The apparent comfort provided by the economic analysis thus fades, even if it does not completely disappear, as a result not of the economic vulnerability of the West but of the strategic vulnerability that dependence on oil from the Gulf implies.

The Relevance of Military Force
The uncertainties and unpredictabilities of third-world developments do not merely impede the analysis of the problem; they also bedevil the search for suitable responses. This is nowhere more obvious than in the context of the traditional instrument for dealing with insecurity: military force. Force is a precise instrument which requires precise planning, but there are no clear-cut contingencies in third-world conflict.

To some extent this is a familiar problem for military planners and justifies the professional tendency to plan for worst-case contingencies: if we can meet the worst threat, we can cope with the lesser ones. But this assumes that the former covers, and does not contradict, the latter. In the Third World preparation for one task – say, a Soviet attack against Saudi oil-fields – by a strong Western military presence could easily undermine the prospects for dealing with another – the strengthening of royal rule. If any confirmation of this point were needed, Sir John Hackett's detailed analysis of the military requirements to protect oil supplies provides it forcefully: to perform the task, the forces needed would have to be so massive that they would impose a considerable strain on the total American military potential – and that already assumes, as he points out, 'abstinence by the other super-power from direct armed interference'. The figures and the analysis in his paper underline this important and probably undisputed lesson: if use of force means fighting, then the chances of success – as defined by the objective – are low and the risks of uncontrollable escalation high. The use of massive military force in the Third World makes sense not in *fighting* but in *weighing* on the situation. If forces are used to fight, this is an admission of failure.

Barry Blechman's paper reviews experience over the past three decades and concludes that military force, applied as pressure, does pay – at least in the short term. It is clear that this generalization, like all others, may be challenged by special circumstances and that the cost of success is not static. The effectiveness of force is linked with political costs; in Iran, for instance, a comparison between 1953 and 1980 shows that these costs have increased.

Military force to deter the Soviet Union in the Gulf, to reassure friendly and to warn hostile parties in the region, yet not to do one at the expense of the other – such is the difficult requirement. That the Soviet threat is not to be discounted was argued strongly by many at the Conference. But Soviet pressure through the threat to use military force, through the weight of power rather than through actual fighting, was regarded as the most likely challenge.

Even those who agree with this definition of the threat and the need for adequate forces will, however, have to ask and to answer a prior question: what is effective deterrence in the Persian Gulf? Here, in contrast to the defined conditions of Europe, the best defence is not necessarily also the best deterrent, since multiple addressees must be considered, each with different sensitivities which often cannot be reconciled in one military option.

The reliability of American support for local regimes, and Soviet respect for American seriousness, would seem to depend on the ability of the United States to be effective more in the (likely) minor incidents than in the (unlikely) case of major Soviet aggression. For the latter, there may be no alternative to threats of not a local but a global response – indeed, if the West did not regard a Soviet attack against Saudi Arabia as a general *casus belli*, American deterrence in support of allies elsewhere would quickly decline in credibility. In minor third-world incidents, however, credibility grows from the effectiveness of the manner in which they are handled. That was the strategic cost of the abortive American raid in Iran in April 1980: if it had succeeded, it would have boosted the general deterrence credibility of the United States throughout the region more lastingly and with less cost than a new Fifth Fleet. And American arms supplies for those who are resisting the Soviet occupation of Afghanistan

might, similarly, promote deterrent credibility in the region as a whole more effectively, more rapidly and more cheaply than the investments that are now being considered. Such *pars pro toto* deterrence would, of course, need the back-up of forces in being, but of a size more compatible with both political conditions in the region and the means now available.

What this suggests is that in the circumstances of the Third World we have to do more than merely transpose the Northern practice of deterrence to the South. Perhaps the rule of thumb – that smaller threats are deterred effectively if one can deter the larger ones – should be reversed: unless force can be effective against minor contingencies, deterrence will not be credible against major ones. The events surrounding and following the revolution in Iran point in that direction and should give pause to those who call for a massive American military presence in the region.

Collective Security Arrangements
Just as we may have to rethink deterrence to adjust it to third-world contingencies, we may have to rethink the potential of formal security arrangements. This is the subject of Shai Feldman's paper. The time for new alliances has too clearly passed, however, not only because the United States would not accept them but also because third-world uncertainties would undermine their effectiveness and third-world insistence on independence and non-alignment has dated such a proposal. Instead – and this is argued in a number of papers, most forcefully by Jusuf Wanandi and Stanley Hoffman – structures of regional co-operation in the Third World should be encouraged, supplemented by economic and diplomatic ties with major outside powers and, possibly, by outside guarantees.

ASEAN is perhaps the most visible and most impressive indication that regional co-operation can at least defuse disputes between the member states, even if it cannot, as yet, deter on its own the power of Vietnam. In the Gulf, arrangements between the conservative states have led to the settlement of a number of outstanding border issues, and the regular contact between Iraq and Saudi Arabia has fostered a pattern of consultation which has served the stability of the region. Precisely because internal sources rather than major aggression from the outside are the most likely causes for conflict, these arrangements need not be formal military alliances. There are limits to the degree to which such arrangements can be encouraged from the outside, but one way might be for major powers to support them by implicit or even explicit guarantees – to deter intervention against and generate confidence within them.

Incentives for Soviet Co-operation

Shai Feldman offers another intriguing rationale for super-power guarantees for specific regions: that this will nudge both the Soviet Union and the United States into a regular dialogue over regional issues. Since the Soviet Union can exploit third-world instabilities to the disadvantage of the West and the Third World, and since effective deterrence will be difficult to provide across the board, incentives to promote Soviet respect for Western interests and agreed rules of behaviour for both major powers are worth seeking, if they can be had. There is another important reason for this, as observers from developing countries point out: their view of Soviet policy is generally not identical to that of the major Western powers. Jusuf Wanandi suggests, for example, that it may be necessary to invite the Soviet Union to join international efforts directed at maintaining some form of regional order in parts of the Third World. These reminders from the developing world must be taken seriously. James Schlesinger's term, the 'grey areas', may make sense to a Westerner, but it is scarcely considerate to those in the Third World whose responsible involvement will be needed to reduce the danger of third-world conflicts for international security.

Can the Soviet Union be persuaded to enter into agreed arrangements for international order which are compatible with Western interests? Many will be sceptical about the possibility of any Soviet–American understanding about the desirability and the definition of stability in third-world regions. There is much evidence to support this view – the Soviet invasion in Afghanistan, Soviet behaviour throughout the Iranian revolution and after, Soviet support for

Vietnam in South-east Asia and for Cuba in Central America, and Soviet action in South Yemen, Angola and in the Horn of Africa. Moreover, the present Soviet leadership, guided both by concern over encirclement and by confidence in its accumulated military strength, with little to gain (in its own eyes) from stability Western-style, does not seem to be a promising partner for agreements on mutual restraint.

But a nagging doubt remains: cannot Western policy contribute to making the Soviet Union more co-operative, at least where vital Western interests are concerned? Is this not preferable to imposing East–West rivalry on local conflicts? Would not a more comprehensive and consistent American attempt at demonstrating to the Soviet Union the advantage of co-operation and the disadvantages of Soviet refusal produce somewhat better prospects? These questions lie behind the view that some rules of behaviour might be agreed between the super-powers. Certainly, Soviet readiness to consider and respect such rules will not come about by itself, only as the result of a consistent Western policy. In the absence of such a policy, present Soviet behaviour provides only partial evidence that the answer would be negative if the offer were to be made.

Uncertainty and unpredictability in the Third World mean not only that the threats and the responses are difficult to define; they also mean that it is unrealistic to call for anything like a comprehensive policy. What there *can* be – to quote Shahram Chubin's paper – is 'respect for diversity, compassion for suffering, and a reputation for steadfastness'. Perceptions and policies are affected not only by the cumulative weight of small defeats but also by the cumulative weight of small victories. The successful solution of regional disputes will do more for regional stability than any other of the imperfect means discussed at the Conference. But breakthroughs like the one over Zimbabwe will be the exception, not the rule. The 1980s will not be a decade when unpleasant and dangerous issues stand aside; on the contrary, such issues will combine with and compound the generally parlous state of international order.

The International Implications of Third-World Conflict: An American Perspective

The theme of this collection of papers is conflict and security in the Third World. To the implicit question that this theme poses about the future, the generic answer is quite simple: the prospects are increased turbulence and instability for the balance of the century. The basic reason is also simple: the relative decline of American power and, associated with it, the reduced will of the American people to play a combined role as international guardian and self-appointed moral preceptor – in short, the end of *Pax Americana*. Though the outlines of the future remain dim, we are in a period of international transition. The balance of the century will have an as yet undetermined character, reflecting the slow unravelling of a framework of international security earlier provided by the United States – partly fortuitously, partly through deliberate policy – for a period of 30 years after the close of World War II.

The ultimate outcome will reflect the resolution of identifiable but unmeasurable forces. The first is the degree of realism among third-world leaders – and their willingness to limit ideological posturing in exchange for concrete, if limited, advantages. Next is the character of the post-Brezhnev leadership in the Soviet Union – whether it will be moderate or aggressive in the use of its new-found power. Third is the orientation of the People's Republic of China – whether she will continue to lean against the forms of turbulence that can be exploited by her arch rival, the Soviet Union. A fourth element will be the emerging policies of the principal European states – whether, having discovered that the United States can exhibit the same irresponsibility and parochialism that has characterized their own policies since World War II, they will gradually abandon the Atlantic

relationship in the futile quest for a Europe that is simultaneously independent and strong. Finally, and perhaps most significant, there is the issue of the future policy of the United States. Will the American people acquire a renewed sense of mission (and of realism), or will they continue in the slough of preachiness and withdrawal? We must bear in mind that, given the realities of power, the evolution of the Third World during this period of transition will be determined to a large extent by forces impinging on it from the outside.

To a considerable degree, the world has become a single strategic stage, its separate strategic theatres inevitably linked, sometimes closely, sometimes more loosely. The policies of the People's Republic of China affect the whole. What occurs in the oil-producing regions of the Middle East will, to a large extent, determine the ultimate outcome. But Middle Eastern developments will, in turn, be significantly affected by the policies, deliberate or haphazard, of the United States and the Soviet Union. Even the outcomes in other third-world regions – the Caribbean, Southern or Eastern Africa, or South-east Asia – will to some, if a lesser, extent affect the overall balance. Yet it remains almost axiomatic that shifts in the Third World, attention-grabbing and suggestive of international trends as they may be, are unlikely in themselves to be decisive.

The Erosion of *Pax Americana*
In order to anticipate the future, one must understand the past and the process by which we have arrived at the present. After World War II developments in the Third World broadly reflected US policies and predilections. Initially, the United States possessed a nuclear

5

monopoly and for a long period remained the world's dominant military power. Under the aegis of that power a framework of security was established in which international trade and investment flourished. As a consequence, there occurred an enormous world-wide expansion of trade, investment and income that affected directly many of the nations of the Third World. That astounding growth of the international economy, shared rather unevenly by nations in the Third World, was based upon more or less unquestioned security and upon the exploitation of cheap energy. It is perhaps unnecessary to add that neither of these former prerequisites for international economic expansion remains fully applicable today.

The oddity was that the American nation never fully understood or even embraced the international order of which it was the principal, if unwitting, foundation. International security was provided by a democratic people whose historical experience precluded a visceral understanding of the meaning of insecurity. For 150 years it had been protected by two oceans and by its remoteness from the centres of international conflict. For the next quarter century, after her emergence as the principal world power, the United States' military position was inherently so powerful that no challenge could be regarded seriously as a direct threat to her own security. Indeed, in the 1960s and 1970s, after the passions of the Cold War had begun to ebb, a generation arose that simply took security for granted – it was an inheritance rather than something that had to be earned anew continuously.

Furthermore, in her long period of gestation the United States had developed the belief that her institutions and values were a suitable model for all mankind. Sporadically breaking out of her isolation, she exhibited – as in the two world wars – a missionary zeal for the redemption of the old world and its conversion from its wicked habits of power politics. In short, the United States considered herself a secular New Jerusalem, her varied virtues to be enjoyed either in isolation or in extension to other people.

After World War II this pent-up idealism burst forth on an industrial world worn down or devastated by war and on a Third World still under colonial rule and generally economically backward. That American idealism became embodied in a steady flow of resources and technology overseas to help resuscitate both weakened allies and vanquished foes. It was reflected institutionally in the Marshall Plan, the World Bank, Point Four and a host of other examples. For the Third World it was reflected in developmental and technical assistance and in numerous institutions for the provision of multi-lateral and bilateral assistance. These economic policies must be borne in mind, though I have insufficient space to develop them; instead I shall mention some of the major political elements bearing on the Third World.

First, true to the American Revolution and to the precepts of Jeffersonianism, the United States pressed steadily for decolonization. Sometimes those pressures were quite direct, as in the case of the Dutch East Indies; more frequently they were indirect. As the process of decolonization unfolded, the pressures from the United States diminished but, even at the close of the period, tacit pressures on the remnants of the French and Portuguese empires could readily be discerned. The process of decolonization was recognizably the chief force in shaping the Third World of today. Middle Eastern nations may boggle at this suggestion and will insist that Israel is a dramatic and, for them, a most painful exemplar of Western colonialism imposed after World War II. Even if one were to accept this somewhat strained interpretation of the introduction of an external population in the creation of the new state, the case of Israel does remain unique. The motivation that lay behind it can scarcely be viewed in terms of traditional motives for colonization. It reflected Western feelings of guilt and the desire for restitution after the tragedies of the period of Hitler's rule. If one puts aside this distinctive and controversial case, one can state categorically that the evolution of the Third World was determined by decolonization, a goal both practical and ethical sought by the United States after the close of the war.

A second goal, pursued somewhat fitfully, was democratization and the enhancement of civil rights. Pressure to promote these ends tended to coincide with Democratic Administrations. Under President Kennedy the *Alianza para el Progreso* concentrated on Latin America and foresaw *measured progress* as the standard for assessing movement towards these political goals. Under President Carter the pressures became more general and more universal, concerned less directly with specific time and circumstance.

A third element, the counter-part of domestic reform on the international scene, was the historic American stress on legality. Subversion or coups might be tolerated, but the sending of forces across recognized international frontiers was considered unacceptable. This continuing emphasis on the inviolability of international frontiers made the United States the natural, if half-conscious, protector of the independence of national states. It led to both the American involvement in South Korea and the unsuccessful attempt to preserve South Vietnam.

Neither friend nor foe, practised in the standards of realism, could anticipate or understand either the American tendency to invest such moral enthusiasm in strict legality or the vehemence of American reactions. Britain and France (and Israel) were nonplussed by what they regarded as the quixotic response of the United States at Suez in 1956. Similarly, the Soviet Union was quite unprepared for the vehement American reaction when her forces crossed the border into Afghanistan in 1979. After all, a far more serious political development – the Taraki Coup in April 1978, which raised the red banner over Afghanistan – had passed virtually without comment in the United States. The Soviet Union might readily believe that a supplementary action, justified as an extension of the Brezhnev doctrine, to sustain a socialist state would scarcely elicit a reaction so sharply different in kind, so plainly at odds with easily recognized 'correlation of forces'. No more than the United States' Allies did she recognize the emotional depth of the American commitment to the sanctity of international frontiers.

Curiously, this neo-Wilsonian moral enthusiasm reached its apogee with the Carter Administration in 1977. Some might suggest that it represented a second attempt by a southern Protestant to redeem this wicked world. Certainly, the Administration came into office rejecting the (sinful) power politics embodied, in its view, in the figure of Henry Kissinger. Other nations, apparently, had simply lacked the opportunity to hear the advantages of

human rights eloquently extolled by the American people. That such nations might be more concerned with the maintenance of order or with political survival was simply ignored. The Soviet Union, so the Administration apparently believed, had until then simply been seeking an opportunity to divest herself of the nuclear weapons in which she had made so vast an investment of national effort. It was just that nobody had approached her in the right manner. In the Middle East the failure to achieve a *comprehensive* settlement had simply reflected a prior lack of necessary will and enthusiasm. The disputes between the industrial and under-developed worlds reflected not concern about interests or resources but rather a lack of communication.

These neo-Wilsonian impulses shaped the initial responses of the Administration through a series of national setbacks and humiliations, including the fall of the Shah and the seizure of the American Embassy in Tehran. They still remain a powerful, if temporarily suppressed, force – even after the Soviet movement into Afghanistan.

The policies of the Carter Administration represented simply an extreme manifestation of endemic American beliefs that had, in large degree, shaped the post-war world. None the less, the decline in the United States' relative position in the world, particularly after the Vietnam war, inevitably meant that the influence of these cherished American views had waned. Perhaps not surprisingly, the American people were the last to recognize this unavoidable reality.

The American nation had long taken security as axiomatic. In part this reflected a widespread conviction that American international influence reflected less American power than the purity of American motives. It was, of course, flattering to hear the purity of those motives praised – as long as the United States' power was pre-eminent.

As a world power, the United States had oddly but steadily neglected the creation of a necessary base structure through which to exercise her military power world-wide. This reflected her firm belief in national sovereignty and a touching faith that in time of trouble other nations would adhere to her banner because of the rightness of the cause, irrespective of the political risks that they might incur. Especially after the Vietnam war, the United States' under-funding of her military establishment, upon which the security of the Free World depended, became almost a case of wilful negligence. The premise of the political left that the United States had been too powerful for her own and the world's good was then put to the test. The outcome is hardly surprising: as the strength of the United States ebbed, so did her influence.

With the decline of American power, the United States' moral impulses were increasingly directed towards those whom she could reach, namely, friendly nations, allies and dependants. Hostile nations – the Cubas and the Soviet Unions – could turn a deaf ear to her exhortations; her associates could do so less readily. The force of her crusading impulses as a practical matter thus were directed against states like Argentina and Brazil, Iran and South Korea, with whose foreign policies the United States had no quarrel – she contested only their internal arrangements.

As a practical matter, the United States could do little to help Soviet dissidents. By contrast, she could effectively, if only temporarily, better the lot of dissidents in Iran. Needless to say, it was only where the United States was most effective that she succeeded in inflicting the most grievous wounds upon herself.

In the practical world of security arrangements, the value of an American alliance, once virtually absolute, was increasingly discounted. Perhaps the most suggestive milestone was the American response to Brezhnev's provocative warning in November 1978 that the United States should not intervene in Iran. To this direct assault on the American alliance system there was no Trumanesque response warning against Soviet intrusion, no reiteration of the United States' fidelity to her ally or reference to the CENTO Alliance that she had been instrumental in creating. Instead, Secretary Vance meekly responded that the United States had no intention of intervening and, by *noting* prior Soviet statements of intent, implicitly called on the Soviet Union to exhibit a similar sense of responsibility. The purpose, no doubt, was to provide reassurance to the Soviet Union, but the mild response provided reassurance to few others.

One wishes to avoid exaggeration. This episode clearly lacked the drama of Munich in 1938. Yet its aftermath offers some remarkable parallels. It was only *after* the Munich Conference that other nations began to edge away from the protection provided by the Western Allies and towards Germany. After September 1938 the Soviet Union abandoned her quest for collective security against Hitler's Germany with the Western Allies and began her approach towards accommodation with Germany, which ultimately resulted in the Hitler–Stalin Pact. Similarly, Romania, Yugoslavia, and Hungary (and later Czechoslovakia) moved away from the Western Allies and towards Germany. Similarly, since the fall of the Shah the United States' partners, in Europe as well as in the Middle East, have edged away to search for other arrangements that may provide security.

Uncertainty in 'Grey Areas'

How should we relate these broader international trends to the prospects for security and conflict in the Third World? In the light of the vast extent and variety of the areas under consideration, generalizations do not come easily. Those generalizations that may be proposed lack concreteness, for they must be distilled from highly distinctive and localized constellations, of income levels, resources, rivalries and power balances. A useful initial observation is that in security matters the term 'Third World' is less appropriate than the older term 'grey area'. The latter provides more accurate imagery, for in these regions questions of security are inherently difficult to define with precision.

None the less, two generalizations do appear relevant. First, the partial dissolution of the security framework provided by the United States for a quarter of a century after World War II makes the entire world – at least, outside the Soviet Union and her immediate satellites – far more unstable. There is no longer so effective a natural protector of national independence and of national frontiers. Consequently, one must anticipate a greater willingness on the part of aggressive nations to move across national borders in the years ahead.

The heightened instability which has followed the decline of American power is perhaps most marked in the region of the Arabian Gulf, for it is on that region that the rest of the Free

World depends for its supply of energy. Yet that region is also noticeably close to the main sources of Soviet power. Until quite recently, the dominance of the strategic nuclear forces of the United States and the clear-cut superiority of her naval and mobility forces provided adequate deterrence for outside threats to the region. Now strategic nuclear superiority has disappeared, however, and American naval and mobility forces no longer possess the clear-cut advantages of times past. As a consequence, the region of the Gulf is susceptible to political-military pressures from the north to a degree unknown hitherto. This heightened vulnerability, combined with the dependency of the outside world on Arabian Gulf energy resources, implies both a degree of risk and a contagion of fear in what has now become the vortex of international strategic conflict.

The second generalization that may be made is that the increased world-wide insecurity that has resulted from the dissolution of the post-war security framework bears with particular force on other 'grey area' nations. Few such nations possess great inherent strength or carry much international weight. Consequently, disruption within such a country, or even its loss to one side or the other, does not immediately affect the vital interests of the great powers or their coalitions. It is a reflection of the 'greyness' of such areas that even shifts of allegiances will not significantly affect the overall colouration of the world's political map. It is this attribute of 'greyness' that allows sharply increased local insecurity without substantially affecting international political risks. In the industrial world, by contrast, clear lines of division and greater political weight imply far greater risks in the event of major change or of bold action.

Quite clearly, if the nations of Western Europe, Japan or China were to shift sides, this would imply a major, if not a decisive, swing in the equilibrium of power. The eastern frontier of the Federal Republic is a clearly demarcated and highly sensitive dividing line. The risks of incursion are consequently staggering. In the case of Berlin the demarcation is clear. There is no 'greyness'. The risks of disturbance are high – far too high in relation to any prospective gains. But in the 'grey areas' the risks are low; incursions, subversion or other pressures may occur without any major impact on the overall

balance of power and, consequently, there is no great likelihood of their inducing major hostilities. Low risk is an attribute of 'greyness', and it underscores the contention that heightened world insecurity will tend to be concentrated in these 'grey areas'.

There is, of course, some limit to the ebb and flow that might be tolerable. Territory implies the possibility of bases. It implies the prospective establishment of advanced positions as stepping-stones. It provides the potential for geographical infection, or falling dominoes. None of these needs to be fatal. By contrast, a threat to Europe, Japan or (for different reasons) the Arabian Gulf could start a process without limit. In the face of the possibility that events may spin out of control, all powers will necessarily remain prudent. That prudence will not inhibit actions elsewhere in the world.

These two points – the heightened insecurity resulting from a weakened international security framework and the concentration of that insecurity in the 'grey areas' – provide the necessary backdrop against which the inner dynamics of third-world countries may be viewed. The direction and pace of such internal developments are critically important. For example, despite the climate favourable for decolonization that was fostered by the United States after the war, the timing and nature of independence movements depended primarily upon indigenous rather than external forces. But after independence third-world nations had to face innumerable internal problems that had previously been subsumed in the cohesion of the independence movement. Ethnic rivalries, for example, were legion, resulting in severe internal conflicts. Alternatively, since boundaries had been determined for the convenience of the colonial powers, the overlapping of international frontiers by specific ethnic groups resulted in unresolved and bitter border disputes. Serious internal disparities of wealth existed, causing further conflict. Too frequently the overall impression was of new states with immature political systems, great internal divisions and weak leadership.

From the standpoint of many third-world nations, a great advantage of the *Pax Americana* had been that it provided a stable background against which temporary compromises could be devised for many of these

9

problems or solutions worked out relatively benignly. A consequence of the decline of the international order represented by the *Pax Americana*, therefore, is that these internal problems come into stark relief. They must now be worked out in the face of heightened competition from other regional contenders and in the absence of any clear international order. Quite obviously, this is a prescription for unrest. For a time it may seem that a confrontation of the South with the industrial North can serve as a substitute for order and a disguise for unrest. But given the disparities within the South that reflect particularly the divergent flows of oil revenues, the North–South confrontation becomes a charade that must ultimately break down. Claims against the North cannot mask for long the discontent, tensions and unrest in the 'grey areas'.

Areas of Tension

Revising Voltaire, a third generalization may be suggested: in the light of the remarkable differences among regions and of local power balances, all generalizations are false. The structure of military-political power is far too variegated and each region too differently affected by the international structure of power for anything other than a differentiated treatment of each region to be attempted. The key ingredients of policy will be proximity to the sources of Soviet or American power, residual influence by European states (as in Francophone Africa) and the presence or absence of a locally dominant military power. Very broadly, the Third World can be divided into the Eurasian periphery of the Soviet Union – with particular attention being paid to the Middle Eastern portions stretching from Turkey to Pakistan and including the Arabian Peninsula – the western hemisphere and other areas visibly less marked by great power influence or threat.

Soviet military power provides a massive threat only to the areas on the periphery of the Soviet Union. These areas have long been the focus of Russian, and now Soviet, imperial ambitions. The rise of American military power after World War II precluded for many years the furtherance of those ambitions, a fact reflected, for example, in the forced Soviet withdrawal from Iran in 1946. But the subsequent growth of the military power of the Soviet

Union and, in particular, the development of her mobility forces have once again created the possibility that she may contemplate movement towards the Indian Ocean. Unlike the case of Vietnam, there can be little question that the vital interests of the West are engaged in this region. It is the coincidence in this region of the possibility of Soviet military action and the existence of vital Free World interests that provides the potential for conflagration. Only the Middle Eastern region provides this potential for an uncontrolled clash between the Soviet Union and the United States. In the unlikely event of a Soviet assault on the oil-fields of the Arabian Gulf the United States would have little choice but to resist with whatever military means were at hand. That is a simple *political* imperative.

Yet one must also recognize that the deterrent posture to forestall such a Soviet move is not now adequate. The Soviet Union may continue to be restrained by political prudence and, perhaps, by the belief that time is on her side. But the military forces presently and prospectively in place in the region are not sufficient by themselves to constrain Soviet moves if the Soviet Union were to become more aggressive. Whether there remains sufficient cohesion and trust between the Middle Eastern countries under threat and the United States to arrange for an adequate military deterrent in time remains to be seen. None the less, an appropriate military deterrent in place remains an indispensable ingredient for avoiding collapse in the Middle East. That is the simple *military* imperative.

In the western hemisphere and on the American periphery conditions are quite different. The United States remains distinctly the dominant military power. Despite the irritations of recent years, most nations in Latin America retain some fidelity to the hemispheric system, as exemplified by the Rio Treaty, and little desire to see the prevailing tranquillity upset. The most notable exceptions are Castro's Cuba, a Soviet satellite, and the ambitions that Castro represents, now quite patently bearing fruit in Nicaragua. None the less, the reality of American military superiority in the Caribbean remains accepted by all. Cuban behaviour exists at the sufferance of the United States, just as prospects for liberalization in Poland depend on

10

the sufferance of the Soviet Union. Indeed, Castro recognizes this reality. His actions over the years since 1962 have been carefully gauged in accordance with what he believes various Administrations in Washington have been prepared to tolerate.

Other regions, especially Africa and Southeast Asia, are therefore perhaps the most interesting. Since the fundamental interests of neither block are obviously engaged, there is a far greater latitude here for shifting relationships and for the tolerance of general unrest. These are regions not readily susceptible to Soviet military action. Despite the growth of the Soviet Union's blue-water naval capabilities and the improvement of her mobility and intervention forces, they remain generally less capable than the military forces of the Western world. Whatever the shifts in the balance of power around the periphery of the Soviet Union, American naval and air capabilities elsewhere remain generally superior. The sustaining of Cuban expeditionary forces in Angola, for example, ultimately remains dependent upon an American disinclination to intervene. Paradoxically, it is the reality of low potential gains and low risks that makes these regions especially susceptible to a set of low-level military activities.

While the Soviet Union has created an immensely powerful military establishment, that establishment remains notably range-limited. Unless the United States permits her forces to erode far more rapidly than now seems likely, the Soviet Union cannot prudently contemplate military moves in these regions in the absence of invitations from inside.

Political penetration will provide the principal means for acquiring positions of influence. Yet such political penetrations will in the longer run depend on the acquiescence of those in the regions. Since political attitudes are notably susceptible to change, it would be wise to anticipate a pattern of shifting allegiances and shifting confrontations over time. The dramatic reversals of allegiances in the Horn of Africa over the last decade represent one likely model for the longer term.

This appreciation is somewhat modified by the presence or absence in a particular region of a locally dominant military power. Vietnam, South Africa and Israel come readily to mind.

Yet each is subject to special constraints. Israel is limited not only by American pressure but also by her sense of siege – and, one may hope, by the recognition that military victory only intensifies problems of control under conditions demographically unfavourable to her. South Africa is limited by her severe internal problems and by the recognition that foreign adventures, if exhausting, could only intensify her problem of internal control. Vietnam is perhaps less inhibited, yet she too must take into consideration the presence of China to the north and the American commitments to Thailand. None the less, these local power balances do pose special problems, and the presence of respectable military establishments implies much higher costs for outside intervention.

Third-World Contributions to Security
Yet, taken all together, we may recognize a high degree of fluidity in these 'grey' regions. Considerable leeway for unrest and for trouble-making will continue to exist. The outcome will depend largely upon the sense of realism in the third-world countries. After the first flush of revolutionary fervour, third-world leaders have generally demonstrated a keen understanding of the need for rational calculation. They have recognized the need to maintain associations with the Western nations, for the latter will remain the principal source of developmental and technical assistance and the principal market for their products. Apart from military equipment, the Soviet Union has persuasively demonstrated that she has remarkably little to offer.

Thus hopes for economic progress will rest on reasonably friendly relations with the industrial world. But these hopes must also be sustained by some degree of confidence in the adequacy of security arrangements. The Western nations have the capacity to provide the minimum semblance of security arrangements that are necessary. No third-world nation can ignore the realities of power. Therefore the perception of military capability does remain important. Third-world leaders will closely, if quietly, examine the question of which nations possess the military chips. The Western nations will be obliged to maintain appropriate forces to provide sustenance to their friends and to constrain the ambitions of those who may be hostile.

11

In the 'grey areas' there will remain great latitude for unrest. But there will also be the knowledge that there may be limits to that general tolerance in the event that gross disturbances are fostered. Unquestionably, direct intervention should be employed very sparingly, if at all. Yet the knowledge that the military capability does exist and might be employed may be the necessary condition for avoiding the descent of particular regions into chaos and for the preservation of reasonable chances for economic progress.

For the Third World there is no longer outside insurance against internal irresponsibility. In the West there should be recognition of the fact that neither universal guidelines nor blanket slogans can guide its policies. Its reactions will depend upon particular times and circumstances.

For progress to be maintained there must be both a minimum of security and a continued association with the industrial world. Neither that association nor economic progress will be much enhanced by continuing illusions and rhetoric regarding a new international economic order or the massive transfer of resources from the industrial to the under-developed world. Neither is going to occur (apart from the continuing and massive transfer to the oil-exporting countries). By and large, resources will flow in accordance with ordinary commercial arrangements based on supply and demand and on the creation of a reasonably promising climate for investment activity. Illusions that run counter to this reality will certainly not foster economic progress. In all likelihood they will only add to a climate of unrest which, in the best of circumstances, will unquestionably remain the hallmark of the 'grey areas' for the balance of the century.

Conclusions

Not only has the partial dissolution of the international security framework increased instability world-wide, but that instability and unrest weighs particularly heavily on the Third World. The era of the relatively benign resolution of disputes ended with the demise of the *Pax Americana*. The Third World has now been left more on its own to grapple with its internal tensions. Given the internal dynamics of the Third World, inevitably the level of unrest will

run high. The degree of success in tamping down that unrest is critically dependent upon third-world leadership. If there is a willingness to avoid feeding the flames, if there is a realistic appreciation of economic opportunities, however limited, and a serious effort to work with the industrial world, then modest economic progress may continue and some minimal level of security maintained. Failure to exercise restraint and patiently to cultivate economic and political ties with the industrial world may result in conditions approaching chaos.

At the outset, I emphasized that the world has become a single strategic stage and that the interlocking theatres affect one another. The future of the Third World depends not only on its inner dynamics and the quality of its leadership but also upon forces impinging on it from the outside; whether the outcome is satisfactory also depends upon whether or not these outside forces are relatively constructive. The world is now in transition, moving towards a new geopolitical equilibrium. The character of that equilibrium will be determined by the future decisions and actions of the more influential players on the international scene.

A major ingredient, needless to say, will be the character of Soviet policy. How will the Soviet Union make use of her enhanced strength and stature in the world? Will she refrain from the direct employment of her forces in the Third World? This question becomes increasingly important as mobility and logistics improve and as the reach of those forces expands. If such forces are employed extensively, then the likelihood of chaotic conflict arises. It is perhaps too much to expect the Soviet Union not to continue to subvert or influence third-world governments. Backed up by an increasingly impressive military capability, that danger will become steadily more serious. The chief responsibility for resisting such efforts will lie with the third-world nations themselves. To the extent that they collaborate with the Soviet Union, the probable result will be the spreading of the kind of trouble observable in Angola or in the Horn of Africa.

A second ingredient is the evolution of European policies and attitudes. Will the major European states allow the drift away from the Atlantic relationship to continue? Given the realities of Soviet strength, along that path lies neither security nor long-term independence. A growing division between the two sides of the Atlantic would encourage further American disengagement from the affairs of the eastern hemisphere. The result would be further to weaken the residual security framework and thereby to affect the Third World. Moreover, growing competition for political influence among Western nations would add to third world unrest. Augmented unrest would intensify those problems that would arise from the further weakening of the international security framework.

Perhaps the most critical ingredient is the future direction of American policy. Will the American people, given the inherent strength of the United States, acquire a new sense of mission and of responsibility towards the outside world? Would such a renewed effort be marked by greater realism and by lessened expectations of long-lived gratitude? Or will the United States follow the path of preachings and injured feelings, the sour fruit of the Vietnam era?

It seems likely that future American policy will be characterized by a higher degree of nationalism. A cynic might suggest that idealism is the luxury of the powerful and secure: American power and innocence seem destined to decline together. The probable result will be a less fervent search for the grievances of others, together with the concomitant belief that if only those grievances could be revealed, they could be satisfied. More painstaking attention will perhaps be devoted to national interests and these will be greater indulgence in traditional types of power policy. All in all, the results may be healthier world-wide than a continuation of high-flown preaching.

Such a change would result in greater clarity in American policy. One can hardly blame others for being confused about American policies, for the United States has contributed to that confusion. When a principal American spokesman refers to Ayatollah Khomeini as 'a kind of saint' or to Cuban forces as part of a stabilizing mission in Angola, it is hardly surprising that others are either bewildered by, or attempt to exploit, this odd combination of guilt and confusion. It was Bismarck who observed that the strong are weak because of their inhibitions. One might even suggest that the United States in this era has been weak because of her illusions and the neuroses that have stemmed from Vietnam.

One final observation on a matter critical to third-world stability. An illusion that has been particularly pernicious has been the hope for instant democratization. The task of dealing with the Third World is more complex than asking it to conform to a checklist devised by the American Civil Liberties Union. Maintaining order in conditions of unrest is not a simple undertaking. Any approach to dealing with the Third World must grapple with the centuries-old issue of liberty and order and the need for striking an appropriate balance between the two. It should be self-evident that an appropriate balance between liberty and order will be bound to vary between one society and another and that consideration will always have to be given to local conditions, historical experience and public attitudes. Yet this has not been self-evident to many Americans, who are inclined to believe that social customs akin to American institutions are not only universally desirable but, more important, universally achievable. It serves the Third World ill to base policies upon this fundamental misconception. In the future the Third World will be better served by a deeper understanding of the relevance to the Third World of that hoary political issue, the reconciliation of liberty and order.

The International Implications of Third-World Conflict: A Third-World Perspective

JUSUF WANANDI

This view from the Third World on the nature of its conflicts and on international security is based on observations and experiences of the South-east Asian region. Subsequently, an attempt is made to draw relevant conclusions for other regions of the Third World. In drawing those conclusions suggestions will be made as to the desirability of an international order for the future and the role of the major powers in that order, as seen from the perspective of the Third World.

Conflicts in South-East Asia

To understand the nature of South-east Asian conflicts and the problems of security one has to look at both the internal and the external dimensions of those problems, as well as the links between them. These links become stronger with the deterioration in the resilience of the individual South-east Asian countries. Thus the greater the threats to security which originate domestically, the greater are the external threats faced by that country. Sources of domestic instability are political, economic, social and even cultural and ideological in nature. Therefore the realm of security in South-east Asia involves a wide spectrum of issues and is not solely a military matter in the conventional sense.

To facilitate a closer look at these problems, the following discussion will be confined to the ASEAN countries. Although many differences among them exist, the following observations hold good for most of them:

—They are concerned with national development with all its side-effects, such as changes in the cultural values of society and the unequal distribution of the gains of development.
—The unity of the state and nation is still a problem for most.
—They are concerned with the establishment and development of political and social institutions as well as improvements in the implementation of the rule of law and human rights.
—Political succession is a major challenge to the stability and continuity of the state and nation.

Each of these aspects will be considered in turn.

National Development

Development efforts must be sustained so that governments can fulfil their promises; at the same time, it is only through their achievements that governments can maintain their legitimacy.

During the last ten years the ASEAN countries have been able to achieve high growth rates in their economic development (between 5 and 10 per cent annually). However, recent uncertainties in the international economy may affect performances of the ASEAN countries. Continuous increases in the price of energy create pressures, especially upon Thailand and the Philippines. Yet because of the abundance of natural resources, the situation over the longer term may not be critical. It is likely that short-term measures could overcome these difficulties. However, it may be less difficult to sustain high economic growth rates than to deal with the side-effects resulting from the very successes of economic development.

The changes in cultural values which accompany economic development generate a search for a new national identity. Ideally, this will incorporate both traditional values and new values from outside. It may take some time to find the proper balance between them. Reform in the educational system could smooth this process. At present, no ASEAN country has

14

achieved cultural identity. In this period of transition it is expected that a certain feeling of insecurity will be quite widespread. However, in view of the history of the South-east Asian people, one can be quite optimistic that this problem can be overcome. Several cultures – Hindu, Sinic and Islamic – have been absorbed in the past.

Development also creates other problems: the explosion of demands, over-consumption and inequalities in the distribution of income. To some extent, these are inherent in the development strategy adopted, namely the adoption of open economies relying upon market mechanisms. Governments have launched efforts to correct these defects by:

—suppressing over-consumption, enhancing national solidarity and fighting corruption. They attempt to control advertisements through television and other mass media as well as other marketing methods. They have also made consistent efforts to eradicate blatant corruption, especially by the ruling few;
—the adoption of a progressive tax system and other social policies, such as increasing public education, public health and public housing, especially for the poor. Thus, even if this group cannot, for the time being, participate directly in economic development, they could nevertheless enjoy many of the fruits of development.

National Unity
The unity of the nation and state becomes a problem because of history. Each ASEAN member country contains many ethnic groups and religious diversities, and this fact tends to have socio-political implications. At present, the Philippines faces problems with her Moslem minorities in the south. Malaysia still faces problems in integrating the Malays and the Chinese population who constitute 45 per cent and 35 per cent respectively of the population. Singapore is still struggling to build a Singaporean nation. Thailand has many minorities within her borders. Indonesia, too, consists of many ethnic groups.

Nation building has thus become a necessary task for all ASEAN governments. Through this effort it is hoped that ethnic or religious minorities may be fully integrated into society. Past experiences have shown that minority groups can easily be exploited by outside forces to create internal unrest and instability with the aim of overthrowing the government.

Religious fanaticism is another disintegrating factor. Initially, the Islamic Revolution of Ayatollah Khomeini in Iran was an inspiration for some Moslems in South-east Asia. However, having seen the uncertain consequences of this revolution, its influence has declined. The majority of the Moslem leaders also acknowledge that the situation in South-east Asia is different from that in Iran and that Islam as practised in Iran is different from that in South-east Asia. More important, they realize that religious elements alone cannot be used as a base for any alternative government.

The crucial factor determining whether a government maintains the support of the population is the degree to which the demands of the people are fulfilled, as well as the extent to which the people participate in all aspects of development. The socio-political implications of religious fanaticism can magnify and complicate the problems faced by governments, but religion alone is not the determining factor in debates on whether or not to replace the government. This was shown by the Darul Islam case in Indonesia.

Some governments in South-east Asia have had to take into account the role of Islam in the formulation and implementation of national policies because the majority of the population are Moslems, especially in Malaysia and Indonesia. Nevertheless, a distinction must be maintained between state affairs and religious affairs, otherwise religion could become a source of disintegration for the pluralistic societies in the ASEAN countries.

National Participation
Political development gives the population a greater sense of participation in the process of policy-making. Yet it cannot be denied that every success creates more diversified demands and greater expectations. Economic gains are not enough. Demands for a genuine rule of law, for political participation and for a wide spectrum of human and civil rights will grow. It should be noted, however, that in a developing country (as elsewhere) it is important to achieve

the proper balance between individual rights and communal rights. This balance depends upon economic achievements, political stability and national unity. Western models and values cannot be adopted indiscriminately, for this would only create new demands which – given the prevailing scarcities and constraints – cannot yet be satisfied.

Nevertheless, it is never too early to embark on the process of establishing political institutions, which provide a mechanism for absorbing or deflecting the side-effects of economic development. Political parties are not the only important political institutions. Other social institutions have important functions – labour and farmer unions, youth and women's organizations, etc. The mass media, students and intellectuals too have to be given special attention because they are the most vocal groups in the society.

In sum, sound political development, adjusted to the stages of economic development, is one way of overcoming the negative implications of development. Governments, with the leaders of society, must design and implement long-term political development plans.

The Problem of Succession
Democracy works when the transfer of power can proceed smoothly and constitutionally. The existence of established socio-political institutions tends to guarantee the continuation of development, with the fate of the nation no longer dependent upon a single person. In the 1980s all ASEAN countries will be confronted with succession problems. For all their shortcomings, the present leaders of the ASEAN countries have been able to further the development of their respective countries. They have exercised strong leadership from a broad base of popular support.

The existing political institutions, which must manage the smooth transfer of power, have not been tested. It is for this reason that in Southeast Asia today the importance of political institutional building has been widely acknowledged by the leadership, by the political parties and by political organizations at large. It is perhaps the Philippines which gives rise to the greatest anxiety.

In solving the internal problems faced by the ASEAN member countries, it would appear that the role of domestic forces will be more important than external factors. Although external factors can exert great pressure in a national crisis, the failure to master the internal situation magnifies and complicates the problems faced by the country as a whole. The military, while important, cannot deal with the complexity of national development, encompassing all aspects of life. It can handle only internal and external security threats.

Anatomy of Third-World Conflicts
Certain features of South-east Asian security may be applicable to other regions of the Third World. Factors which constitute sources of international conflict in the Third World differ from one region to another because of differences in geographic location, strategic position, history, the dynamics of internal developments and natural resource potential. None the less, those factors which are relevant to the internal development of the ASEAN countries ought also to be relevant to other third-world countries. The intensity and complexity of third-world problems differ according to the stages of economic development, the establishment of socio-political institutions and the degree of national unity. The ASEAN countries are in this respect somewhat ahead of the majority of third-world countries. In terms of the existence of an inter-country mechanism for conflict resolution, too, ASEAN may be well ahead of other groupings, such as the OAU for Africa, the Arab League and the smaller (and perhaps more effective) co-operative structures in West and East Africa.

Conflicts in the Third World are basically reflections of internal weaknesses, which may be exploited by the big powers for their own interests. Internal weaknesses may be the result of the troublesome process of gradual or sudden decolonization (recent examples are Angola, Mozambique and Zimbabwe); they may arise because of political struggles among various groups, whether based on ideological, religious or ethnic grounds (Ethiopia and Afghanistan provide examples); they may also be brought about by social revolution, focusing on the problems of change in the country's leadership coupled with an ideological movement such as Islam (in Iran) or leftist socialism (in Nicaragua).

Conflicts between countries in the Third World also arise because of territorial disputes, often dating back to the arbitrarily drawn boundaries of the colonial period or traditional ethnic rivalries of the pre-colonial period. Many ethnic groups which, for historical reasons, have become separated and are living as minorities in neighbouring countries have found a new urge to seek unification (*irredenta*), largely because of their dissatisfaction with the governments of the countries in which they are now living. These problems are often allied to internal instability and political struggle and are complicated by the involvement of neighbouring countries. Such situations prevail in Indochina, in East Africa (Ethiopia and Somalia), and in South-west Asia, between Afghanistan, Pakistan and Iran, in connection with the demands of the Baluchis to have their own nation-state or at least a substantial degree of independence.

Third-world conflicts involving outside powers which compete on the basis of ideological antagonism may not be of an East-West type alone, but the involvement of the big powers, either because of challenges created by their global rivalries or because they are invited to become involved by the conflicting parties, tends to worsen the situation. However, the presence of the great powers does not necessarily increase internal or regional conflicts, provided that they agree to maintain regional or international order in the area. In the case of Zimbabwe the great powers have shown some restraint in involving themselves in the internal conflict. In the Korean Peninsula all the big powers in the region have an interest in maintaining the existing balance.

National vulnerabilities tend to result from a blend of unfavourable internal factors. Because of the complexity of the domestic scene, conflict resolution in the Third World has become a very delicate and difficult matter. It has become even more complicated in areas where the regional environment is not conducive to solving the problems, and where the East–West and the East–East conflicts are most pronounced. Given the vulnerabilities of many third-world areas, it is in these that the East–West conflict is likely to find its outlets, not only for politico-strategic reasons but also increasingly because of economic interest. The Third World has become a more vital source of energy and raw materials as well as a market for industrial countries' products.

As noted above, conflicts in the Third World involve the complex interplay of political, economic, social, cultural and ideological factors, and therefore they can be resolved by the dynamism of indigenous socio-political forces; resolution depends to a large extent on national resilience, which can be promoted or destroyed by the involvement of outside powers. Both the exercise of unreasonable and unnecessary pressures upon third-world countries and intervention, whether or not undertaken within the framework of super-power rivalry, will tend to be damaging to national resilience.

Conflicts among third-world countries have their roots in nationalism and problems associated with the survival of the nation-state. They are often no longer ideologically motivated, and thus major conflicts between Communist countries can arise, as in Indochina. These conflicts are based not only on political motives but include economic interests and the struggle for resources.

The big powers are obviously able to play either a positive or a negative role in such conflicts, yet interventions by the big powers can be of only limited value, for three reasons. First, their capabilities are not always suited to the resolution of third-world conflicts. Secondly, world opinion will always be against the use of force by a big power in conflict resolution in the Third World. And, thirdly, the use of force by the big powers in local conflicts could escalate into a global confrontation. It follows that efforts to resolve third-world conflicts should be undertaken by domestic or regional forces. Outside powers can help the situation by exercising restraint themselves and by restraining others from becoming directly involved by example or persuasion. In the process it may well be that the big powers are asked to provide help, but this is best given through diplomatic means, humanitarian aid or economic assistance.

A more urgent need, however, is to find ways of preventing third-world conflicts from arising in the first place. Given the tendency of East–West rivalry to increase, the creation of regional order in third-world areas may be the most profitable avenue to explore. Initiatives should preferably come from the third-world

17

countries themselves, although there might be a role for the big powers to play in helping to maintain regional order in many parts of the Third World. Even intervention can become the subject of negotiations, as long as there is a shared understanding of the circumstances in which such an instrument could be applied (its terms and forms), and if this is acceptable to third-world countries, intervention can become a legitimate instrument. Increased East–West conflict, however, may not help in the creation of such an understanding. There are even strong fears that growing East–West conflict will tend to magnify local and regional conflicts in some parts of the Third World and will also encourage new conflicts to arise. Thus, a kind of detente is seen as a prerequisite for the creation of stability in the Third World, although it should have a much broader base than hitherto.

The use of military force, the establishment of military alliances and large sales of military hardware will neither by themselves prevent third-world conflicts from arising nor resolve them. Sound relations between countries of the Third World and the big powers, in the political and economic fields as well as in the cultural field, are much more profitable goals to pursue. It cannot be denied that a military balance is often a necessity in preventing big-power intervention in a particular area or the invasion of a third-world country by a neighbour, but in the long run third-world conflicts are unlikely to be solved by military means alone.

East–West Conflicts, the Third World and International Security

Recent international tensions seem likely to encourage a new round of East–West competition, and thus to increase the likelihood of conflicts in the Third World, largely because no clearly defined spheres of influence of the super-powers have been established.

Increased tension between the United States and the Soviet Union results from charges by each side that the other does not abide by the rules of detente. The United States accuses the Soviet Union of continuing her strategic and conventional arms build-up and of having a greater propensity to intervene in third-world areas to upset the global balance. The Soviet Union charges the United States with not fulfilling her promises in the area of trade and

finance and with failing to ratify the SALT II Agreement. The Soviet Union believes that the erratic policies of the United States are responsible for emerging misperceptions. Given the mood of the American public, a new round of the arms race seems a far from remote possibility.

The majority of third-world countries formally adopted a neutral or 'equidistant' aitude with regard to the East–West competition. In practice, however, most of them retain quite intensive and extensive relations with Western countries. In the political field the relationship is somewhat ambivalent in nature because many third-world nations are ex-colonies of the West. In the immediate post-colonial period they strove for complete political independence, implying an anti-Western attitude, and thus were attracted initially to the Soviet Union. But the second generation of leaders in many of these countries, having been through the various revolutionary stages of national development, are now more pragmatic and politically more neutral towards the West. Relations will become even easier if the Western countries make more effort to understand (and to take a less inflexible attitude with regard to) social systems, systems of government, societal values and the dynamism of changes in the Third World.

Relations in the economic field are already quite extensive. It is obvious that the West possesses great leverage *vis-à-vis* the Third World in this respect. The need to restructure economic relations, as stipulated in the Report of the Brandt Commission, is an important task for both sides. Although the Soviet Union has herself almost nothing to offer in this field, dissatisfaction on the part of third-world states with their economic relations with the West can easily be exploited by the Soviet Union for her own political gain.

The West is also a major source of science and technology for the Third World. Yet the ransfer of science and technology is a delicate matter, for it touches upon the socio-cultural values of the receiving society. This calls for close co-operation and great understanding between the Third World and the Western countries.

As stated above, relations in the military field are not likely to be the dominant factor in East–West competition. From the third-world perspective, it is expected that the United States and her Allies will try to maintain a level of military presence which balances that of the Soviet Union. It is also hoped that the West could become a 'consistent' source of military arms, but the old pattern of military relations, whether in the form of military pacts or of overseas bases, has become outmoded from the third-world perspective. Thus there is a need to find new forms of military co-operation which are both more flexible and respect the sovereignty of third-world countries.

The relationship between the Third World and the West needs broader foundations, and this implies, first, that Western countries (and especially the United States) should formulate more comprehensive, consistent, credible and long-term policies towards the Soviet Union because the relationship between the United States and the Soviet Union remains the most important factor in maintaining world peace and security. It is a relationship that must be handled with great care and sensitivity, for a host of contradictions are embedded in it; the need to co-operate must coexist with inevitable competition. Specifically, the conclusion of SALT II and preparations for SALT III are urgent tasks, because they touch upon the main issue in the relationship between the super-powers. Arrangements to ensure a balance in conventional weapons and to regulate arms sales to the Third World are also needed. Relations in the economic fields should be promoted with a view to lessening the tensions between the two countries. Last, there is a need to seek arrangements through which both sides could support the creation of regional order in the Third World. These would limit the rights of outside powers to intervene and would aim to prevent either super-power from achieving dominance.

At the same time, the United States and her Allies in Western Europe and Japan must restructure their relationships to conform to the new realities. The United States is no longer the dominant power that she was, in either political or economic terms, and must share responsibility with her Allies, which implies placing the relationships on a more equal footing. Structuring this relationship may not be easy because, at least in the area of defence, both Western Europe and Japan are still critically dependent upon the United States. This dependence could be circumvented, however, if new mechanisms of consultation could be developed between the United States, Western Europe and Japan. The issues affecting the relationships between these countries has expanded beyond their traditional concerns. For example, the security of the Arabian Gulf can no longer be separated from the security of Western Europe and Japan. The EEC and NATO cannot cope with new areas of interest outside Europe. The Summit Meeting in Venice in June 1980, at which political and security matters were discussed, may indicate a desire to reshape the Western (and Japanese) relationship.

It is equally encouraging to see the emergence of a division of responsibilities between the United States, Western Europe and Japan. France is attempting to take care of the security of French Africa and maintains a naval squadron in Djibouti on the Indian Ocean. West Germany is providing greater economic assistance to Turkey and Pakistan. Japan is increasing her political role and has supported ASEAN in its efforts to bring about the stabilization of South-east Asia.

Overall, it can be said that the capabilities of the Western countries are still very credible, provided that they can co-operate constructively and can formulate workable policies regarding the division of responsibilities between them in the political and economic fields, in the transfer of science and technology and in the military field. Because the division of labour includes an increased defence commitment by Western Europe and Japan, the resources of the United States can more readily be diverted to maintain a power balance in the Arabian Gulf.

Finally, relations between the Third World and the Western world in various fields must involve more concrete co-operative programmes. To ensure long-lasting co-operation, mechanisms of dialogue and form for consultation must be permanently established, ASEAN, for instance, can be most useful in this respect for the South-east Asian region. Also, the division of labour among the Western countries and Japan must be extended to their relations with the Third World. The United States alone cannot take care of all the areas of the world. Furthermore, the too obvious presence of the United States might be disadvantageous in some circumstances.

19

The foregoing proposals will depend to a large extent upon initiatives originating in the United States. It is there that adjustments are taking place, and they will affect the processes of decision-making and the American political dynamic. To cope with these adjustments, the United States needs a more consistent leadership and a better relationship between the Executive Branch and the Legislative Branch. Equally important is the performance of the American economy. In all these respects the Allies and friends of the United States must give support. It should not be forgotten that the United States has contributed massively to the maintenance of an international order which has brought relative stability to the world for the last 35 years. In the years to come the United States will face great challenges and it is in the interests of all that she should be able to cope with them.

The Soviet Union, on the other hand, does not have the potential to assist the Third World in its search for prosperity. The Soviet Union is respected only for her military might. Newly independent countries may be attracted to the Soviet Union initially because of the anti-colonialist flavour of her political propaganda, but most third-world countries see her only as a balancing power, when such a balance is considered necessary, or as a source of military hardware.

It is likely that a decreased American presence and credibility in a particular area could create a situation in which the countries of that area feel the pressure of the Soviet Union directly. Such has been the case after the Soviet invasion of Afghanistan. This invasion was seen by most third-world countries as a violation of the sovereignty of an independent, non-aligned, developing country. Whatever the reason for the action, most third-world countries reacted strongly against it.

Nevertheless, this does not mean that the Third World will not admit the *legitimate* presence of the Soviet Union, for she is a superpower that cannot be discounted. It may even be necessary to invite the Soviet Union to join international efforts directed at maintaining some form of regional order in parts of the Third World. She could become a balancing factor in certain regions, such as East or Southeast Asia, especially with respect to China.

On the other hand, concern is expressed in the Third World with regard to the future direction of Soviet global policies. Great uncertainities arise from the fact that the military power of the Soviet Union could be used to obtain distinct advantages, especially in the second half of the 1980s, when the Soviet Union is expected to undergo many difficult internal changes, perhaps involving radical adjustments in policy, whether arising from a change in leadership, from economic stagnation, from resource scarcity or from demographic shifts which may create imbalances in the ethnic composition of her population.

Therefore many in the Third World tend to argue that all must have the courage to continue to work towards the creation of an environment in which detente could work. In such an environment the Third World could find the opportunity both to develop and to participate in international affairs. The development of national resilience will help to guarantee world stability, for it could prevent the East–West conflict from escalating through the exploitation of the national vulnerabilities that exist in many parts of the Third World. Consequently, the Third World could become a stabilizing factor in the world as a whole.

Sources of Third-World Conflict

UDO STEINBACH

The Soviet invasion of Afghanistan and the deterioration in East–West relations which accompanied it have clearly shown just how important parts of the Third World are for the development of international relations and for the global balance of power. If there is any substance in the comparison between the present situation in international politics and that of 1914, it is the fear that a global conflict involving the super-powers could be sparked off by events in a remote corner of the world and that regional political tension could, by means of a largely unpredictable process of escalation, develop into a major international confrontation. The Third World is the scene of numerous conflicts with a wide variety of antecedent causes and varying degrees of importance. In this paper conflict is used in the broadest sense of the term and embraces wars between states, revolutions and social, political, ethnic and sectarian tensions which, even if they have not developed into open crises, have international implications.

In any attempt to discover common denominators among the profusion of conflicts, potential conflicts and sources of conflict in the Third World, one is faced with a particular and fundamental problem – bewildering variety. The causes of conflicts in the Third World (in Africa, in the Middle East, in South and Southeast Asia and in Latin America) result from cultural, social, economic and political factors of such a specific nature that it is only through generalizing to a very high degree that common features can be determined. Whether operationally useful conclusions can be drawn from these findings for a policy directed towards the Third World may be highly questionable.

It is only comparatively recently that we have become conscious of the problem of regional conflicts and of their sources as vital elements in international politics. This awareness is symptomatic of a steadily increasing interest on the part of the great powers in the Third World as a factor of political importance for East–West relations. Political influence or a military presence in the key regions of the Third World can have a lasting effect on the global balance of power and East–West relations.

How can the sources of regional conflicts be categorized? And in what circumstances can regional conflicts and potential conflicts influence international politics? Moreover, what prospects are there for settling conflicts, eliminating their causes and thus achieving the long-term stabilization of the Third World? This paper sets out to provide answers to these questions.

The Categories of Conflict

The numerous causes of third-world conflict might be summarized in four main categories: national fragmentation, inequitable development, cultural clashes, and liberation movements. This categorization may imply greater clarity and precision than is either intended or demonstrable, but, for the purposes of analysis, the causes would appear to be separable.

National Fragmentation Within the Third World

The structure of the Third World along national lines forms the political framework within which conflicts there arise and then come to a head. National structures used not to be a part of the political or cultural traditions of either the Middle East or Africa. The concept of 'nation', introduced by the colonial powers or by small elites who saw in it the prerequisite for the fulfilment of their own political aspirations, materialized in a way which, in many cases, went against territorial, ethnic, religious, geographical or culturo-historical traditions. During a long historical process characterized by numerous conflicts, the driving forces of nationalism in Europe led to a sort of land consolidation in which the national state was largely an expression of 'national' pretensions, and this has resulted in the inner consolidation of single states. In the Third World, however, externally imposed divisions of national states have set going processes in which newly created 'national' pretensions come into conflict with traditional structures. What this means in practice in the Middle East, to take one example, is that the division of the community of Moslems and Arabs into numerous nation states since World War I has not only to a large extent ignored the traditional ethnic and religious groupings but has also resulted in the governments of the various national entities starting to lodge claims which are almost bound to lead to conflict with other countries. The fragmentation within these emerging nation-states coincides with the geopolitical fragmentation of the Third World itself. Ethnic minorities and sectarian divisions are the consequences of this development, as are many of the conflicts between states as well as the domestic conflicts within particular countries, in particular demands for autonomy.

The Problems of Development

This term covers a whole range of problems of an economic, social and political nature. On the one hand, there is the fact that the majority of the third-world countries are barely capable of reaching a level of economic development at which even the basic needs of the population are met. This conflicts with the fact that no government in the Third World can escape the need to pursue the socio-political and politico-economic values and objectives of the industrialized countries. They must try to increase per capita income, provide for a fairer distribution of income and wealth and, at least to some extent, move away from dependence on the industrialized nations. Thus the Third World becomes the scene of unrest and impatience, which causes renewed power and political struggles and intensifies the conflict between rival ideologies.

Yet the problems of development are not only to be found at an economic level. Many of the tensions and conflicts arise from the inability of ruling elites to pay due regard to the demands of individuals, social groups or religious and ethnic communities for greater participation in political life, demands which arise

as a result of the process of economic and social transformation, itself a by-product of industrialization. In most cases such a process of modernization has not been accompanied by a strengthening of appropriate political institutions or by a fairer distribution of social and economic assets in favour of the individuals, groups and communities which comprise the state.

Cultural Clashes

Patterns of conflict are developing at the cultural level also. These have found their most extreme expression in Iran and can only be detected distantly in other parts of the Third World. For the present such patterns are most clearly expressed by the catchword 're-Islamization'. Although the emergence of tensions at a cultural level cannot be separated from the main body of development problems, culture and religion do constitute unique factors as mobilizing elements. The survival of cultural traditions in a rapid process of modernization and the manner in which the masses are mobilized differ from revolutionary processes with a purely social or economic background. Western-style economic rationality, the cultural foundation of the Western course of development and Western civilization are all rejected. Instead the aim is to revitalize the native culture and to adapt it to the needs of the modern state. This conflict of cultures is expressed within a country itself in the confrontation between native chauvinism on the one hand and Westernized elites on the other. An international dimension is added to the domestic through the rejection of all external influence and power. However, the experience of developments in Iran teaches us that even within a chauvinist movement new frictions can arise.

Liberation Movements

Although many aspects of liberation movements overlap or border on the first three categories, it may be helpful to introduce liberation movements as a fourth – and thus separate – cause of conflict in the Third World. Generally speaking, liberation movements aim to remove political frameworks established during the days of colonial rule. They include such diverse aims as the achievement of independence, the shaking off of the rule of white

22

minorities, the breaking away from existing national entities or the instigation of upheavals of a socio-revolutionary nature. A characteristic feature of liberation movements is that they are often supported by a group of third-world countries, the reason being that the objectives and intentions of liberation movements themselves often reflect the unsolved political problems which are characteristic of many parts of the Third World.

Theory and Reality

Categorization of the sources of conflict in the Third World shows how the elements of conflict are present in, and between, many third-world states. Actual examples of conflict illustrate that these elements can be seen singly or in combination. The pattern of conflict based on nationalism can be seen both in wars between states and in domestic struggles in which the government of a country is at war with parts of the population living within the country's boundaries. There have been too many wars between states and too many tense confrontations in the Third World since the end of World War II to make it necessary to enumerate them all. In the last decade alone troops occupied part of Kuwait in 1973; there was border conflict between the two Yemens in 1979; and there is war between Iraq and the new regime in Iran. In Africa there has been war between Ethiopia and Somalia (1977–78) and the invasion of Uganda by Tanzania and of Chad by Libya. In South-east Asia the persistent conflict between Vietnam, Cambodia and Thailand reflects the fact that the political boundaries left behind by the colonial powers concealed unresolved disputes and cut across ethnic lines.

The internal conflicts arising from nationalism have nearly always been concerned with the problems associated with the integration of ethnic or religious groups. Generally speaking, the pattern of states which has grown up in the Third World during the past decades has not been consolidated. Bangladesh's break from Pakistan was the most profound manifestation of separatism, but in the Middle East the problems of ethnic and religious groups have recently increased. The extreme tensions or open conflicts in Iran, Turkey, Pakistan and Lebanon (to mention only the most dramatic cases) have subjected the constellation of nation states in the Middle East to a severe test. Looking at Africa, although the Sudan stands as a rare example of a (so far) successful solution on the basis of autonomy for ethnic groups, in the Horn of Africa an explosive crisis has developed as a result of ethnic separatism in Ethiopia and Somali irredentism in the Ogaden. Chad and Zaire are further examples of just how endangered Africa still is by the risk of ethnic conflicts, at times heightened by religious differences. A lack of participation in decision-making, the fact that all do not enjoy equal rights and the absence of autonomy are the main reasons why many minority ethnic groups have not identified themselves with the states to which they belong.

To a considerable extent, internal conflicts and tensions in third-world countries arise through failures in economic and political development. Putting it briefly some or all of the following phenomena are observable:

—The economy's weakness leads to discontent, provoking 'impatient' groups in society to attempt to seize power.
—Weak political institutions are destroyed by rival forces within the state.
—Existing socio-political and ideological concepts are called into question and new 'revolutionary' ideas are introduced.
—Out-of-date, traditional social structures are replaced by the forces of modernization.
—The participation of the various ethnic or regional groups in the economic and political life of the state is neglected, leading to an intensification of tensions.

Latin America offers classic examples of the interaction of economic weakness, structurally flawed political systems and political lability. The most recent evidence of this is supplied by Bolivia. One can also point to examples in the Middle East during the 1950s and 1960s and in Africa the *coup d'état* in Liberia in April 1980 is only the latest of a whole series of conflicts. The origins of all these are to be found in this 'development deficit'. One could also add to this list the revolution in Ethiopia, the two coups in Afghanistan (1973 and 1978), the uprising directed against Idi Amin in Uganda and the overthrow of a number of other dictatorial African potentates in the recent past. In many of the examples mentioned the army was involved because the armed forces enjoy a privileged position as a result of the training and education of their members and because, as one of the relatively few organized bodies, the army is in a position to play a decisive role in countries which have, in many cases, weak and unstable political systems. Just how severely an economic crisis can upset the fabric even of countries with relatively mature political systems is shown by the recent destabilization of Turkey.

The 'development problem' intrudes into foreign policy and international politics generally when the attempt is made to export a particular ideology, or *Weltanschauung*, as with Nasser's attempt to export his version of Arab socialism to all parts of the Arab world as the necessary prerequisite for the modernization and resurgence of Arab countries. Nasser's disciple, Colonel Qaddafi, is following in his footsteps, although he is operating with a more limited agenda.

Cultural conflict has arisen as a reaction against a course of development which has too often been based on the Western model. Such conflict has reached a critical stage in the shape of so-called 're-Islamization' and has indeed, for the first time, broken out into an open conflict in Iran. Islam, with its synthesis of religious beliefs and social organization, offers a political alternative which claims to be able to catch up on the West in the field of development. Certain elements of the conflict which has broken out in Iran can also be observed, in a more or less pronounced form, in many other Islamic countries. The Islamic revival has resulted in the destabilization of large parts of the Middle East and the symptoms of this process can also be seen in Egypt and Syria, as well as in the secular state of Turkey.

Liberation movements in the Third World have always attracted considerable world-wide attention. In addition to the 'classical' liberation movements such as the Eritrean Liberation Front (ELF) and the Palestine Liberation Organization (PLO), which were founded in the early 1960s, many other organizations have emerged in the course of the process of decolonization with widely differing aims: for example, numerous movements operate in Ethiopia for the overthrow of 'Amharic colonialism' (in other words, the destruction of Ethiopia). Liberation movements in Southern Africa call for the termination of white supremacy, and the *Polisario* are fighting for the independence of what used to be the Spanish Sahara. However, in the main all liberation movements which are directed against the former white colonists, either directly or indirectly, enjoy the vocal and sometimes practical support of a large part of the Third World. In contrast, the movements which aim to destroy particular political structures in the Third World find themselves in an ambiguous position. Polarization within the Third World follows, and this can lead in turn to the aggravation of conflict as, for example, in Ethiopia. This is also evident where the political regime has existed only for a very short time, as in Morocco's take-over of what was previously the Spanish Sahara. Generally speaking, however, it remains true that the agents most likely to bring third-world conflict into the international arena are liberation movements.

Nevertheless, conflicts in the Third World can rarely be traced back to a single cause. It is much nearer the truth to say that in most cases various causes intermingle and are mutually reinforcing. For example, the so-called 'Islamic revolution' in Iran grew out of a socially and politically based conflict, but it was only after the religious element had been introduced that it was possible to mobilize the masses in active opposition against the Shah. In the case of conflicts involving ethnic or sectarian groups, the national conflict pattern is often related to shortcomings in the process of development. Nationalist pretensions and interests are conjured up only in order to legitimize the pretensions of a particular party or individual as, for example, in the case of Afghanistan's recurring claims to Pushtunistan, or when the armed forces of a country dress up their seizure of power in the cloak of 'national interests'. Conversely, power politics at the national level are quite often legitimized by demands for social change in other countries; for years Nasser linked his claim that Egypt should play a special role in the Arab world (with him as leader) with the propagation of the progressive doctrine of Arab socialism. In the conflicts in Indochina, particularly with regard to Vietnam's policy towards Cambodia, a mixture of aggressive nationalism and ideological justification can be discerned.

Attempts to categorize the causes of conflicts – in any case a questionable undertaking – become totally inadequate in the case of a regional conflict as complicated as the Arab–Israeli confrontation. The underlying pattern of conflict reflects, without doubt, the structuring of the Middle East along national lines which took place after World War I. The division of the Arab region into nation-states and the creation of the state of Israel meant that two mutually exclusive sets of interests had been created. The Islamic view that the 'territory of Islam' is indivisible and cannot be subjected to any foreign rule resolves itself into the Palestinians' claim to a state of their own. The undertaking to settle the Jews in the 'Promised Land', which forms the basis of Zionism, meant the existence of the state of Israel. As if this were not enough, the internal instability of the majority of the Arab regimes, the causes of which are to be found in their 'development problems' in the broad sense of the term used above, further complicates the issues. On many occasions during the recent past these regimes have tried to use the fact of the existence of the state of Israel and the Palestinian problem to legitimize their own rule. The Palestinian liberation movements represent an attempt – in view of the inability of the established Arab states to solve the problem in the interest of the Arabs – to undertake to solve the problem on their own.

Darkening Prospects

The prospects for a long-term stabilization of the Third World are not encouraging. There are certain symptoms which point to a general deterioration of stability. One is that the number of people who, as a result of bilateral conflicts or domestic violence, have been forced to leave their homes to become refugees has reached an unprecedentedly high level. Vietnam, Cambodia, Thailand, Somalia, Ethiopia, Sudan, Djibouti, Chad, Uganda, Afghanistan, Iran and Pakistan are all involved in more or less serious refugee problems. Palestinian refugees greatly complicate the politics of the Middle East. On the one hand, this is evidence of the use of more radical methods on the part of some regimes in the Third World when pursuing their own interests or in seeking solutions to existing problems. On the other hand, the flood of refugees brings enormous economic problems for most of the countries which admit them, problems which these countries cannot solve on their own and which their own precariously balanced economies cannot withstand.

Despite a nominal increase in development aid from the industrialized nations of the West and from the oil-producing countries, investment remains much too low to maintain a rate of development in the Third World that would 'solve' the 'development problems' these countries face or to have a fundamentally stabilizing effect. Only very few of the developing countries have the resources to reach the stage of 'take-off'. The majority will remain underdeveloped. The gap between these countries and the industrialized nations can only grow wider, and tensions between many third-world countries are likely to increase.

The high price that the developing countries have to pay for oil is also an indication that the oil-producing nations, despite their belonging (in most cases) to the group of developing countries, are chiefly concerned with furthering their own interests. A sort of 'third-world solidarity' aimed at solving the existing 'development problems' appears virtually non-existent. For the foreseeable future, impatience and disappointment will grow, leading to further conflicts.

The inherent and persistent instability of the majority of third-world states has meant the establishment of armed forces of relatively large dimensions to enable regimes to hold on to power, to hold the state together and to defend it against the competing claims of other nations. Perceptions of greater threats at home and from abroad lead to the assumption that in future an ever-increasing share of national expenditure will be spent on armaments. This is true not only of the oil-producing states which can afford the colossal sums involved (Saudi Arabia, Libya, Iraq, the Sheikhdoms or Indonesia) but also of poor countries (such as Ethiopia, Somalia, India or Pakistan). This entails an increased economic burden, and it heightens the perception of mutual threat with a wide range of political consequences. On the one hand, external threats can be exploited to distract attention from internal tensions and 'development problems'. This clearly has the effect of further aggravating mutual threat perceptions. On the other hand, an army always represents a danger to fragile political structures, such as those that exist in the Arabian Peninsula or in Africa. The heavy expenditure by the Shah on the armed forces of Iran was used ultimately as a weighty argument against him, for they came to be seen more as an improper waste of money and as an instrument of a hated regime than as contributing to the country's security.

Great-Power Rivalries

The intervention of the great powers in regional or local conflicts is no new occurrence. The history of the 1950s and 1960s is full of interventions of a direct or indirect nature by the United States and the former colonial powers. Iran (1953), Suez (1956) and Lebanon (1958) form a chain of events which came to a climax in Vietnam. Yet these interventions were not able to stop forces of liberation from gaining power in many parts of the Third World, forces which associate the West with imperialism and colonialism and see in favourable relations with the Soviet Union the chance of pursuing an independent political course or more rapid economic development. By the beginning of the 1970s the Soviet Union had built up a military capacity (combined with the political will to play the role of a world power) which made it possible for her to safeguard her influence in the Third World by direct means with the help of a variety of political, economic and military tools. It was no accident that it was in the Middle East that the two super-powers first came to face each other directly. The occasion was the fourth Arab–Israeli War in 1973, when the American armed forces were put on alert in order to deter a possible Soviet intervention on the side of the Arab states. The Soviet-Cuban intervention in Angola, which settled the power struggle among the rival liberation movements in favour of the Marxist MPLA, was the first indication of a new interest on the part of the super-powers in developments in the Third World. Since then, the United States – after some years of non-involvement in the Third World as a result of the Vietnam experience – has begun to show considerably more interest in Africa and elsewhere. The analysis of the sources of conflict in the Third World has taken on a new dimension.

Super-power rivalry is increasingly affecting what used to be simply regional affairs, and the rivalry is likely to intensify the conflicts which already exist. However it is also true that because the super-powers regard the Third World in the context of East–West relations, regional conflict is likely to increase the danger of a deterioration of relations between them because of their involvement.

The rivalry between the super-powers in the Third World varies. It is obviously at its most intense where political or economic interests are deeply involved. It is again no accident that it was in the Middle East that the super-powers first competed for influence. This is easily explained by the geopolitical significance of the region and, especially for the West, its importance for energy supplies. In the 'Northern Tier', in the Gulf and in the Arabian Peninsula there are very direct connections between fundamental regional instability and international interest. The potential for conflict is great, and the causes are likely to be extremely complex. Social and political conflicts, both open and below the surface, are present in Turkey, in Iran and in Pakistan. Border incidents between Iraq and Iran were commonplace for many years and have now resulted in open warfare between them, and there is a great deal of speculation about the stability of the Arabian Peninsula in view of the increasing strains between economic modernization and social and political conservatism. Through the invasion of Afghanistan the Soviet Union has shifted the political and military balance of power in the whole region somewhat in her favour. Any further destabilization of any one of the countries of the 'Northern Tier' could result in fundamental changes in the international power balance. The Soviet Union is interested in perpetuating this sense of crisis for she tends to favour the forces which want to abolish the existing political structure in favour of socialist-orientated systems.

In the past there seems to have been some sort of unwritten agreement concerning the spheres of influence of the super-powers in the Third World. According to this 'pact', Latin America was just as much a part of the American sphere of influence as the Gulf or Saudi Arabia. Afghanistan, on the other hand, seems to have been treated as if she lay within the

Soviet sphere of influence long before the recent invasion. Africa was, to a large extent, an unmarked map. The West has been alarmed by the Soviet invasion of Afghanistan, viewed, as it were, against a backdrop of the Soviet interventions in Angola and Ethiopia, the long-standing Soviet presence in South Yemen and the rapid destabilization of Iran. It would, seem therefore, that a new era is being ushered in, characterized more by rivalry than by accommodation; both sides appear to be seeking to increase their influence in areas which they consider politically and economically vital – no matter where. The possibility cannot be ruled out, therefore, that the Soviet Union will make efforts to exploit the growing instability in Latin America in order to expand her influence there.

More than the West, the Soviet Union has used conflict in parts of the Third World as a means of exerting influence. The growth of Soviet arms deliveries to Africa during the 1970s (and in particular since 1977) is a significant indication of Moscow's determination to increase its influence over the regimes involved. The Soviet Union, in following this policy, is prepared not only to accept the conflicts that arise but even to take some risks, for she sees conflicts as a way to promote the establishment of centralized, socialist-orientated states.

This willingness on the part of the Soviet Union to exploit conflicts in order to extend her influence has increased tension in many parts of the Third World. This is true for practically all of Africa, for the Middle East (where the Soviet Union has intervened in recent years) and for Afghanistan, where the internal resistance to the Soviet presence threatens to involve neighbouring states. In Ethiopia some Arab states are involved through their support for liberation movements, especially in Eritrea. In Indochina, Vietnam, supported by the Soviet Union, is in conflict with almost all neighbouring countries, including the People's Republic of China. Even if one may justifiably ask how long the Soviet Union will be able to pay the high costs of such a policy, there are no reasons to believe that she will now give up what has been, until now, a quite successful strategy.

A Blueprint for Stability
Despite the determination of the super-powers to increase their influence over certain countries in the Third World, the forces of change defy, to a considerable degree, the control and direction of external powers. But because almost all internal conflicts in the Third World are between groups seeking to change the *status quo* and other groups fighting to maintain it, the Soviet Union has developed remarkable flexibility in managing to side with the forces of change. The West, on the other hand, as has become perfectly clear in the case of Iran, tries to collaborate with regimes which are facing growing internal opposition for the sake of the stability of the region. This dilemma is likely to emerge again in Africa, elsewhere in the Middle East and maybe even in Latin America. This raises the question of whether the Western concept of stability (in the sense of maintaining the *status quo*) is, in fact, adequate in view of the structural changes which are bound to take place in the Third World. In the past the Western nations (and especially the United States) have tended to focus exclusively on stability as the desirable aim, which has led to efforts to maintain existing and superficially stable political systems at the cost of losing influence over alternative political figures and movements.

It is obvious that a military deterrent alone cannot prevent conflicts from breaking out in the Third World. It is much more important to reduce the local and regional tension and so the conflict potential in the Third World. Three long-term prospects are worth considering in this context.

First, it would be particularly helpful if the regional organizations could be strengthened. For all its weaknesses, the Arab League for example, has repeatedly proved during recent years that it enjoys at least some moral authority, which has enabled it to influence the management of certain conflicts of both an internal and external nature. This is true also of the Organization for African Unity (OAU), for the principles contained in its Charter reduced the tensions which surfaced when former colonies gained their independence. Many potential boundary disputes have not developed into conflict. In Latin America, too, multilateral organizations have enjoyed a fine record. Finally, in South-east Asia ASEAN has demonstrated the stability which can be achieved when states which have similar interests work together to reduce conflict.

27

The second avenue to explore should be guarantees of the independence of the countries of the Third World and of the non-involvement of external powers. Although there are few grounds for optimism, this much is clear: only genuine independence and a 'hands off' attitude on the part of the great powers can put an end to the vicious circle in which local instability brings super-power interference which then increases instability. Such a policy would have to be based on a system of agreements not to intervene and respect for the sovereignty of other states. Only through a reduction in the level of regional tension and perceptions of threat can arms races in the Third World be controlled or reduced.

Finally, it is necessary to attend to development needs as a decisive step towards the stabilization of many countries of the Third World. Since it is hardly possible for most of them to develop on their own, it is vitally important that development aid be increased considerably. In the long term it is possible that aid will prove to be the West's strongest suit as far as relations with the Third World are concerned. Development aid should proceed within the context of the North–South dialogue and should aim to set up a new world economic order which would give the Third World a fair share of the world's resources and would open up the prospects of comprehensive development.

Realistically, one must assume that, for the time being at least, regional conflicts will continue and that the West will endeavour to prevent the emergence of changes which are believed to be detrimental to its interests. Nevertheless, the West should try to gain a better understanding of local and regional factors and should acquire a credible capacity to help friendly groups or regimes. The West must realize that its interests are being affected more and more in the Third World. It can no longer afford to stand back and watch the situation deteriorate to its disadvantage, while the Soviet Union makes political capital out of the conflicts and tensions which continue to plague the states of the Third World.

Outside Military Forces in Third-World Conflicts

Assessing the utility of military power in the Third World is complicated by a number of factors: uncertain data, vague public statements of objectives and methodological shortcomings are all debilitating; most important, however, we lack a commonly understood standard by which to measure its usefulness.

One could assess utility narrowly on the basis of the immediate operational objectives of the decision-makers who choose to make use of military strength. Take the Soviet intervention in Angola in 1975, for example. With the aid of naval forces, Cuban combat troops and their own logistical services, Soviet decision-makers sought to ensure the victory of the MPLA in the Angolan civil war, to defeat the factions backed by the West and to cause the South African troops that had intervened in the conflict to withdraw. On the basis of these operational objectives, one would conclude that Soviet military power had been useful: the Western-supported UNITA and FNL factions were defeated; the South African troops retreated; and the MPLA now constitutes the official Angolan government. Of course, such assessments are perishable; there continues to be lively conflict in Angola, at least in the south, in which South African forces at times intervene and which requires the continuing presence of Cuban troops and Soviet advisers to ensure the MPLA's continued success. So Soviet immediate operational objectives were attained, but for how long?

Moreover, in judging the utility of military power, one should pass beyond the strictly subjective criteria of the decision-makers' own purposes to a more comprehensive and objective assessment. Interventions, like the Soviet intervention in Angola, have consequences which should influence judgments, if not of the immediate utility of military power, at least of the wisdom of its use over the medium and the longer term.

For example, looking again at the Soviet Union's Angolan intervention, one might list the following consequences on the positive side:

—Continued Angolan dependence on Soviet and Cuban military assistancé for security has resulted in the accretion of Soviet political influence with the Angolan government. For example, Angola was one of the very few non-Warsaw Pact nations to vote in 1980 against UN condemnation of the Soviet occupation of Afghanistan.
—Soviet influence has resulted in more tangible benefits, including (intermittently) staging rights for Soviet reconnaissance aircraft flying between bases in the Murmansk area and Cuba.
—More broadly, Soviet willingness to aid a nationalist movement under attack by South African forces seems to have provided certain positive benefits in terms of African perceptions of the Soviet Union's willingness and capacity to aid in the continuing struggle for African liberation.
—Less tangibly and even more broadly, Angola was the first of several incidents that helped to create perceptions among political leaders throughout the world of Soviet military competence and decisiveness which, over the long term, could cause some to think twice before taking positions that could conceivably precipitate new Soviet interventions. This reputation for military competence could be a decisive factor in crises. Perhaps more important, some believe, it could subtly influence countless decisions of a more routine character.

The Soviet intervention in Angola was not without its negative consequences, however, among which were the following:

—Soviet political influence in Angola has not

29

been sufficient to prevent sporadic political flirtations between Angola and the West or mutually beneficial economic relations. To take the most obvious example, among their other chores Cuban troops help to protect the Gulf Oil Company's efforts to exploit Angola's petroleum resources in the Cabinda area.

—Tangible Soviet military gains in Angola have been rather limited and compare unfavourably even with the *direct* costs of the operation. This situation may change and may have as much to do with Soviet preferences as Angolan choices, but so far the Soviet armed forces have given far more than they have received in Angola.

—In Africa more generally the influence acquired by opposing South African forces may have been offset, to a certain extent, by concern over Soviet interventionary propensities. Much as most African leaders may have applauded Soviet assistance to defeat South African forces, this demonstration of the new global reach of Soviet armed forces must have inspired trepidation in the hearts of many.

—Finally, in the global arena it seems evident that the Soviet intervention in Angola had a marked negative effect on relations between the United States and the Soviet Union and initiated a political process in the United States which has all but destroyed any hopes Soviet leaders might have harboured of economic and political gains as a result of co-operation. It will be recalled that the Angolan intervention, because of its effect on Republican party politics in 1976, caused the Ford Administration to defer conclusion of the Vladivostok Strategic Arms Limitation Accord. This process was replayed among a bipartisan political constituency later in the 1970s, causing the Carter Administration to continue to delay the conclusion of SALT and otherwise contributing to a broad deterioration in American–Soviet relations.

Many other costs and benefits of the Angolan intervention could be described. How then, does one assess the balance? On the whole, was it 'useful' for the Soviet Union to deploy military power in Angola in 1975? The answer, of course, depends on the value assigned to each consequence. Was the Soviet Union's greater reputation for military competence more or less important than the incremental degradation in American–Soviet relations? Obviously, individuals differ in such judgments.

Moreover, any such judgment is susceptible to change as events continue to unfold and is coloured vividly by events that have already occurred. Isolating the consequences for American–Soviet relations of the Angolan intervention alone, abstracting its effects from subsequent Soviet interventions, like that on the Horn of Africa, is an extraordinarily difficult task. In essence, one must look at the stream of history and ask: if this one incident had not occurred, what might have ensued? And would that alternative course of events have been better or worse, both from the perspective of the nation making use of military power and from the perspective of the overall interests of mankind?

Obviously, these are not questions that can be answered in this short paper; we have to settle for something less. In the past several years a number of empirical studies have been completed which describe and assess the post-war history of American and Soviet military operations.[1] Among other issues, these studies have addressed the question of the utility of military power in the Third World. What I propose to do is to highlight briefly the major features of these military operations, to discuss what seem to have been the determinants of their successes and failures and to examine some implications of these findings for future policies of the Western Alliance.

The Record
There have been literally hundreds of incidents since 1945 in which external powers have sought to influence the outcome of events in what we now call the Third World through the use of military power. The history of these incidents seems to divide rather neatly into three phases: 1945–56, 1957–66 and 1966 to the present day.

Between 1945 and 1956 relatively few such incidents occurred but those that did often involved sizeable military operations. The 1950 North Korean invasion of South Korea, for example, prompted a significant use of American and Western armed forces but led to a decline in American involvement elsewhere, as both the demands of the war on military resources and the subsequent adverse political reaction caused American decision-makers to consider new commitments only reluctantly. Britain, France and other Western nations also contributed military units to the Korean conflict, of course, and in addition utilized their armed forces in various colonial wars in Southeast Asia and Africa. Soviet armed forces, on the other hand, were only rarely seen outside Europe during this period. A few incidents in China soon after the war, a possible supporting role in the Korean conflict and the brief occupation of Azerbaijan were the only instances of Soviet military deployments in what is now the Third World until the late 1950s.

During the second phase, from 1957 to 1966, there were both a steep rise in Western activism and the first stirrings of Soviet involvement. American armed forces figured in a sharply rising number of incidents each year, particularly in South-east Asia and the Caribbean. This trend peaked in 1965, when, repeating the pattern of the 1950s, the beginnings of a massive American military involvement – this time in Indochina – resulted first in a reluctance to commit military resources elsewhere and, subsequently, in a policital deterrent against new involvements overseas.

The armed forces of the other Western powers were also heavily involved in the Third World during most of this period. To name only a few examples: France fought in North Africa until 1963; Britain and the Netherlands confronted Mr Sukarno's Indonesia until 1965; and British forces were seen in support of various regimes in the Middle East. Even after independence was granted to many nations in Africa, British, French and Belgian troops were used to influence, and sometimes to determine, the outcome of local political conflicts. France particularly seems to have defined a special role for herself in this regard. According to Information Minister Alain Peyrefitte, French armed forces intervened in Africa on 12 occasions between 1960 and 1964, a trend which seemed to be gathering momentum until an awkward incident in Gabon led to a temporary respite in French activism.[2]

The Soviet Union experimented with the use of military power in the Third World during this phase. The Kaplan study[3] identifies 16 incidents during the period, in such widely disparate locations as the Congo, the Levant, and South-east Asia. No real muscle was applied in these incidents, however, and for the most part the activity constituted a futile attempt to demonstrate that, like the United States, the Soviet Union was a great power to be reckoned with throughout the globe.

The post-1966 phase has been marked by a relative decline in American and other Western interventions in the Third World and a much greater frequency of Soviet military activity. The United States, of course, was not entirely quiescent during this period; apart from the war in South-east Asia, there were several major deployments of American military forces, particularly in connection with events in the Middle East. American armed forces were also used in less dramatic ways to underscore changing US relations with a number of states in Africa and South-west Asia, particularly in the vicinity of the Arabian Gulf. Yet it was not until 1976 that the Vietnam-induced restraint on American military activism began to ease, and then only gradually until the twin shocks of the hostage crisis in Tehran and the Soviet invasion of Afghanistan in late 1979.

Other Western powers also tended to remain militarily aloof from events in the Third World. There were isolated incidents, such as the use of Belgian troopers in Zaire's Shaba Province in 1978, or the rescue by German commandos of a hijacked Lufthansa aircraft in Mogadiscio in 1977, but such events provide little more than interesting footnotes. France remains the one exception, particularly in Africa. Since the mid-1960s French forces have been involved in actions to maintain order in Chad, to restore order in Shaba, to preserve political authority in Mauretania and, most recently, to install a new government in the Central African Republic. France has made plain that she intends to pursue such activities as are necessary to protect French interests and the interests of her allies.

The Soviet Union, too, has made it clear that she sees continuing utility in the use of military power in the Third World. The June 1967 Middle East War seems to have marked a turning-point in Soviet policy; Kaplan identifies more than 50 incidents of Soviet military involvement in the Third World since that date.[4] Initiation of this new activism coincided with a significant change in Soviet politico-military doctrine. It was at roughly this time that the Soviet Union seems to have concluded that super-power military competition, confrontation and even conflict was possible in the Third World without excessive danger of escalation to nuclear war.

Apart from Afghanistan, the Soviet Union has concentrated her military activity in two areas. She has been heavily involved in the Middle East, particularly in the Arab–Israeli conflict and in those disputes among Arab nations and sub-national groups in which there appeared to be significant risk that the United States might become involved, such as the 1970 Jordanian Civil War. The Soviet Union has also been quite active in Africa. In addition to her substantial operations in Angola and Ethiopia, she has utilized naval visits and other forms of seemingly benevolent military activity to influence political developments and military conflicts in the Western Sahara, Somalia, Sudan, Sierra Leone, Guinea, Ghana and elsewhere. The deployment of some Soviet forces in Cuba, at least on an intermittent basis, and Soviet support for Vietnamese operations against Cambodia and China round out the picture.

A new interventionist power also emerged during this period. Cuban military forces continue to be heavily engaged in the Angolan and Ethiopian conflicts and, at various times, have been reported to have been deployed on the Golan Heights in support of Syria and in the Arabian Peninsula in support of South Yemen. Cuba also maintains advisory military missions in many other nations. The Cuban presence in Africa dates back to the earliest days of the revolutionary regime, and results at least as much from her own revolutionary fervour as from Soviet attempts to use Cuban troops for Soviet purposes; it is misleading to term Cuba a 'Soviet proxy'. Indeed, a case can be made that Fidel Castro led, rather than followed, the Soviet Union into a policy of military activism in Africa.

What did the external powers hope to accomplish in these incidents? Typically, several specific objectives at once, which could generally be catalogued as attempts to influence the outcome of political conflict within a target nation, to protect the interests of a client state in conflict with a local rival or to signal an interest in a local situation for the purpose of influencing the global competition between the great powers.

It is important to note that only in very few incidents, such as the April 1980 American attempt to free the hostages in Tehran, could the objectives of the military operation be secured directly by the armed force itself. In most of the incidents the purposes of the external power's military activity could only be served indirectly; that is, the operational goal of the use of military power was to persuade a foreign decision-maker to take some action (or not to take some action) which, in turn, would result in the achievement of the external power's fundamental objective. These indirect applications of military power constitute 'political' uses of force. In these 'political' incidents armies may have marched and fleets may have sailed, but when all was said and done the utility of entire enterprises depended on the impact of the military operation on the minds of very few individuals. This is a key point in determining the utility of military power in the Third World. It means, of course, that the individual psychology of the targeted decision-maker(s) – his or her goals, prejudices and values, to say nothing of strength of character – will have a major effect on the consequences of an entire operation.

Next it is necessary to consider what types of military forces are most often used in these incidents. Generally, they involve only small units of military force; major deployments are rare. Most often, the forces involved are naval forces. The Navy has taken part in four out of every five incidents in which the United States has intervened in the Third World since 1945. The Navy has been the pre-eminent instrument of Moscow's military diplomacy in the Third World as well. Indeed, it was only after a continuous Soviet naval presence had been established in the Mediterranean, the Indian Ocean and the South Atlantic that relatively frequent Soviet military involvement in these regions began to take place.

This reliance on naval forces results from several factors. First, ships can be moved at less cost and with less logistical difficulty than can ground-based units. Additionally, of the military services, only navies traditionally think of diplomatic operations as part of their mission and thus train for such contingencies. Most important, the employment of naval forces in these situations is less difficult politically than would be the movement of ground-based forces, as it implies less of a commitment. This is also a key factor which bears significantly on the question of utility.

What did the armed forces of external powers actually do in these situations? Very little. In most cases, they established a presence. They moved closer to the scene of conflict or increased their alert status so as to inject the fact of their interest and potential capability into the deliberations of local policy-makers. Only in a few incidents did the external powers' armed forces actually engage in combat or forms of military activity other than manoeuvre.

Finally, we might note that on the whole the United States and the Soviet Union have tended to stay out of each other's way in these incidents; confrontations have been rare. Of the several hundred incidents in which American military forces have played some role since 1945, the Soviet Union has been involved in only one-third. More often than not, when she has become involved, intervention has taken the form of diplomacy and political rhetoric. Soviet military forces – even the threat of Soviet military intervention – has been a factor in less than half of the incidents with any Soviet involvement, or one-sixth of the total number of incidents involving the United States. Of the far fewer number of incidents in which Soviet military forces have been involved, the United States played some part in two-thirds.

Most important, with the exception of the 'Linebacker' operation in Vietnam in 1972, every major confrontation between the United States and the Soviet Union in the Third World has resulted from their mutual entrapment in situations initiated by others. Although in each of these cases both super-powers have made sizeable military deployments, the likelihood of deliberate, violent conflict between them has probably never been very great. Each has seemed to recognize that although they were involved in an intricate and significant minuet, it could be extremely dangerous to provoke the other, and that it was always important to retain the flexibility to permit each other a graceful exit. This fact, too, bears importantly on the question of utility.

Determinants of Success
It is evident, therefore, that decision-makers in many nations believe that military power is often an effective way to secure their objectives in the Third World. This perception is supported by the findings of the three studies mentioned above.[5] It should be emphasized, however, that it is also evident that the pay-off from these military activities tends to decline over time. Even when viewed from the narrow perspective of the decision-makers' own operational objectives, favourable outcomes become less likely as time passes beyond the initial application of military power.

Moreover, the relative effectiveness of military power in the Third World varies markedly with a number of factors. For one, it is essential to distinguish between incidents in which military power is applied primarily to secure objectives directly through military means and those 'political' incidents in which the operational objective of military activity is to cause others to take decisions that, in turn, will secure the mission's primary purposes.

It seems clear that in incidents involving the direct application of military power the decisive factors are the sufficiency of the quantity and the appropriateness of the character of the armed forces applied to the problem. If the forces used by the external power are adequate to the task in sheer military terms, if they are applied with some finesse and if luck doesn't intervene significantly on the other side, then the immediate objectives of the nation intervening in this way are likely to be obtained. As a general rule, this would seem to mean that the direct military operations which are most likely to succeed are those with narrowly defined objectives that can be accomplished rapidly and decisively with relatively small forces.

There are also longer-term consequences of such direct military operations, which are probably beneficial on the whole. In an anarchic international system such as ours, a reputation for military competence and decisiveness is an important good. Not that such a reputation will deter all assaults on a nation's interests, but to some extent such a reputation can cause responsible decision-makers in opposing nations to think twice before taking actions which they believe may provoke a new use of military power. One need not belabour the complement of this rule: continued evidence of military incompetence or indecisiveness can result in others taking liberties with the interests of the faltering military power.

Of course, one cannot wield military power indefinitely (or even successfully) without suffering some adverse consequences. Profligate use of military power, unjustified by reasonable assessments of real interests, can create adverse political effects, as France discovered after a number of successful interventions in Africa in the 1960s and as the Soviet Union may now be learning. Yet on the whole, assuming that military interventions are not too frequent and that minimum necessary force is applied, it would seem to be beneficial in the long term, as well as in terms of the operational objectives of decision-makers, to be able to utilize military power in the Third World in direct defence of legitimate interests.

As already noted, however, the more common interventionary incident is of the 'political' type. This means that the utility of whatever military activity is undertaken will be determined, in the first instance, by the judgments of one man or at most of a few individuals. Let us for example, say, that instead of seeking to free the hostages directly through a commando raid the United States had decided to use military power against Iran in April 1980 but had chosen to apply it indirectly – to threaten or actually to inflict punishment on Iran so as to persuade the Iranian authorities to release the hostages. Assuming that the Soviet Union steered clear of the situation militarily, the United States clearly would have had little difficulty in applying sufficient military power to destroy whatever she believed to be necessary in Iran. But a question would still remain, quite apart from the potential longer-term consequences of such an action: would such military activity have been successful when judged by the operational objective of American decision-makers (i.e., to free the hostages)? Would Ayatollah Khomeini have been persuaded to release the hostages if Iran's petroleum industry had been destroyed? If Iranian ports had been blockaded? If the Iranian armed forces had been decimated? If Iranian holy

places had been targeted? If his own life and the lives of his closest associates had been jeopardized? These are imponderables; yet it is obvious that the character of the particular individual in authority can have a major impact on the utility of military force when applied indirectly for 'political' purposes.

These idiosyncrasies aside, there are certain broad generalizations concerning the utility of military power in the Third World which, while not necessarily valid in any particular situation, do provide some guidance as to likely outcomes.

Indirect applications of military power are more likely to be effective when the specific operational objectives of the external power fit closely with previously established patterns of policy. When the objectives deviate significantly from historic expressions of the intervener's interests, 'political' applications of military force are less likely to be successful; prior expressions of interest include formal treaty commitments, repeated statements by high-level officials over considerable periods of time, routine deployments of military forces and prior applications of military power in similar situations. Essentially, what seems to happen is that the messages that are meant to be transmitted through the activity of military forces are received with more or less credibility depending on the policy context in which they arise. When the military activity seeks to articulate a new commitment, for example, there may be a tendency on the part of its targets to be sceptical of the external power's seriousness and, therefore, a greater reluctance on their part to take the desired actions. On the other hand, when the external power's military activity seeks only to signal a reminder of historic commitments, targets are more likely to find the threatened action credible, and therefore the military demonstration is more likely to achieve its purpose. For example, all other things being equal, reinforcement of the US Sixth Fleet to deter a threat posed to Israel is more likely to achieve its desired end than would such a reinforcement to deter a threat posed, say, to Egypt. Such American actions in support of Israel are well-rehearsed and therefore credible, while Egypt is only recently an ally. This is not to say that it would be impossible for the United States to utilize military power effectively, and indirectly, in defence of Egypt – only that it would be more difficult and therefore would require more dramatic military actions.

The credibility of transmitted messages can also be lesser or greater depending on the character of the military action itself – what Thomas Schelling has called 'the idiom of action'.[6] The firmer the commitment expressed by the military activity, the more likely is the activity to be effective. For example, the insertion of ground forces (or land-based air units) into a situation, which is more difficult politically for an external power, would be more likely to lead to the achievement of the external power's operational objectives than would be the movement of naval forces alone. This is why, for example, the US has in recent years made increasing use of land-based aircraft for political objectives in the Middle East. Deployments of four AWACS aircraft to Saudi Arabia and F–4 squadrons to Egypt seem to have had considerable impact – far more than routine deployment of massive naval forces into the Indian Ocean.

The fact that the external decision-maker is willing to bear the political costs associated with putting troops on the ground in an area of conflict indicates the seriousness with which he views the situation and thus strengthens the credibility of the commitments which the 'political' use of military force is designed to signal. Conversely, in other situations the external power may not value the stakes highly enough to warrant such political costs, in which case the application of naval power makes perfect sense.

Similarly, when the military forces of the external power actually do something beyond establishing a presence, they are more likely to be effective. Engagement in operations of one sort or another seems to express firmer commitments than do military preparations without specific purposes. Establishment of a naval blockade is clearly of greater political significance than a simple naval presence.

An implication that the external power might be willing to run the risk of nuclear war may also help to establish credibility. Historically, in those cases in which American strategic nuclear forces have been involved in third-world operations, American operational objectives have been more likely to be achieved.[7] It would appear that a willingness to imply a risk of nuclear war signals that a greater seriousness is attached to the situation and thus strengthens the credibility of the messages being transmitted. However, most of these incidents have occurred during the period of American nuclear superiority. The potential utility of a demonstrated willingness to manipulate nuclear risks in an age of strategic parity requires further consideration. Moreover, the longer-term consequences of such actions, to say nothing of the risks involved, should contain enthusiasm for the use of this means of strengthening credibility.

Finally, utility seems to be related to the nature of the objectives of the intervening power. There is a very simple rule to keep in mind. When the objective is to alter a target nation's existing behaviour, a 'political' use of military power is less likely to be effective than when the objective is to reinforce existing behaviour. This is true whether the military activity is coercive in nature (i.e., designed to compel a real change in the target's behaviour or to deter a threatened change) or supportive in nature (i.e., designed to induce a new action by an ally or to persuade the ally to continue some existing activity). The reasons for this should be clear. First, individuals, in both their personal and public lives, typically face the known risks and benefits of existing behaviour with greater equanimity than they view the uncertain risks and benefits of an altered state of affairs; 'political' uses of military power, in the end, succeed or fail depending on the decisions of few individuals. Secondly, political leaders cannot afford to be seen to be responding to the desires of foreign powers, particularly when the blandishments of those powers take the form of military threats. Few, if any, political leaders, whether in authoritarian or democratic political systems, can survive long when they must moderate their nations' behaviour in response to the public demands of external powers. Thus in one sense, at least as concerns indirect applications of military power, utility can be strengthened to the degree that external powers' objectives are congruent with preservation of the *status quo*.

This brings us to a special sub-set of these indirect or 'political' applications of military power in the Third World – the incidents in which both super-powers intervened simultaneously in third-world conflicts. In some ways these are the most interesting incidents, just as they appear to be the most dangerous.

Over the years the armed forces of the United States and the Soviet Union have been involved simultaneously in a sufficient number of incidents in the Third World to indicate certain patterns of behaviour. While their military activities in these local conflicts were ostensibly directed at one another and, perhaps to a somewhat lesser extent, at their respective clients and clients' adversaries, in a sense they played to a much larger gallery. Both super-powers, at times, seem to have felt compelled to take part in situations in which they perceived very little in the way of substantive interest because of their belief that to behave otherwise could have had adverse political impact on their relations and standing with other nations. In short, in certain situations there is a presumed consequence of inaction for the global competition for political influence between the United States and the Soviet Union. As a result, quite apart from whatever specific operational objectives each may have harboured *vis-à-vis* the local participants, in these incidents both the United States and the Soviet Union had three overriding objectives:

—to avoid the development of situations in which the risk of nuclear war might become significant;
—to avoid the appearance of being limited significantly by the actions of their rival;
—to appear successful in defence of their own clients' interests.

More often than not, both super-powers seem to have been able to emerge from these incidents with each of these fundamental interests secured, a fact which attests to their complementary perspectives as well as to the existence of certain tacit mutual understandings about appropriate behaviour.

James McConnell has termed these understandings, which he has inferred from the empirical behaviour of the United States and the Soviet Union in a large number of incidents, 'the rules of the game'.[8] Adherence to these 'rules' makes it possible for each super-power to make the necessary political impact without excessive risk. Most important, the 'rules' determine for any specific situation the latitude which each nation will have for military action or to threaten military action.

While they are commonly cited, neither overall military capability nor tactically relevant military strength accounts for the actual outcomes of these super-power confrontations; latitude is not determined by the military balance. Indeed, for the most part, at least in their third-world naval confrontations, the United States and the Soviet Union seem to have deployed forces which, considering their differing missions, had roughly equivalent capabilities. As McConnell puts it:

The proper forces deployed in the proper place at the proper times are a necessary but not a sufficient condition for [success] . . . and beyond a certain level – the level, it turns out, of mutual credibility – force competition at the local level does not drive the competition as a whole.[9]

This squares with the finding of my own study that there is no significant relationship between relative effectiveness in these types of situation and either the overall strategic nuclear balance or the size of the forces explicitly deployed at the scene of the conflict.

A second factor that is commonly cited, native resolve, also fails, upon close examination, to explain why in one situation the United States will act with greater latitude while in another the Soviet Union will dominate. Historically, the achievement of dominance is too inconsistent to be related to the native resolve or toughness of American and Soviet leaders.

Rather, it is a fourth factor that appears to be decisive – each super-power's perception of the stakes involved in the situation. In turn, this seems to consist of two components: the inherent value ascribed to the specific interests in question, and the fact of possession. A close study of actual confrontations in the Third World shows that time after time the super-power which dominated the situation, the one which assumed the greatest latitude in its behaviour, was the one whose client was defending the strategic *status quo*, the one whose client was on the strategic defensive because interests in its possession were being challenged. Thus, for example, in the 1970 Jordanian crisis the Soviet Union deployed substantial forces in the Mediterranean in support of Syria but more or less stood by while the United States – together with Israel – dominated the situation in defence of Jordan, which had been attacked. Conversely, during the 1969–70 war of attrition on the Suez Canal, the United States acquiesced in the deployment of major Soviet air defence units in defence of Egyptian territory against Israeli incursions, limiting her support of Israel to fierce rhetoric, naval gestures and aircraft sales.

This is not to say that the more passive super-power, the one whose client is attempting to breach the strategic *status quo*, plays no role in the situation; the fact of the second super-power's involvement itself tends to limit the freedom of action of the first super-power's armed forces.

When the United States and the Soviet Union have both deployed forces in the Third World they have always played quite distinct roles. The intervener whose client has been on the strategic defensive has tended to dominate events, as its client has been in possession of the interests being challenged, and it has thus perceived a much greater latitude for action. The second super-power has served as an armed bystander, in order to limit the threat thereby posed to its own client, which would otherwise be open-ended, and thus to prevent a reversal such that the *status quo ante* would then be threatened from the previously defensive position. In this sense, both super-powers have acted as guarantors of the *status quo*, ensuring that neither was in a position to breach previous understandings of international equilibrium.

Obviously, all this is too orderly, rational and static; reality is more complicated. Respective definitions of what actually constitutes the *status quo* may change either as a result of small acts of local origin that do not precipitate confrontations or because of more decisive actions; thus at times there may be uncertainty as to what constitutes proper behaviour by each of the guarantors of the *status quo*. Moreover, numerous factors – including the misperceptions of decision-makers in Washington and Moscow, to say nothing of those in local capitals – can complicate decisions. There are dangers as well as opportunities for political impact.

Still, there does appear to be a mutually acceptable definition of what is and what is not appropriate super-power behaviour in third-world confrontations which has stood substantial tests. James McConnell sums up the situation well:

> The realistic aim of both sides, then, is not to maximize gains but to reduce losses. The patron threatening intervention is limiting the losses of his own client against the other client; the countering patron is limiting the scope of the threat to his client by the other patron. The patrons do not neutralize each other, either politically or militarily . . . each has a role to play . . . and each makes a political impact; this is no zero-sum game.[10]

The utility, then, of the super-powers' military activity in the Third World, simply put, can be seen at two levels: first, such activity can serve to protect the specific interests of client states and, presumably, whatever values cause the super-power to seek or to accept such a patron/client relationship to begin with; second, use of armed forces serves to demonstrate to a global audience the strength and resolve of each super-power and thus the value of their patronage, thereby contributing to their continuing quest for political influence throughout the world. As long as the United States and the Soviet Union continue to attribute great importance to this competition, the use of their military forces in the Third World will continue to be seen as inherently important, regardless of the substantive interests at stake in specific situations.

Indeed, there has recently been an emipirical test of this proposition. For much of its term, the Carter Administration deliberately refrained from military confrontations with the Soviet Union in Africa, not so much because of moralistic concerns, as has so often (though erroneously) been noted, as because of a belief that it was a serious mistake to permit the dictates of East–West competition to dominate American policies *vis-à-vis* the Third World. Take the Soviet and Cuban intervention on the Horn of Africa in 1977–78, for example. In this case the Soviet client, Ethiopia, was on the strategic defensive; the Soviet Union clearly had the greater latitude for action. In a purely competitive model, the United States would have come to the aid of Somalia. The standard response, which the United States could have made, would have been to deploy naval forces in the region but to stand by passively, thus appearing to prevent the Soviet Union and her client, once defended successfully, from reversing the situation and threatening Somalia. However, to have done so would have been to place the United States in association with a nation whose actions had been strongly condemned by virtually all other African states. Moreover, this would have occurred at a time of (and would have adversely affected) delicate, secret negotiations through which the United States was seeking, with the co-operation of the Front Line States, to bring about a peaceful resolution of the Rhodesian conflict. Thus a deliberate decision was made to decline the standard super-power role, with the expectation of thus strengthening the position of the United States *vis-à-vis* other African issues.

Similar decisions were taken at other times – as concerns military sales, for example. In the end, though, the political consequences of this refusal to play the super-power game overwhelmed such a deliberate reordering of priorities. Domestically, the Administration came under heavy fire for not 'standing up' to the Soviet Union. Internationally, non-African nations with whom the United States valued close relations, such as China, Israel and Saudi Arabia, expressed concern about the apparent free hand thus given to Soviet military power in the Third World. As a result, well before the Soviet occupation of Afghanistan the United States was shifting back towards a more active confrontational stance.

This experience thus confirms the basic judgment that conflicts such as that in the Horn constitute necessary opportunities to make local and global political impact and that a refusal to participate can have significant adverse political consequences. Whether this confirmation results from immutable factors intrinsic to the international system or from specific debilities of the Carter Administration is a moot point. The fact remains that the experiment has been tried and, having failed, is unlikely to be tried again soon. In the future, both super-powers will continue not only to see utility in the exercise of military power in the Third World for direct purposes but also to perceive the need for mutual participation with armed force in a wide range of contexts for indirect or 'political' objectives.

Policy Implications

The West brings considerable advantages to the continuing struggle with the Soviet Union for influence in the Third World. Whether as a model for economic development or as an ideal of how to organize society, the Soviet Union has failed; the inhumanity, inefficiency and stultifying bureaucracy of the Soviet state is widely recognized. The West, on the other hand, has much to offer the people of the Third World: automobiles, electronics, markets, capital, dynamic political models, organizational skills, blue jeans, TV programmes, music, technology and agricultural know-how. Whatever people of the Third World need or crave is more likely to be found, in greater quantity and higher quality, in the West.

There is but one instrument of policy in which the Soviet Union has an advantage – the acquisition and utilization of military power. In the contemporary world only an authoritarian society like that of the Soviet Union can allocate resources to the armed forces with contempt for the competing needs of its people, and only an authoritarian society can make use of that power without taking careful account of the desires of its own citizens.

It is thus to the West's advantage to seek to define the terms of competition so that its military aspects are de-emphasized. This is not always possible, and when such occasions arise the West can, and must, compete effectively. It is crucial to maintain at least a rough balance of military power. At times it is necessary for Western nations to employ their military forces in confrontations with the Soviet Union or to defend interests in the Third World unrelated to the competition with the Soviet Union. Still, to rely too heavily on military power in the Third World, to permit the Soviet Union to define the terms of the competition such that the armed forces gain an increasingly important role would be a strategic blunder that played to the Soviet Union's one comparative strength. Neither in abstract terms nor in terms of the relative advantages of Western societies can Western armed forces be expected to serve more than temporary, marginal and largely cost-minimizing functions in the general context of the Third World.

The exercise of Western military power in the Third World cannot, therefore, be a substitute for the development and implementation of broader and longer-term strategies, strategies which orchestrate a variety of policy instruments in ways that both take advantage of the strengths of the industrial democracies and reflect realistic assessments of contemporary political and economic conditions in the developing world. The West must come to a hard-headed understanding of what its real interests are in the Third World and then articulate those interests with credibility, backed up by military strength in being, so that situations which may require the actual exercise of military power arise less and less frequently.

This will not always be easy. The world is not orderly. Perceptions of interests change; local political and economic realities are transformed; great powers neglect their military strength; villians or fools rise to high office and pointlessly challenge existing arrangements. Any of these developments can lead to situations which demand the exercise of military power. The fact that such situations arise, though, signifies failures of policy. Military power can be used to attain certain specific operational objectives, but in effect the exercise of military power can only buy time so that the problems which have led to the policy failure can be understood and solved and new policies adopted which can lead to renewed security for Western interests over the longer term.

In utilizing military strength decision-makers should be quite clear about these limitations. Military strength can be used directly by external powers to accomplish certain specific operational objectives – to recover seized assets, for example, or to topple tyrannical governments. In general, however, external military power cannot maintain unpopular governments in the Third World over long periods of time.

Military power can also be used indirectly to persuade third-world policy-makers to take steps which lead to the achievement of certain operational objectives. But here, too, what can be accomplished is generally limited in scope and perishable. Military power can be used to remind third-world policy-makers of historic Western interests and commitments relatively

easily, but only with difficulty can it be used to articulate and make credible new commitments. Military power can be used relatively easily to defend the *status quo* and to retard change in existing patterns of behaviour, but only with difficulty can it be used to compel sustained or significant changes in the behaviour of nations. It can also be used as part of the competition with the Soviet Union in the Third World, but here, for the most part, its realistic objectives can only be to avoid the adverse consequences of unrestricted Soviet activity. In the continuing minuet of super-power competition confrontations in the Third World offer plenty of risks but few opportunities. The position of neither the Soviet Union nor the West *vis-à-vis* the Third World has been permanently affected by the confrontations which have punctuated post-war history.

Whatever its objectives, the exercise of military power in the Third World can be done with greater or lesser skill. It is exceedingly important that the character of any action taken should fit the character of the objective and the importance of the interests involved. If, for example, Western decision-makers see no real gain in intervention but merely wish to avoid the appearance of a free hand for the Soviet Union, them any planned military operation should be quite ambiguous. One could then afford to pay greater attention to minimizing the risks implicit in any East–West confrontation and should thus tailor the military operation to maintain maximum flexibility. In other circumstances, however, the West's interest may be compelling. In these cases the idiom of the military action itself should aim to remove any possible ambiguity about the seriousness of the commitments made.

One way to signal resolve, of course, is to stress the risk of nuclear war, as the United States did during the 1973 Middle East crisis. There will be more and more temptation to take this route as long as the balance of conventional military power continues to erode. This is a temptation to avoid; the risks are great, and there are alternative ways to make commitments credible. Greater attention might be paid to the use of land-based air power as an instrument of diplomacy, for example, as the United States has done recently in deploying squadrons of F–4 *Phantoms* in Egypt for temporary 'training' missions. Moreover, the actual operations undertaken by the military forces which do intervene can have much to say about the credibility of the positions taken. More care might be taken to ensure that these activities reflect a certain seriousness of purpose.

NOTES

[1] Barry M. Blechman and Stephen S. Kaplan, *Force Without War* (Washington: The Brookings Institution, 1978); Bradford Dismukes and James McConnell (eds), *Soviet Naval Diplomacy* (London: Pergamon Press, 1979); and Stephen S. Kaplan, *Diplomacy of Power: Soviet Armed Forces as a Political Instrument* (Washington: The Brookings Institution, 1981). All three studies owe a considerable debt to the pioneering work of Alexander George. See Alexander L. George and Richard Smoke, *Deterrence in American Foreign Policy* (New York: Columbia University Press, 1974); and Alexander L. George, David K. Hall, and William E. Simons, *The Limits of Coercive Diplomacy* (Boston: Little, Brown, 1971).

[2] Cited in Pierre Lellouche and Dominique Moïsi, 'French Policy in Africa: A Lonely Battle Against Destabilization', *International Security*, vol III (Spring 1979), pp. 108–33.

[3] *Diplomacy of Power, op. cit.* in n. 1.

[4] *Ibid.*

[5] See n. 1.

[6] Thomas C. Schelling, *Arms and Influence* (New Haven: Yale University Press, 1966).

[7] A list of incidents in which American strategic nuclear forces have taken part since 1945 can be found in Blechman and Kaplan, *Force Without War, op. cit.,* in n. 1. p. 48.

[8] *op. cit.* in n. 1.

[9] Dismukes and McConnell, *Soviet Naval Diplomacy, op. cit.* in n. 1, p. 243.

[10] *Ibid.*, p. 277.

Protecting Oil Supplies: The Military Requirements

SIR JOHN HACKETT

The reduction to acceptable limits of the uncertainties inherent in continuing reliance upon Gulf oil to meet minimal Western and Japanese requirements is a clear need. The best way of meeting this need is by no means as clear. Options under study include military action. This paper now looks at the military option, chiefly in respect of the Middle East. That area, however, is not the only one of interest in the study of military possibilities, and some reference will be made to others.

It cannot be too strongly emphasized that military action can *never* be rationally undertaken except for identifiable political ends and in an environment in which political factors are of paramount importance. The world has paid dearly for adherence, up to the end of World War II, to the view then dominant in the major partner of the Western Alliance that wars are to be won by the military, to whose interests all else must be subordinate, and the resultant situation is to be handed over to the politicians for resolution. It would be difficult to imagine a situation in which the possible military options were more highly charged with political complexities than that currently prevailing in the Arabian Gulf.

The General Aspect
Oil as a Source of Energy
The importance of oil as a source of energy for the United States, Western Europe and Japan is shown in the following table, which gives figures for 1977.[1] It will be seen that nearly half of all energy consumed in the United States comes from oil. Fifty per cent of this is imported and one-third of the whole (8 per cent of the total energy consumed) is from the Arabian Gulf. The European need for petroleum from the Middle East is even more pronounced. Most of what is consumed in Europe comes from there. Japan and other industrial centres of East Asia depend more heavily still upon the same source.

	United States	Western Europe	Japan
Oil as percentage of total energy consumed	47	55	73
Percentage of oil imported	49	96	100
Percentage of oil imported from Arabian Gulf	34	61	72
Arabian Gulf oil as percentage of total energy consumed	8	32	53

The Soviet Union currently produces a surplus, but in the late 1980s she is quite likely to be joining the ranks of the customers for Middle East oil.

US Threat Analysis
In his State of the Union speech on 23 January 1980 President Carter declared that the United States would be prepared to use force if necessary to protect her vital interests in the Gulf, including the supply of petroleum. The so-called Carter Doctrine (which was backed by the President's Chief Security Adviser) identified the greatest threat to peace in South-west Asia, and thus to the oil flow, as Soviet military adventurism. On 28 January 1980 Secretary of Defense Brown produced a variant. He saw a greater and possibly more realistic danger in regional turbulence. Whether the USSR was likely to intervene or not, 'the threat of violence and the use of force remain widespread'.[2] According to this argument, the Soviet Union will certainly foment, and may even cause, destabilization in the area generally but is unlikely to undertake direct military intervention in the

41

Gulf if this would lead to a major military confrontation with the United States.

Tass reported Georgy Arbatov as saying on 7 April 1980, 'despite the panic-mongering allegations of US propaganda, no one will see Soviet tanks and soldiers on the shores of the Persian Gulf or other warm seas'. This statement can be taken with a pinch of salt. After all, the People's Democratic Republic of Yemen took in the greater part of a Soviet division airlifted there in 1978. None the less, it can probably be accepted that among possible threats to stability in the Arabian Gulf area direct Soviet military intervention is not the most likely.

Types of Threat
The magnitude and duration of military operations to secure the oil flow, wherever these might take place, and the size and nature of the forces necessary to undertake them would depend upon, among other considerations, the choice of areas within which they would be carried out and the types of threat which would be thought to make them necessary. Three types of threat are distinguishable: domestic disorder, blockade and intrusion (whether by an independent local power, by a Soviet proxy or by the Soviet Union herself). According to the Brown variant of the Carter Doctrine, the last would probably be considered the least likely.

United States policy, logically enough, accepts that rapid reaction forces may be used to deter action by others and not merely to respond to it. In December 1979 Brzezinski referred, in a little noticed address to the Chicago Economic Club, to the desirability of being able to respond 'quickly, effectively and *even pre-emptively*' (my emphasis).

Choice of Objective Area
In choosing an area of operations it would first be necessary very clearly to specify the requirement. This can be identified in four degrees:

—to supply US needs alone;
—to supply US needs plus those of Japan;
—to supply US needs plus those of NATO allies;
—to supply US needs plus those of NATO allies *and* Japan.

In order to supply American needs alone, without regard to those of Japan or allies, there are several options open to the United States, by no means all of which concern the Arabian Gulf.

Venezuela (Maracaibo) and Nigeria could between them meet US demands (which can be estimated currently as some 7 million barrels a day) if strict conservation were to reduce demand by rather more than one-sixth. Both areas are much closer than the Middle East, and transport does not need to go through choke-points like the Straits of Hormuz. In neither area could more than token resistance be offered by local forces. Threats of Soviet military intervention would be negligible in both.

On the other hand, action here to assure oil supplies would necessitate separate operations 4,500 miles apart, with serious strains on resources and very heavy costs. To explore the political repercussions of any such move lies outside the scope of this paper, but these would certainly be severe. Venezuela, for example, is an ally of the United States in the Organization of American States (OAS).

Maracaibo and Libya (whose production is one-third greater than that of Nigeria) could satisfy the requirements of the United States and some of her allies. Intervention by Soviet naval elements would now become a possibility, and there are choke-points at Gibraltar and in the Sicilian narrows. Politically, it might just be possible to extract advantage from Libya's equivocal position in the Arab world, especially where relations with Egypt were concerned.

To guarantee to meet all United States needs plus those of NATO allies and Japan, by American military means, must be regarded as impracticable. To supply American needs together with those of NATO allies *or* Japan would double the demands on the United States. To supply all three would treble it. Japan might be in a position to help herself by action in Indonesia, for which the United States would have to furnish an impressive degree of sea-lift and logistical support. In that event Maracaibo, Nigeria and Libya could meet all the United States and the balance of Japanese needs, under conditions of strict conservation. The addition of even some of the needs of NATO allies inevitably directs attention to the Middle East, where alone can be found supplies in sufficient quantity to meet all requirements. Here, however, choice of target areas demands very careful thought.

The Object of Operations

Such operations could only be said to have succeeded if they satisfied five requirements:

—to seize the vital oil installations virtually intact;
—to secure them for weeks, months and even years;
—to restore wrecked resources rapidly;
—to operate installations with little or no co-operation from the owners;
—to guarantee the safe passage of petroleum products from the area and supplies to it.

It would be idle to pretend that there are not truly formidable difficulties to be faced here.

For the purpose of this study it is assumed that the ground and air forces actively engaged in the area of operations will be exclusively those of the United States and that the naval forces will be largely so. It can, of course, be assumed that allies will do what they can to help, if only because their own interests are concerned. The assistance of allies, however, is likely to be offered more by way of taking up the slack in other areas than by furnishing forces in the actual area of operations itself. Nevertheless, some active intervention can be expected – for example, from Britain and probably France and Australia. Allied naval assistance would be indispensable to guarantee safe passage and could almost certainly be counted on. It simplifies this study, however, and is by no means unrealistic to consider the mission, as far as ground forces and air operations are concerned, in terms of United States forces alone

For the seizure and securing of vital installations American airborne troops are too few to cover all essential objectives, if there is anything like effective opposition, even with surprise. Amphibious forces are slow, while opportunities for demolition before any forces could arrive would be extensive. The plugging of 100 wells (there are 775 in Saudi Arabia and 1,040 in Kuwait and the Neutral Zone) would take out more than a million barrels a day. Pipelines (of which there are, for example, some 2,000 or more miles in the Saudi core area) offer rela-

tively unrewarding targets for sabotage. Wellheads, pumping stations, refineries and transshipment points are more promising, particularly where facilities depend on central installations. Taking the Arabian Gulf again as an example, 60 per cent of all oil passes through three facilities – those at Ras Tanura and Juaymeh in Saudi Arabia and at Kharg Island off Iran. Eighty per cent of all Gulf oil passes through five facilities. The vulnerability of oilfield installations is high, particularly where vital links such as pumping stations are concerned. One electrical power plant supports all pumping operations in Saudi Arabia. In addition, the fire risk is serious. A well-blown pumping station (Abqaiq) has been known to shut down a pipeline for 90 days with a repair cost of $100 million; light oils mixed with volatile materials (in separators or stabilizers, for example) are easy to ignite and hard to extinguish. A big fire in Kuwait's Burgen field burned for two months before being brought under control in the summer of 1978. Buring oil could block beaches and port facilities needed by assault forces. Explosions in loading areas could devastate shore installations. One super-tanker carrying liquefied natural gas (LNG) or naphtha, set on fire at a jetty, could do immense damage.

It is, however, possible to exaggerate the dangers and difficulties arising out of demolition. Demolition is an expert's job, demanding specialized personnel and material, neither of which is currently in plentiful supply. It also demands careful planning and early decision-making. Inadequately planned or insufficiently prepared demolition, as every specialist operator (a member of a special force like the SAS, for example) will know, can be abortive or can cause only slight and short-term damage. Special operations to prevent damage, undertaken in good time by the United States, could be of immense value. Saudi wells, moreover, are mostly of moderate depth, and redrilling would not be unsuperably difficult.[3] Damage, none the less, could not fail to be considerable, and restoration is likely to be costly and time-consuming. It should be said here that success in an operation to assure the flow of oil would depend above all on two conditions: slight damage to key installations and abstinence by the other super-power from direct armed interference. Neither of these two conditions is impossible.

The Structure of an Operation

United States force structure is intended to be capable of meeting one major crisis (say, in the NATO area) and one minor crisis at the same time. This is somewhat loosely known as the 'war-and-a-half' concept. Whatever forces are to be employed in an operation of the sort considered here will have to be found from those already in being. The force to be used must be tailored to the requirements, from the resources likely to be available at the time, in the context of the 'war-and-a-half' concept. This would be the 'half' war. Escalation out of it into full and unrestricted war with the Soviet Union is beyond the scope of this paper. It should always be borne prominently in mind, however, that the Soviet Union is unlikely to regard escalation into total world conflict with any more enthusiasm than the United States.

The operation would fall into three phases, not always sharply distinguishable one from another but differing in essence. There is, first, pre-hostilities action. This would be intended to bring about the creation of an appropriate infrastructure in the theatre to allow for rapid deployment from home bases. In present circumstances the size and nature of the available lift is more important than the size and even the availability of forces and deserves more urgent attention. A demonstrable ability to deploy United States forces rapidly and then to sustain them may prove to be the most effective stabilizing factor and the best deterrent to intrusion by others. This would depend more than anything on pre-hostilities preparation and a demonstrable strategic life adequate for the forces required. It would mean also a high degree of pre-positioning of equipment.

The second phase would see the actual establishment of a force in the chosen area, with forward operating bases and assembly and logistical support areas in the region in question.

In the third phase there would be the requirement for the establishment and conduct of an area defence as far forward as tactically feasible and for the maintenance of the oil flow. This last is likely to be difficult. It would almost certainly involve the reopening of facilities blocked, destroyed or in other ways rendered inoperative. It would also necessitate the security of maritime movement. The reopening of facilities would make heavy and unusual demands upon American resources, which certainly could not be met out of those at present available to the military. It is difficult to see how the drafting of conscript civilian personnel from oil-producing operations in the United States could be avoided. Moreover, the personnel and material required for reopening obstructed or vitiated facilities, even when these were found, would take up a good deal of the maritime transportation also needed for the support of the military operation.

Phase One, initially, would be an almost entirely political operation. The second part of Phase One (the setting up of the lift capability) would take time and be costly.

The force would clearly have to be tailored to the requirement. There is no such thing as a rapid-deployment force suitable for any and every task. What is presently available can be quickly summarized. There is the 82nd Airborne Division (strength 15,200); the 101st Airmobile Division (17,900); two Marine Divisions (19,800 each); 600–1,000 combat aircraft (fighters, ground-attack aircraft, bombers and other types); 700 cargo-carrying aircraft, including tankers and troop carriers; and two to four aircraft carrier groups, with a command vessel and destroyer escorts. The United States naval presence in the Arabian Gulf area has, until last year, consisted of a command and support vessel and two destroyers, though occasional visits were paid by aircraft carriers from the Pacific. It has recently been very considerably increased. There is also a French naval force in the Indian Ocean, and a British force has conducted visits to the region. Again until recently, these were together considerably greater than the United States presence, though the latter can be more readily increased than the others or that of the Soviet Union.

In Phase Two fast deployment would be essential. Indeed, it is upon speed that the success or failure of the mission would be likely to hang. The meeting of this requirement would depend, as already noted, on pre-hostilities activity to secure the required presence and facilities in the chosen area to allow a rapid build-up and on the bringing into being of the sea- and air-lift which would be necessary to deploy an adequate force. Of this more will be said later. At this point it is worth noting only that Phase Two might easily merge into Phase Three, with the initial deployment to secure the oil running in parallel with subsequent reinforcement.

A Test Case

It is now important to the argument to be more precise in the indication of a possible mission, in order to quantify requirements.

A relatively recent study by the United States Congressional Research Service chose, for in-depth analysis, what is known as the 'Saudi Core' as the most promising target area. 'Results reveal the feasibility of applying US armed force in that specific area but readers should recognize that companion studies of alternatives might reach quite different conclusions in many regards.'[5] The 'Saudi Core', as a target area, offers advantages as a focal point of study and will be so used in this paper.

'The 'Saudi Core' consists of four on-shore fields – Abqaiq, Dammam, Ghawar and Qatif – together with Berri, a big off-shore producer. No other complex of comparable size has comparable capabilities. These fields would satisfy all American and most Allied requirements from a single centre in a single country. A tight perimeter around all of the vital area would take in about 10,000 square miles, roughly the size of Yorkshire and Lincolnshire together, or twice the size of Connecticut. This would present United States military forces with a not impossible problem, though the occupation of such an area would tie up certainly not less than two and probably four divisions for as long as it was needed.

Crude petroleum from all fields converges on Ras Tanura through a pipe system containing well over 2,000 miles of pipe. The area is mostly desert, with virtually non-existent water supplies (though deep drilling would almost certainly yield water), sparse population and climatic conditions which, especially in summer, would tax United States or European troops to the utmost. A military occupation might well also have to take in the Saudi Arabian capital, Riyadh, which could be expected to be a source at least of dissidence and perhaps a forceful opposition. The two oil ports at Ras Tanura and Juaymeh constitute the world's foremost oil port facilities. Between them they have a throughput capacity of some 12 million barrels per day.

In addition to Riyadh, the United States forces would need to seize, or at least to control the following elements to operate successfully in the 'Saudi Core' area: well-heads and associated facilities in four widely separated oil fields, some situated off-shore; choke-points at Ain Tar, Abqaiq, Dhahran and Qatif; the Ras Tanura complex; the Juaymeh complex; Dammam port; Dhahran airbase; the Straits of Hormuz.

US Military Resources
It must be emphasized that the 'Rapid Deployment Force' has created no new troop resources. It is, in essence, a reorganization of forces already available.

Army: Of the seven divisions available in the Continental US after the deduction of forces with NATO (or other) strings attached to them (such as the requirement in any situation short of all-out war of a workable rotation base) planners could use for operations in the Persian Gulf: 82nd Airborne Division; 101st Airmobile Division; one light armoured division; 25 Infantry Division, which is the Pacific Reserve in Hawaii.

If NATO needed all those forces which are not only assigned but also earmarked, and the Pacific Command (PACOM) had to deal with a crisis in, say, Korea, the United States could furnish no more than one contingency division. The favourable case is considered here as the only feasible one for the carrying out of an operation of this sort.

Marines: Of the existing Marine Amphibious Forces (MAFS), either I (in California), or II (in North Carolina) but not both could be committed in South-west Asia without a Presidential and Congressional declaration of a state of emergency which would enable the activation of IV (Reserve) MAF. The division known as III MAF, with its associated air wing, logistic support and command element, is the only flexible US ground force in the Western Pacific. *Neither* I nor II MAF would be available for sustained operations in the Arabian Gulf if trouble in Europe demanded a division/wing force or if a second division/wing contingent were required in the West Pacific. This paper assumes the continued availability of at least one Marine division/wing force for sustained operations in the Arabian Gulf, though in the best case a second should be available.

Air: Of the United States Air Force 81 fighter-attack squadrons, after subtracting 26 assigned to the European command, the ten supporting American forces in the Pacific, the two earmarked (but not assigned) to NATO, the three with strings on them to support the permanent squadron in Alaska and the requirement for a rotational base, Tactical Air Force Command (TAFC) could dispose of about 31 squadrons for tasks in the Arabian Gulf. This assumes no call on reserves earmarked for Europe and Alaska and no major crisis in Korea.

Naval forces: The critical operation element in the naval component of a force for the Arabian Gulf would be aircraft carriers. Fast patrol boats, minesweepers and anti-submarine resources would be important, but the carrier forces would be critical. Requirements for a maritime lift are referred to below.

Of the 12 fully equipped American carriers (the 13th, the USS *Coral Sea*, has at present no air wing), seven are assigned to the Atlantic and five to the Pacific. Two of the Atlantic carriers are committed to the Sixth Fleet in the Mediterranean, although one of these is temporarily in the Indian Ocean. Two carriers operate with PACOM in the Seventh Fleet along the shores of East Asia. One of these periodically reinforces the American naval presence in the Indian Ocean and is currently on patrol in those waters. A Fifth Fleet is a possibility, though this would affect only the distribution and not the total number of carriers available. A Fifth Fleet could include the two carriers now in the Indian Ocean supported from Subic Bay in the Philippines, with one deployed forward with facilities at Diego Garcia (which is more than 2,000 miles, it should be remembered, from the head of the Arabian Gulf) and the other held back. A contingency force could, under favourable conditions, be raised to the level of three-carrier task forces if another were taken from the Western Pacific. A fourth might be made available if the USS *Coral Sea* could be furnished with an air wing.

Factors Affecting the Operation
The chances of achieving surprise, in view of the distances involved and the certainty that preparations for an assault could not be concealed, must be reckoned low. One airborne division would be insufficient to seize all key points,

though the main choke-points in the collecting system – the Ras Tanura and Juaymeh complexes, Dammam port and Dhahran airfield – could probably be secured. The closest Marine Division at Okinawa would take 12 to 14 days to reach Ras Tanura after embarking on amphibious vessels. Half the required sealift is normally stationed somewhere in the Pacific, but only one squadron of eight ships with the Seventh Fleet is readily available. The balance of the 48 ships required for a divisional lift are scattered from the Marianas to the Mediterranean. The time required to assemble, load and move a division-sized assault force to the Middle East could be about two months.

As a measure of what is required (though it would be misleading to apply this as a precise template), the security of one oil well-head would perhaps be furnished by a five-man fire team. There are 243 eleven-man rifle squads in the 82nd Airborne Division. Each contains two such fire teams. The 82nd could therefore cover 486 of the 544 oil-producing wells in the 'Saudi Core' area. Fire teams from the United States Army's sole separate airborne battalion, if this were detached from duty with NATO, could probably secure 54 more. This would bring the total to 540. These figures are quoted only to show how tight initial airborne troop security cover would be, with nothing in hand for more active operations or as a reserve.

Combat Mobility
It has to be conceded at once that the strategic airlift and sealift forces which, until very recently, have been available (though urgent steps are now being taken to improve this capability) are barely adequate to support division-sized airborne and amphibious assaults in the Saudi Core area.

Assault airlift: To move the essential combat elements of the 82nd Airborne Division (roughly 11,000 men out of the total of 15,200) the required distance (that is to say, half-way round the world) with a basic load of ammunition and five days of rations and fuel would, it is thought, use up more than 700 C–141 'equivalent sorties'. The operation would take 10 to 15 days from a standing start, although this could be reduced to under seven days if it were possible to make certain prior preparations. If a parachute assault were intended, the requirement would be for nearly 1,200 'equivalent sorties', including aircraft for heavy dropping. The United States has some 70 C–5As and 234 C–141s in operational squadrons. It is difficult to estimate what force would be available for an assault as opposed to a strategic lift. Some of the 500 C–130 tactical transport aircraft in the regular Air Force and National Guard could participate in parachute assaults, provided the troops were moved overseas by other means. They would then board the C–130s at forward mounting bases. Most of the Airborne Division would in any case have to be airlanded, which means that the Dhahran air base, the only suitable entry point, would have to be seized and secured early on. This should not, however, present insuperable difficulties in the face of light opposition.

Assault sealift: Mention has been made of the requirement for 48 ships to lift one Marine amphibious force. These are made up as follows:[6]

Command/control ship (LCC)	1
Amphibious assault ship (LPH)	5
Amphibious transport (LPA)	2
Amphibious transport dock (LPD)	10
Landing ship dock (LSD)	9
Amphibious cargo ship (LKA)	5
Landing ship tank (LST)	15
Amphibious transport submarine (LPSS)	1
Total	**48**

Meeting this requirement would certainly strain American amphibious capabilities, even though these are now being improved. The 48-ship requirement set out above constitutes more than three-quarters of the whole operational inventory of these types of ship which is available to the US Navy.

Certain elements of heavy non-divisional troops normally expected to operate with an independent corps could be thinned out considerably. In an operation of this sort, for example, heavy armour would not be a critical requirement. To take an even more obvious example, bridge companies would hardly be required. On the other hand, construction resources needed for roads and airfields and for other communication requirements would be considerable. Ammunition would probably not be needed to anything like the extent that it was in Vietnam,

with a very great saving in cargo weights and bulk. Petrol and water, however, would be more important. Twelve gallons of water a day per man, for all purposes, would be required and roughly the same quantity of fuel. The climate could be expected to cause a high level of medical casualties.

It can be assumed that a two-division corps set up under conditions such as these would total nearly 80,000 men. If four divisions were to be deployed, the total would double. This assumes, of course, that security could be maintained on a routine basis. Military operations of higher intensity would generate greater requirements.

Air Cover and Air Support
The closest land bases suitable for United States Air Force fighters which could conceivably be available (though this can by no means be guaranteed) are in Israel, 1,000 miles from the 'Saudi Core' area. That is double the normal unrefuelled 500-mile combat radius of F–4s carrying two 370-gallon wing tanks and typical ordnance loads. Any additional fuel carried externally would reduce payload and increase time spent over target areas. Refuelling from aerial tankers is feasible, but – to give an idea of the size of this problem – a strike wave of 40 F–4s would take ten tankers to serve them outbound, ten more on their return. Back-up to account for aborts and other abnormalities would run the total up to two full squadrons of 25 to 30 tankers. Tankers, moreover, might need fighter cover themselves.

Conditions for aircraft operating from carriers would also be difficult. The Arabian Gulf is too congested for carrier operations, and it is assumed that the carrier force would have to operate no closer than the Gulf of Oman, some 1,000 miles south-east of Ras Tanura. This would involve in-flight refuelling requirements similar to those for aircraft operating from Israel. Most of these difficulties could disappear, or at least diminish, however, following the establishment of a firm foothold and the provision of forward airfields within the area of operations.

Air Defence Forces
On the basis of an allocation of one *HAWK* surface-to-air missile (SAM) battalion to each

division, with another to cover corps units, between three and five *HAWK* battalions would be required. There would be further requirement for *Vulcan* battalions for point defence at the rate of one for every three critical targets, plus one for general support. This would suggest that four *Vulcan* battalions would be needed for the operation. The main air-defence task would be to deter (and, if necessary, defeat) Soviet and outside Arab air threats. Unless Soviet fighters were moved forward, they would be at the limit of range.

Taking a position somewhere between an optimistic and a pessimistic outlook, it would seem that the requirement for Air Force F–4 aircraft would be two wings of three squadrons each, with two other wings on call. Currently, 16 F–4 squadrons are assigned to TAC. This mission would take up 12 of these. Taking rotational and maintenance requirements into consideration, this is a dangerously high level (75 per cent) of employment.

Logistic Air- and Sea-lift

Military Airlift Command's active force of C–5s and C–141s, backed up by the Civil Reserve Air Fleet (CRAF), would be tied up from D-Day to D + 10 or D + 15, delivering parachute and air-landed assault echelons of one airborne division, together with some corps-level support and Air Force elements. No additional division could even begin to deploy by air until at least D + 15, perhaps even later. An Airmobile Division with top priority would take about 20 days thereafter to deploy to the operational area with its organic equipment. This move might be completed by D + 35. The follow-on infantry division would need another 27 days (assuming the aircraft were still available) and so could be fully deployed some time after D + 62.

A MAF, embarked in the Amphibious Task Force shipping, could begin marshalling in advance of the order to commit the force. Transit time for the lead elements of the force would be about 30 days from the East Coast of the United States or about 21 days from the West Coast. Final elements of the MAF could close the area about six weeks after the alert. Essential back-up for all supporting requirements additional to these assault elements could be expected to be available by about D + 60 or very soon after.

Cargo Requirements

A force of two divisions (one airborne, one marine) on an austere scale would need about 1,760 short tons of supplies daily for its maintenance. The Military Sea-Lift Command (MSC) inventory at present includes six Government-owned and 25 Government-chartered dry cargo ships, the latter including 14 fast break-bulk ships. The cargo capacity of 5,215 short tons for each of these 14 fast break-bulk ships would be inadequate to meet the demands of two divisions. Assuming an average speed of 21 knots, it would take 53 days to make the 23,000-mile round trip from Norfolk to Ras Tanura and back, with four days for turn-around at either end. Eighteen such ships would be required to sustain the force.

It is not necessary to take this analysis further (more details can be found in sources referred to) to demonstrate that shipping would be tight. Charter ships from the US Merchant Marine would be essential, but it is worth noting that the Merchant Marine is now half the size it was in the late 1960s and is facing increasing obsolescence.

Protection of Sea Lines of Communication

Although shipping would be at peak vulnerability in the Arabian Gulf and adjacent narrow seas, its protection would be less difficult here, where it would be concentrated, than during the long haul (11,000 miles) from the Straits of Hormuz around the Cape of Good Hope, to the East Coast of the United States or Europe.

It would not be as easy to block the Straits of Hormuz as is often claimed. The actual Strait itself, in terms of navigable water, is some 50 kms wide. This is wider than the English Channel between Cap Gris Nez and Folkestone. It is not feasible to obstruct this passage by sinking shipping (as it is, for example, in the Suez Canal). The most favourable area for laying mines shows a depth of water between 60 and 80 metres. Elsewhere, in the most commonly used channels, depths are commonly nearer 100 metres. There are alternative channels which could be used by shipping in the event of blockage. Mining would have to be kept topped up and does not in any case present an insuperable problem to available mine-detection and minesweeping equipment. Shore batteries (except in conditions of hostile air dominance, which would render them superfluous and the whole operation impossible) could be suppressed with no great difficulty by fast patrol boat and air action.

In 1977 2,500 million barrels per day, or 32.3 per cent of all American oil imports, travelled around South Africa, with 288 tankers (average size 80,000 deadweight tons) at sea at any time. It is outside the constricted areas in the Gulf itself and its vicinity that attrition could be very great, unless convoy protection were provided. The provision of adequate convoy protection from United States naval and air resources unaided is impracticable. It is here that Allied resources would be indispensable, and even then there would be very great difficulties in the face of Soviet submarine or air attack.

Concluding Comments

It is not proposed to pursue further, with the aid of the mass of material now available in open sources, the illustration of the considerable difficulties that would attend military intervention in the Arabian Gulf. The assertion by Secretary of Defense Schlesinger that 'it is indeed feasible to conduct military operations in the Persian Gulf' might be thought to have been based on somewhat optimistic assumptions at the time it was made, in January 1975.

Improvements to the posture of readiness have been made since then. Maritime mobility has improved in some respects (for example, in the provision of new dry cargo tonnage) but not in others (for example, the decline in numbers and the ageing of the United States Merchant Fleet); improvement in forward base facilities and in pre-positioning has taken place, but the level of forces to be drawn on has not increased.

This is no place for the exploration of political implications. It must be pointed out, however, that the ability of the United States, even with Allied support, to intervene in the Arabian Gulf for the securing of oil supplies depends in the very highest degree upon two closely interrelated factors. The first is that timely action is scarcely possible without the willingness of countries in the area either, at best, to accept the basing of American forces on their territories or, as a second best, to accept the presence in the vicinity of pre-positioned material and amphibious base resources which could be brought into use without the long delays involved in bringing them from their normal deployment areas. The key country, of course, is Saudi Arabia. There is little doubt that there is here a tangible awareness of the value of American support, coupled with a deep reluctance to ask for it. This reluctance will certainly persist – and may increase – as long as United States policy is deemed in the Arab world to be hostile to the interests of the Palestinians.

The second factor is the vital need for the pre-positioning, with appropriate facilities, of troops for early action and of equipment for the follow on, together with the provision of adequate air and sea mobility for the rapid deployment of a main force. Action is proceeding in the United States for the expeditious creation of an adequate sealift, though whether this is being given the political support which, in the national interest, it would appear to deserve is questionable. Closely allied to this consideration is the high importance of the maintenance of a presence in or close to the Arabian Gulf area sufficient to demonstrate the ability and willingness of the United States and her Allies to contribute in an effective and acceptable fashion to the maintenance of stability in the area. It cannot be too strongly emphasized that the presence of naval and amphibious forces in the vicinity is of the utmost importance. It would be wrong to suggest that nothing is happening in this respect. The United States naval force which has been maintained in the area since the 1940s (but amounted last year to no more than two destroyers and an amphibious transport dock ship, the *La Salle*, converted as a flagship, to which has been added, from time to time, a carrier task force from the Seventh Fleet for a one month cruise in the Indian Ocean) has been recently considerably increased. Of friendly countries it is important to recognize that France has clocked up more ship-days of deployment in the Indian Ocean in recent years than either the United States or the Soviet Union. With base facilities at Réunion, Mayotte and especially at Djibouti (where there are also 4,500 infantry troops), French naval forces in the Indian Ocean usually consist of a helicopter carrier with marines embarked, two or three destroyers and an occasional submarine, together with assorted minesweepers, landing craft and support ships. The British squadron of up to four frigates which deploys to the region periodically is a very welcome and valuable contribution. The Australian Government has also been taking an increasing interest in the maintenance of a naval presence in the area and has been holding joint naval exercises with the United States, France and Britain. Australia may make naval facilities available to the United States at Cockburn Sound in South-west Australia and airfields at Learmouth, Pearce and Cocos, of which the last is near enough to be of considerable value.

Finally, it should be emphasized that distance is the real enemy. Subic Bay is 6,000 miles from the entrance to the Arabian Gulf. Guam is 1,500 miles further off. Norfolk in Virginia, via the Cape of Good Hope, is 11,000 miles away. On Diego Garcia the improvements first proposed in 1972, which made no more than slow progress until 1976, have now progressed so far that most of what is required is operational. Diego Garcia, however, is 2,300 miles from the head of the Gulf. There is still some possibility of the use of facilities on a visiting basis at Bahrain, and United States patrol aircraft now

use with advantage the old Royal Air Force station on the Omani island of Masirah. Negotiations have been concluded for American facilities in Kenya, in Oman and at Berbera in Somalia. Egypt, too, will be very important and the acquisition of US base facilities on Egyptian soil (such as Ras Banas) cannot be ruled out, though much here will depend on the attitude of the United States to Israel. There are reports that airborne early-warning aircraft have already exercised from Egyptian bases, and four American AWACS deployed to Saudi Arabia at the start of the Iran–Iraq War.

There can be no substitute in an emergency for the very early arrival of a military force, even if this were to be no more than relatively small and lightly armed. As General Volnay F. Warner, Commander of the United States Readiness Command (of which the Rapid Deployment Joint Task Force at McDill Air Force Base is a part) puts it, the important thing is to get 'US combat boots on the ground' – and to get them there first, so as to place the onus of removing them on the USSR.

Appendix A: Background to Rapid Reaction Planning in the United States

The Kennedy Administration, in which McNamara was Secretary for Defense, faced with a choice on the one hand between stationing forces and material more or less permanently overseas, in areas where national interests might be threatened, or maintaining, on the other, a mobile fire brigade to be sent to trouble spots as required, opted for the latter. Global mobility was to be assured by the provision of the new C–5A transport aircraft and Fast Deployment Logistics (FDL) ships. Involvement in Vietnam damped down enthusiasm for distant interventions in the years that followed, returned the emphasis of American defence preoccupations to NATO Europe and increased American dependence on allies (e.g. Iran) for regional security. Secretary Brown's 'Rapid Deployment Force' (RDF) can now be seen as a resurrection of McNamara's fire brigade. The new monster transport aircraft (as it is popularly described), the C–X, is only an updated version of the C–5A;[7] the Maritime Pre-positioning Ships (MPS), upon which the mobility of equipment depends, are little more than facsimiles of McNamara's FDL vessels.

The scenario, too, is similar. The fire-brigade troops would be flown in C–5As, (or, when they are in service, C–Xs), to friendly airports near the combat zone, where they would pick up their equipment

from the MPSS and move to the battlefield.[8] What has changed radically is United States Government support. A special defence vote of some $580 million has been provided to establish the American military base system in the Indian Ocean. Assistant Secretary of Defense Claytor is reported to have said that the United States naval supply shipping at present afloat there 'would provide for in-theatre unit equipment and supplies to support a marine brigade of about 12,000 men and several air force fighter squadrons'.[9]

The United States Navy has also now coming into service new amphibious assault ships (LHA) upon which would be embarked Marines and AV–8A VTOL aircraft.

The forces available, out of which the fire brigade in the early version and the RDF in the later would be found, have changed little over the years. A recapitulation, in summary, may be helpful. They comprise:

82nd Airborne Division at Fort Bragg, North Carolina (15,200: air assault element, 11,000)

101st Airmobile Division at Fort Campbell, Kentucky (17,900)

One or two Light Divisions (10,000 to 15,000 each, depending on task and make-up)

One or two Marine Divisions (19,800 each, with their own fighter/attack aircraft wing, each forming part of a Marine Amphibious Force)

600 to 1,000 combat aircraft

700 (approximately) cargo aircraft: there are 70 C–5As and 234 smaller C–141 transports, plus several hundred KC–134 tankers for in-flight refuelling

Two to four Aircraft Carrier Groups

Fast patrol boats, minesweepers, ASW craft and a command vessel escorted by, say, three destroyers.

NOTES

[1] John M. Collins and Clyde R. Mark, 'Petroleum Imports from the Persian Gulf: Use of US Armed Force to Ensure Supplies', Issue Brief No. 1B 79046, last updated 8 January 1980, p. 2.

[2] Quoted by Klare, in *The Nation*, 8 March 1980.

[3] 'Oil Imports: A Range of Policy Options', Congressional Research Service, Committee Print 96 IFC 36, 1979.

[4] See Appendix A.

[5] Committee on International Relations, United States Government Print, USGPO, 21 August 1975, p. 42.

[6] 'Oil Fields as Military Objectives; A Feasibility Study', prepared for the Special Sub-Committee on Investigation of the Committee on International Relations by the Congressional Research Service, presented 21 August 1975, p. 61.

[7] According to *Army*, July 1980, p. 19, the C–X, even if fully funded, will not be deployable before 1987.

[8] 'Have RDF, will travel', Klare, *The Nation*, 8 March 1980.

[9] *Observer*, 17 August 1980.

Internal Change and Regime Stability

MICHAEL NACHT

When the Shah of Iran was forced to leave his country in January 1979 two knowledgeable and prominent Americans publicly offered strikingly different interpretations of what had caused his political downfall.

Henry Kissinger, former Secretary of State and a personal friend of the Shah's, argued that Iran's fundamental problem was a mismatch between economic development and political modernisation. As Iran experienced an enormous influx of petrodollars into her economy as a consequence of the quadrupling of oil prices after the 1973 Arab–Israeli war, forces for economic development were set in motion that were felt in every corner of the society. These forces were accompanied by a desire for increased political participation that the Shah was too slow to appreciate. When political demands went unheard opposition to the Shah's regime grew. Then, according to Kissinger, mismanagement of the situation by the Shah, coupled with extraordinary demonstrations of weakness and vacillation by the United States, led to revolution and the collapse of authoritarian rule.

George Ball, former Under-Secretary of State, who had been called in by the Carter Administration, in December 1978, to provide an independent assessment of the Iranian situation, saw matters differently. He claimed that the Shah had a severe case of megalomania that had led to his systematic alienation of most of the key elements in Iranian society. Ball judged that the principal cause of this behaviour was the enormous quantity of sophisticated weapons that Iran had received from the United States since the early 1970s. By placing great reliance on Iran to be the policeman of the Gulf, as part of the Nixon policy of using 'regional hegemonies' to protect American interests, the United States had unwittingly, according to Ball, transformed the Shah from a minor despot to a leader with great-power aspirations. In the

process, the Shah became intoxicated with his own power, surrounded himself with sycophants, encouraged corruption that became pervasive, promoted domestic, economic and social policies to suit his own purposes, isolated himself from the cross-currents developing within Iranian society and, thereby, sowed the seeds of his own destruction.

Obervers of the Iranian scene without political axes to grind or reputations to protect would readily admit that all of the features cited by both Kissinger and Ball were prevalent in Iran. There *was* rapid and disruptive economic development that, in part, clashed with traditional norms and values. The growth of political participation did *not* accompany economic progress, and there was little evidence that it was likely to in the near future. The Shah *was* perceived by many Iranians as a corrupt, autocratic ruler, installed with American initiative, who permitted and even encouraged the use of secret police to root out and torture political opponents. He *did* have great-power aspirations, encouraged by the growth of potent military forces armed with the most advanced American weapons; he *was* out of touch with sources of dissent in the society; and he *was* confused and ultimately disappointed by conflicting advice and declaratory policies offered by high-level American officials. What is far less clear, however, is what was decisive in leading to the Shah's downfall and what was peripheral. What mixture of economic, social, political and military developments really determined the Shah's fate? How, if at all, could the United States have acted more effectively? More important for the long term, how does the Iranian illustration of political instability in a developing society relate, if at all, to other manifestations of the same behaviour? Are there common threads between the Iranian case and Somoza's experience in Nicaragua, for example? What can we learn from the demise of

Haile Selassie in Ethiopia or even from Castro's success in Cuba 20 years ago? Indeed, are there discernible patterns to political instability in developing countries, or is every case *sui generis*?

Most important, what can these historical cases tell us about the future? What is the likelihood of political instability in Turkey,[1] Saudi Arabia, Mexico, the Philippines? What changes in domestic conditions or in the policies of external powers could reduce the probability of instability? And is the reduction of this probability uniformly desirable? These are enormously important questions for the student of economic and political development, for international business executives, for the citizens and governments of developing countries and for policy-makers in the United States, the Soviet Union and other major powers. This paper does not provide the answers to these questions. It does, however, offer a way of structuring the issues and provides a set of propositions that would appear to deserve further investigation.

Clarifying Some Concepts

Because the problem of political instability in developing countries is, on the face of it, one of overwhelming complexity, it is useful to clarify what is relevant to our concerns and what is not. The political systems of the world's roughly 150 nation-states can be divided into three categories: democracies (about 25), Communist states (about 20) and authoritarian states (about 100). More than 90 per cent of the developing countries of Asia, Africa and Latin America have authoritarian governments which, according to Webster, 'relate to or favour a concentration of power in a leader or an elite not constitutionally responsible to the people'. There are no provisions for the legal and orderly transition of power in authoritarian governments, and their leaders must necessarily, therefore, rely on force of arms to retain power. This in turn means that any demonstrable sign of discontent or opposition to the ruling elite is in itself a threat to the existing social and political order. Strikes, anti-government demonstrations, riots, major Cabinet shifts and crises, vocal questioning of the ruling political party's legitimacy and arrests of opposition leaders can all be classified as manifestations of 'political instability' in authoritarian states.

But these actions take place all the time in developing countries, and most often the ruling elite rides out the problem without great difficulty. Therefore 'political instability' *per se* is not the principal focus of our concern. What is of interest is leadership change that is followed by significant alterations in the domestic and foreign policies of the state. Authoritarian regimes have traditionally been prone to two forms of leadership change. The first, 'political revolution', may be defined as a major alteration in government and society, usually embodying a departure from the old order and typically carried out with violence. The second, the *coup d'état*, whether by an individual or by a small group, usually occurs with only limited violence and sometimes with none at all. The *coup d'état* usually results in the abrupt replacement of leading government personalities but, unlike a revolution, it generally does not alter basic economic and social policies.

Coups d'état occur with great frequency in developing countries – in Latin America in particular. Bolivia, for example (depending on how one counts), has had almost 200 coups in its less than 200 years of history as a state. But, apart from Captain X replacing Colonel Y, very few substantive changes in domestic or foreign policy have followed as a consequence of these government changes. Because of their frequency, because they most often affect little of note in social, economic or foreign policy and because they involve few individuals, usually acting with little advance notice, *coups d'état* are not at the centre of our concern.

It is the phenomenon of 'political revolution', carried out over a period of months or even years, that is our main concern. It is this form of extra-legal regime change in developing countries, involving the use or threat of force, that leads to social transformation and fundamental policy shifts often adverse to Western interests. It is this form of protracted political upheaval that provides both sufficient data for analysis and time for governments to act and react.

Consider, therefore, the multitude of possible combinations facing the analyst:

—manifestations of political instability that

fail to lead to social or economic transformations or to extra-legal regime changes – the seizure of the Mosque in Mecca, Saudi Arabia, the armed insurrection against the Marcos Government in parts of the Philippines, or the student strikes against the South Korean military government are recent examples;

—*coups d'état* that, after significant time delays, lead to major domestic societal changes and foreign policy shifts – the actions subsequently taken well after initial seizure of power by Nasser in Egypt in 1952 and Qaddafi in Libya in 1969 are examples of this;

—major domestic social change and foreign policy shifts without any extra-legal regime change – Sadat in Egypt in the 1970s is a prime example;

—political instability that leads to extra-legal regime change, social transformation and foreign policy shifts – the Iranian revolution of 1978–79 is the latest illustration of this, as the Nicaraguan situation after Somoza is perhaps not yet clarified fully enough to be included in this category.

We are not concerned with Westernized, developed countries, and therefore the experience of the American, French and Russian revolutions are not likely to be of help in the analysis (although technically, of course, these revolutions took place when the United States, France and Russia were not developed societies). Nor are we concerned with centrally planned economies, because the political and economic structure in such states is markedly different from those of authoritarian systems and because, in most cases, they are peculiarly susceptible to the threat of direct Soviet involvement. Hence, present difficulties in Poland and possible future troubles in Yugoslavia, for example, are outside our purview. We are not concerned with major domestic or foreign policy shifts initiated by standing governments, and therefore the problem of 'realignment' is not what we are addressing. We are most directly concerned with the first and last combinations listed above: we wish to know what mixture of characteristics of states in the last category permitted the flourishing of successful revolutionary movements,

and how governments in the first have been able to weather severe political storms.

Causality, Prediction and Multiple Indicators
Students of political revolution have traditionally sought to understand the revolutionary process in different social contexts and, from their analyses, to derive the 'causes' of revolution. Despite a voluminous literature, however, the explanatory power of the postulated theories remains low and the predictive power virtually non-existent.[2] Intimately connected with the study of revolution has been the effort to examine the process of political modernization more generally. Some observers have argued that the process is complex, systemic, global, lengthy, phased, homogenizing, irreversible and progressive. But even the most intellectually compelling analyses of political modernization provide little guidance as to how the Shah could have avoided his fate, or why President Marcos, facing apparently similar problems, has stayed in power so long.

Since theorists of revolution and analysts of political modernization have failed to provide much useful policy guidance, those interested in such matters have resorted to either *ad hoc*racy or selective comparative impressionism. In the former category are many government officials, intimately familiar with a particular society, who argue that every case is unique and that there is nothing to be learned from, for example, an examination of the Iranian case that could be of any use in understanding and assessing the internal situation in the Philippines. Since it is obviously the case that every state has certain unique features – its geographical location, the cultural composition of its populace, its relations with foreign powers – there is some merit to this perspective. But at the same time policies must be formed on the basis of the most sensible predictions that governments can formulate ('We will do X because we expect Y'), and their expectations should not be restricted to the characteristics that are peculiar to a particular state. They should be informed by a search for patterns that cut across the multiplicity of modernizing societies. Only if a systematic effort to uncover such patterns fails to identify any meaningful conditions of commonality can the emphasis on *ad hoc*racy be sustained.

54

Recognizing intuitively that some common characteristics may be present between states in the categories listed above, some writers have leaped to the use of analogies based largely on astute, but none the less impressionistic, observations.[3] By selecting points of commonality and ignoring crucial differences a case can be built to support many persuasive arguments. But it is largely a political shot in the dark that could hit or miss its target. Moreover, this is no way to conduct informed policy analysis. The problem is complicated by the realization that countries that have experienced extra-legal regime changes are incredibly heterogeneous (they include large and small states, those at the richer and at the poorer ends of the economic spectrum, those with populations with varying religious orientations) and are located in virtually every region of the globe, exhibiting a wide variety of topographical features.

Given the difficulties experienced by others in tackling this formidable intellectual problem, certain guidelines emerge.

—Given the presence of certain conditions, it is easier to derive probability estimates of regime change than causality. Just as meteorologists do not have to understand fully the interaction of complex atmospheric and environmental conditions to be able to predict the weather with a reasonably high degree of accuracy, policy analysis of political instability should emphasize the conditions that most often accompany regime change, and it should not focus on the development of an all-encompassing theory that seeks to identify the precise causal relations among a set of complex and dynamic phenomena.

—Economic, socio-cultural, political and military indices pertinent to the society and measures of the role of external powers must all be considered potential contributors to the likelihood that any state may experience an extra-legal regime change within a specific period of time. Multiple indices, rather than a single dominant issue or 'force', are most pertinent to the assessment of the significance of political instability.

—Multiple indices of a dynamic rather than a static nature are more helpful in assessing the likelihood of regime change. It is not the absolute value of the state's GNP or GNP per capita but trends in these statistics over time and the expectations these trends create among the populace that are important. A population that has long been ruled by a regime widely known to be very corrupt – the norm rather than the exception in many (even most?) 'developing' countries – is often indifferent to corruption as a political grievance unless, because of new-found wealth, the corruption spreads while certain segments of the population remain outside the reward system.

—The examination of a wide range of indices for each developing country over a one- or two-decade historical period is required to develop the most statistically robust estimations of likelihood.

—Two levels of analysis are important in anticipating regime change. With the aid of the historical record, macrostatistical data and Bayesian probability formulations are useful to generate the probability of regime change, given the presence of certain conditions (after all, we know which states in the last two decades had extra-legal regime changes and which did not). Then, utilizing these probabilities, the future likelihood of regime change can be calculated if a given set of conditions is present. These probabilistic formulations (not statistical correlation coefficients) are in turn refined in the light of work undertaken at a second level of analysis: detailed case studies of states. The richness of detail of historical case studies provides major insights inaccessible to the first level of analysis. These cases reveal the cumulative effects and non-linearities among indices. They identify catalytic events that, in retrospect, seemed crucial in igniting opposition to regimes in power. They also assess the roles of external powers in the states' economic, political and military affairs prior to, during and after the regime change.

Country-specific expertise and reasonably sophisticated data-handling and analytic capabilities are required for such work.[4] But there are problems of data quality and availability and significant intellectual minefields in link-ing results from the two levels of analysis. There are normative problems if, in addition to predicting regime change, the orientation of the work is exclusively to suggest policies designed to thwart social change in developing societies.

The goal of such efforts is to offer the following observation based on the analysis of two decades of historical data and the generation of perhaps a dozen detailed case studies.

Given that conditions x_1, x_2, x_3, x_4 and x_5 are present in Country X, the probability of political revolution in the next year is P_1. These probabilities, in turn, may then be grouped into qualitative categories such as 'virtually certain', 'highly probable', 'highly unlikely', etc. Probabilistic formulations can be offered for a large number of states. Besides those analysed correctly, the classical two types of statistical error would be committed: some revolutions would occur that were not predicted, and some revolutions would be predicted that would not occur. By constantly updating the database and refining the probability estimates, improved estimation capabilities can be perfected over time. Subsequently, in focusing more explicitly on the role of outside powers, results take the following form:

Given conditions $x_1 \ldots x_n$, the probability of political revolution in Country X in the next year is P_1. But if Country X takes action j_1, thereby eliminating condition x_1, the probability would be reduced to P_2 (where P_2 is less than P_1).

Failure to identify patterns of conditions leading to regime change and the corresponding generation of estimates of likelihood consistently low in accuracy would reinforce the intuitive notion, held firmly by some, that only country-specific expertise is helpful in tackling this problem.

Some Preliminary Insights

Researchers into political phenomena should be as agnostic about the directions in which their research takes them as those into the natural sciences, although this is an admittedly formidable request that is complied with far too infrequently. In an initial phase of research on this problem that has been completed several preliminary insights have emerged that are guiding further efforts. These are summarized below.

The Ideology of Opposition

A regime is effectively challenged by an opposition movement only if the opposition can articulate both a set of convincing grievances against the regime and a body of ideas directed at rectifying these grievances. Jorge Dominquez, who analysed the Cuban revolution in great detail, identifies the necessary ingredient as an 'ideology of opposition'. In the preliminary work completed to date it has become apparent that an ideology of opposition can be based on one of the following: rectifying the trampling of religious customs and traditional norms, as was the case in Iran; providing a preferred economic alternative to existing economic inequities, as was the case in Nicaragua; or providing a more 'just' political alternative to the present system, as is the case in Taiwan. The major point is that an opposition movement must be able to make a persuasive case that its grievances are 'valid' within the given social context and that it has an effective remedy for these grievances.

The Origins of the Regime

A vital tool for opposition groups is to play on the illegitimacy of the ruling elite. This illegitimacy argument is strengthened greatly if the leader is not a home-grown product, if he has been 'installed' by an outside power or if he has characteristics clearly alien to important segments of the populace. A French-speaking, Catholic, urban elite controlling a Vietnamese-speaking, Buddhist, peasant society in South Vietnam, for example, did not ease Saigon's problem of winning the 'hearts and minds of the people'. This charge of illegitimacy, therefore, cannot be levelled easily against Sadat in Egypt or the Royal Family in Saudi Arabia, whereas the case was much easier against Shah Pahlavi (a 'product of the CIA').

Economic Performance

There are a large number of indices worthy of detailed study in this category, including the extent of rising inflation rates, the rate of increase in unemployment, fluctuations in food production and certain measures of income distribution. In several instances (Cuba, for example), a revolutionary movement was greatly strengthened after a period of sustained economic growth had been halted and a significant economic downturn had set in. This behaviour is closely related to the 'J curve' phenomenon identified in the literature on economic development. It would appear that improving economic conditions raise people's expectations greatly. Once the downturn sets in, a great sense of disappointment prevails and the credibility of the regime becomes very suspect, providing fine recruitment opportunities for opposition groups.

Social and Demographic Indices
Preliminary research suggests two important indicators in this category: the growth of urbanization and the growth of university enrolments. The seeds of several political revolutions are to be found in the large influx of population from rural to urban areas and the tremendous overcrowding that ensues, with attendant shortages of housing and jobs. Urban slums are natural breeding grounds for political unrest. The more rapid the rate of urban migration, the greater the likelihood that the existing economic and social structure will be unable to accommodate the demands made of it. Concomitant growth in university enrolments is important, since institutions of higher learning serve as intellectual bases where the ideology of opposition can be formulated, refined and then promoted to target populations.

A third indicator within this category is ethnic conflict. Many states are ravaged by divisions between ethnic groups. But in many instances the clash is between a ruling elite representative of an ethnic majority and a disenfranchised ethnic minority. The opposition of such ethnic minorities usually takes the form of a separatist movement that seeks the establishment of its own ethnically homogeneous, sovereign state – as has been the case with the Ibos in Nigeria, the Basques in Spain, the Croats in Yugoslavia, the Kurds in Iran and Iraq. Such groups rarely pose a state-wide challenge to a regime's authority.

Corruption
Corruption (that is, 'impairment of integrity, virtue or moral principle', or 'inducement to wrong by bribery or other unlawful or improper means') is certainly very widespread through-
out developing societies and is not necessarily a potent force to be levelled against ruling elites. The corruption argument does become potent in certain conditions: if the corruption is restricted to a small circle of friends, relatives and colleagues surrounding the leader, and this state of affairs, formerly confidential, becomes widely known to the urban elite; if the corruption is pervasive and well-known but then grows suddenly in magnitude, yet selected groups remain outside the reward system; or if a ruling elite bases its legitimacy in large measure on theocratic piety but then becomes widely acknowledged to be also highly corrupt. Either 'selective corruption' or the contrast between professed religious morality and demonstrated economic immorality (the latter seems to be a growing phenomenon in Saudi Arabia) can make the corruption issue an explosive political force.

Repression
Repression, like corruption, is pervasive throughout developing societies. The use of secret police, the imprisonment of political opposition leaders, methods of torture, cruel and inhumane punishment and summary executions carried out in secret are the norm in many 'developing' countries. A sudden departure from practices long extant, however, can promote opposition. If the circle of represssion widens, it can generate animosity among groups formerly thought to be safe from recrimination or to be part of the establishment. The easing of repression, especially by a leader under siege, may often encourage opposition movements to believe that the leader is weakening and that a revolution might succeed. Indeed, leaders who appear to ease repressive measures solely to satisfy the demands of other governments, as both Shah Pahlavi and President Somoza did at the urging of the United States, may have weakened rather than strengthened their regimes as a consequence.

The Catalytic Event
Just as budding young actors often need a break to make it into the big time – the star becomes ill, and the understudy steps in and gains stardom – so revolutionary movements usually benefit from an unplanned event that triggers the growth of political opposition. Such a cata-

lytic event can be the imprisonment or execution of an opposition leader, a gross violation of ethical or religious norms by the leader of the regime or the demonstration of spectacular economic extravagance. It is extraordinarily difficult to identify such an event before it occurs, but in retrospect analyses of a regime change often point to a single excess by the ruling elite that triggered its downfall.

The Behaviour of External Powers

A crucial contribution in this area is the provision of arms or even combat forces by an external power to an opposition group. The role of military assistance to contending groups in a domestic political struggle is an important and complex subject. In preliminary analyses of a few selected cases there is a striking contrast between the Soviet ability to deliver large numbers of high-performance weapons at short notice to contending groups within developing countries and the much slower and less reliable response rate by the United States in similar circumstances. Moreover, the Soviet Union's use of proxy forces and military advisers has been a major determinant of the outcome of some political struggles and has placed the United States at a significant disadvantage in several cases.

Many additional indices within each category require further investigation, and it remains to be demonstrated how crucial regional differences are in influencing the pattern of regime change in developing countries. Moreover, the complex pattern of interaction and influence among several of these characteristics has yet to be addressed but attempts to generate useful predictors will persist. Both *ad hoc*racy and selective analogizing ought to be relegated to positions of insignificance by those concerned with political and economic stability in developing countries in the 1980s.

NOTES

[1] Turkey is a peculiar case and, arguably, should be omitted from this analysis. In economic terms, as measured by gross national product per capita in US dollars in 1977, it fell near the mid-point among 54 states classified as 'middle-income countries' by the World Bank. Its GNP per capita is less than that of Mexico, Jamaica, Lebanon, Chile, Panama, Iraq, Iran, Trinidad and Tobago and many other states in this category. But it is largely a European society; traditionally it had (until 1980) a democratic form of government; and it is, of course, a member of NATO.

[2] A useful summary of the evolution of this literature may be found in Jack A. Goldstone, 'Theories of Revolution: The Third Generation', *World Politics* (April 1980), pp. 425–53.

[3] See, for example, John B. Oakes, 'Like the Shah, President Marcos', *New York Times*, 6 July 1980.

[4] For more detail on a continuing effort that follows these guidelines, see Steven E. Miller, Stephen M. Meyer, and Michael Nacht, 'Everything You Ever Wanted to Ask about Patterns of Political Instability in Developing Countries and their Implications for American Policy but Were Afraid to Know', mimeo, Harvard University, June 1980.

Security in an Age of Turbulence:
Means of Response

STANLEY HOFFMANN

Dissociation and Insecurity
International security is both a relative and an uneven notion. In an 'anarchic society' of nations that live in a condition of troubled peace or in a 'state of war' – depending on whether one takes a more Lockian or a more Hobbesian view of world affairs – there will always be a modicum of insecurity. Not all the actors can be simultaneously secure as long as we have not reached the unlikely stage of living in a world without threats and enmities or the distant stage of inhabiting a world so well organized that its members are both deprived of, and saved from, self-help. Moreover, the scope of insecurity is not fixed; the security of the world as a whole is threatened only by some perils, whereas certain regions, or individual members, can be endangered also by threats that do not affect the security of others.

For the purposes of this paper, I will define international insecurity as the sum of all the factors that can lead to serious confrontations between the major powers (those whose resources and policies are such as to shape the fate of a large number of other actors), to increases in the threat or in the reality of contagious or uncontrollable violence and to such a deterioration of, or such an increase in the unpredictability of, international economic transactions as to threaten the economic lives of large numbers of countries. I will argue here that there is a likelihood of considerable international insecurity in the 1980s, for reasons described below. I will then examine the general problem of how to cope with it and will finally discuss specific means of response.

The major factors that contribute to insecurity in the 1980s are not new. For many years now the international system has been characterized by three contradictions that breed tur-

bulence. The first is the contradiction between the universal cold war and the growing complexity of the system. It creates a serious dilemma for the super-powers. How far should they go in injecting their rivalry into a region? Non-involvement spares one the risks of confrontation and the costs of economic or military presence. Involvement, however, yields opportunities for influence. The dilemma creates uncertainty – especially as local circumstances or domestic factors may, at times, facilitate or invite the involvement of one super-power and inhibit that of the other. The American attempt, in the 1970s, to find a middle way by relying on regionally influential states has been disappointing – their leaders turned out to have clay feet, like the Shah, or pursued their own interests.

The second is the contradiction between what Raymond Aron once called the 'unity of the diplomatic field' – the existence of a single international system – and the multiple heterogeneities of the field. These relate to:

—the types of actor – they range from peoples in search of a nation-state (Palestinians, Kurds) to states in quest of a nation (Africa), to nation-states, to empires; hence there are innumerable opportunities for conflict;
—the regimes and ideologies which despite universal lip-service to two principles – self-government and self-determination – turn out both to have multiple interpretations and to create insoluble problems;
—the economic and social systems and levels of economic development (here, heterogeneity has been and will keep growing);
—the nature of power: one observes a func-

59

tional fragmentation of international politics, in which different games are played not only in different regions but over different 'issue areas' (to borrow the language of Nye and Keohane).

As a result, we live in a world marked by three features:

—First, considerable asymmetry between the actors. Very few can be considered 'full powers', endowed with a complete panoply of power; many actors have only one dimension of power – for example, economic but not military (Saudi Arabia), or military but not economic (Vietnam), or no power other than a good geographical location or a potentially usable vote in an international or regional organization. Even the two super-powers are asymmetrical, given, on the one hand, both the weaknesses of the Soviet economy (despite huge resources) and the Soviet Union's absence (on the whole) from the open international economy and, on the other hand, the Soviet Union's willingness, in recent years to resort to self-help and ability to use proxies on a considerable scale.
—Second, by a double transformation of the international hierarchy. It is being subverted, in so far as the super-powers are often inhibited in the full use of their power by a variety of factors (the risks of collision, their inability to achieve collusion, the inadequacy of their forms of power to deal with local circumstances and the ability of their clients to manipulate them), and in so far as states with limited power (such as Saudi Arabia or even West Germany) can achieve considerable influence in certain 'issue areas'. The international hierarchy is also being fragmented, since the pecking order varies from one 'issue area' to another.
—Third, a contradiction both between the principle of sovereignty, which remains the basis of international law and international order, and the restraints which weigh on all the actors and provide the only safety nets in a very dangerous system devoid of common values, and between the concern for survival and the quest for development and welfare. In the realm of security this contradiction takes the form of another paradox: the coexistence of stable deterrence at the global level (despite the difference in military arsenals and strategic doctrines between the United States and the Soviet Union) and the search for 'usable' nuclear strategies (i.e. for war-fighting rather than for pure deterrence), as well as a continuing drift towards nuclear proliferation. In the realm of development and welfare the contradiction creates two acute problems: the problem of inequality, or the revolt against the international economic system largely created by the leading capitalist powers, and particularly by the United States, and the problem of monopoly, or the attempt by developing states endowed with key resources to exploit their advantages. In other words, the international system is characterized by the constant manipulation of the two restraints: it is a permanent and multiple game of chicken.

Until now, international insecurity has been kept at tolerable levels by different factors which have had the same result: they have prevented causes of turbulence from joining, or trouble in one region or 'issue area' from spreading to the others. Fragmentation or dissociation has prevailed. First, in the super-powers' competition this has taken the form of a sort of division of the world into relatively autonomous sub-systems, each one with its own 'rules of the game', which depend on the configuration of local forces and of the super-powers' forces in the region. The limits of Soviet power, both in the economic realm and, until recent years, in the military domain, and the stability of the 'balance of terror' provided by the chief rivals' strategic nuclear weapons have contributed to this fragmentation.

Domestic Politics and Foreign Policy
A second kind of dissociation has always been more fragile. The distinction between domestic politics and foreign policy has never been rigid in practice, and throughout the 1950s, 1960s and 1970s we have witnessed inter-state conflicts over a regime, or over the application of self-determination, or over the combination of the two – this is what the wars in Korea and

60

Vietnam were about – as well as domestic revolutions with international repercussions (as in Cuba and China). But again these explosions have been kept separate, and a great deal of domestic turbulence has not provoked international involvement or conflict.

A third dissociation, which lasted through the 1960s, was that between the open international economy and the strategic-diplomatic chess-board: the 'two-track' system analysed by Richard Cooper.[1] To be sure, that dissociation itself resulted from a political design – the United States' conception of a global order – and from the kinds of political bargain that Robert Gilpin has described.[2] And it was never total: the Marshall plan had strategic-diplomatic goals, and the West used economic warfare against the East. Nevertheless, within these limits it allowed for the reasonably successful management of the world economy – brilliantly, indeed, in relations between advanced capitalist states, less brilliantly in North–South relations. Deterioration, whose causes began to operate in the late 1960s, set in in the 1970s. However, despite inflation, recession and the multiple ramifications of the oil crises of the 1970s, a major disaster comparable with the Depression of the 1930s has been avoided.

The problem of the 1980s is the risk of an end of dissociation or fragmentation, for reasons that can be found within each of three realms just mentioned. In the first place, the factors of regional fragmentation of the super-powers' contest are weakening. The key development here is the Soviet ability to project military power abroad, and the Soviet determination to exploit Western weaknesses in the Third World in ways different from, and more effective than, the earlier Soviet methods that led to serious reversals not only in the Congo in 1960 but later in the Sudan, in Egypt and in Somalia – not to mention China. The Soviet Union, while continuing to support forces more promising than subservient Communist parties in places where these are insignificant, now prefers to help movements whose social goals and method fit within Marxist–Leninist orthodoxy; and the Soviet Union sees to it, when her client gets to power, that his dependence is great enough, and her own presence weighty enough, to prevent a repetition of what had happened in Egypt in July 1972. Moreover, for reasons best analysed by Seweryn Bialer,[3] the Soviet Union may, in the 1980s, be increasingly tempted to compensate abroad for domestic weaknesses and tensions: declining growth, serious economic inefficiencies, one or two succession periods, a growing need for oil from the outside, changes in the demographic composition of the Soviet Union – all may lead to a quest for external triumphs. There is an interesting asymmetry here: turbulence in Eastern Europe would obviously affect the Soviet Union more profoundly than the West, but the desire to avoid Soviet repression (as well as another burst of tension and another display of Western helplessness) incites the members of NATO to prudence and counsels of moderation for the malcontents. Turbulence in third-world areas affects the United States and her Allies far more than Moscow, and Moscow shows little reluctance to exploit it whenever the circumstances seem favourable.

Another development dangerous for regional disconnection is the activity of Soviet client states with important military means and ambitions of their own: Cuba in Africa, and Vietnam in South-east Asia. A third development is the new American determination to contain more vigorously than in recent years such advances by Soviet proxies and by the Soviet Union. The final threat comes from strategic considerations. Regional fragmentation presupposes either a military balance (as in Europe), or such an imbalance that (as in Latin America) one super-power actually has the field to itself, or a willingness on the part of the rivals to compete primarily by means other than military (or merely by providing arms to local clients). But when both super-powers – or one super-power and the close allies of the other – decide to compete more vigorously and with armed forces, and when, in addition, there is a regional imbalance in conventional forces, the temptation for the loser to compensate either by exploiting his superiority elsewhere or by exploiting whatever advantages he may have (or believes he has) in the strategic nuclear realm will be considerable. In this respect, the gradual shift from the stability of mutual assured destruction, plus some arms control, to the instability of counter-force, war-fighting strategies – likely to be detrimental both to deterrence and to crisis stability – minus arms control is a last nail in the coffin of regional fragmentation.

Fragmentation in the Third World

In the second place, the collapse of the distinction between domestic and foreign affairs is likely to become universal. To put it as bluntly as possible, domestic affairs are likely to become the stake of international politics and intervention the empirical norm. We have almost reached the end of the protracted period of decolonization (only Southern Africa is left). What we now find is a scene marked by the following features.

Many states are endowed with artificial borders and are racked by destructive internal communal conflicts between tribes, ethnic groups, religious sects, cultural factions, or by violent clashes between ideological opponents or rival army cliques, or a combination of all these. Recently Iran, India, Burma, Zimbabwe, El Salvador, Bolivia and South Korea have all been in the news for such reasons. A state with a badly or only partially integrated society or a tyrannical regime is likely to be a target for meddling, either by a great power or by a neighbour intent on ensuring his security or on expanding his influence by removing a hostile regime or by exploiting internal dissensions next door. In recent years Vietnam's move into Cambodia, Tanzania's overthrow of Idi Amin, Somalia's war in Ethiopia, Iraq's intrigues against Iran and Syria and her war on Iran and Libya's probes in Chad all give us a taste of things to come. Finally, revolutions are likely in many places – it is through force that governments and regimes tend to change in the Third World – and many of these carry a risk either of realignment in the global cold war or of withdrawal from a present pro-Western alignment, as in the case of Iran in 1979.

Why should the threat of greater internal fragmentation in third-world countries, and of more inter-state conflicts resulting from it, lead to international rather than to mere regional insecurity? Partly because some of the countries that could be in trouble occupy important strategic positions (Egypt) or provide vital resources (Saudi Arabia); partly because internal factions or external meddlers seek and obtain outside support (think of the POLISARIO case: the guerrillas have Algerian and Libyan help; Morocco has American assistance); partly because of the way generalized turbulence affects the great powers' definition of their security. They always tend to oscillate between two poles. The narrow definition practically equates security with survival: national security means the protection of the nation (and of nationals abroad) against physical attack and the safeguarding of its economic activities from devastating outside blows. The broad definition tends to equate national security and foreign policy or national interests. This is excessive (and dangerous, either when such interests vastly outrun the nation's power or when they lead to so formidable an expansion of that power – in order to match the interests – as to frighten or threaten other states). And yet an expansive definition of security is inevitable, for two reasons. The first reason is valid for all states, major or not. Since the state is represented in world affairs by its regime, the latter will consider its own self-preservation as a matter of national security, a fact that tends to be neglected by authors who write in countries with legitimate and stable governments. Secondly, major actors, almost by definition, project their power abroad in order to provide their physical and economic security with a kind of *glacis*, and they do so in the two modes distinguished by Arnold Wolfers, when he wrote about possession and milieu goals.[4] They tend to equate their own national security with that of close allies – of states whose physical and economic survival is deemed indispensable to their own. And they define as essential to their national security the preservation either of a clientèle of states (without whose physical and economic survival they could most probably live) or of international rules and regimes whose loss would markedly affect their influence and their status.

In a sense, the scope of a major actor's definition of his national security depends on two factors. One is his power – the greater it is, the more widely he will throw the net, the more interests will be equated with security and national security with foreign policy. This happened in the United States in the late 1940s and the 1950s; it is happening now in the Soviet Union. The other factor is external threats: when they multiply or become sharper, and even if national power is limited, the notion of national security tends to become more expansive; it expands to meet the threat, rather than the other way round. If we look at the post-war United States, we find that the first half of the 1970s was a kind of golden period in which the definition of the scope of national security relaxed somewhat (not all *that* much, as Allende found out). Earlier the scope was huge because of American power. Now it grows again, because of the rise of threats and also because of the recent dynamics of the super-powers' contest. Many Americans believe that the turbulence in the Third World and the rise of radical movements hostile to the West there are due partly to a perception of declining American power or will, and they are determined to reverse the trend. But in the meantime the Soviet Union has deepened her own involvement and has to protect her own investment or act in such a way as to become a necessary factor in most important disputes and an unavoidable counterpart for the United States.

Economic and Political Dissociation

The third dissociation that is vanishing is that between the economic and the political 'track'. Here again there are several reasons. The most obvious is the international economic crisis. International insecurity is increased by the persistence of inflation and recession in major industrial countries; by the brutal politics of oil, which, through the complicated bargains of OPEC, result in higher prices (partly as a reply to the industrial powers' inflation) as well as in uncertainty about levels of production (an uncertainty compounded by revolutions and wars in the Middle East); and by the enormous threat which the rising debt of the oil-importing developing countries creates for the international financial system. The outcome is both an intensified contest among states for resources (particularly those of the seas and oceans) and domestic tension everywhere: a weakening of the ability of governments to meet the demands or needs of citizens, the rise of protectionist pressures and the necessity for many governments in poor countries to cut back on social expenditures and development plans. Another factor is the contribution made by economic development itself to internal disruption, social dislocations and political turbulence in many

third-world countries – particularly in the oil-producing states, where sudden wealth has spread corruption and has heightened the tensions between a crumbling traditional order on one side and its two very different kinds of foe – modernizers who often turn to socialist or Communist models, and traditionalists intent on restoring threatened values.

If there ever was a line separating economic from political affairs, it has now been crossed at all points, and this is likely to continue. Economics has become a political weapon – for those oil-producing 'radical regimes' that want to use higher prices and cuts in production as weapons against the United States or Israel because of the Palestinian issue; for the United States, which has resorted to economic warfare against Idi Amin, against Iran after the seizure of American hostages and, after the invasion of Afghanistan, against the Soviet Union; and for the international community as a whole, which used economic sanctions against Ian Smith's Rhodesia and may do so again against South Africa. Economic frustration can also have political consequences: we have seen that, on a small scale, in Britain's recurrent ultimata to the EEC; a much more disturbing case was seen at the Havana Conference of the non-aligned nations and in the success of Castro's speech, centred on North–South issues, at the UN General Assembly in 1979.

Competition and the Diffusion of Power

Let us combine these different trends. We obtain the image of a world that is becoming much more dangerous and unmanageable because of the interaction of two contradictory trends. One is the renewed commitment of the super-powers to global competition. There are serious disagreements about the nature of Soviet ambitions, but there can be little doubt about Moscow's determination to be a world power, about its accumulation of military means (whether for actual use or, like money in the bank, as a guarantee of influence), about its determination to exploit – albeit at low risk – promising opportunities and about the decline of the inhibitions that the hope for detente's benefits had temporarily induced. In the Third World, the Soviet Union now has important assets: she can turn against the West the very strong anti-racist and anti-imperialist resentments and can provide liberation movements, or national leaders, or both with material help and with a kind of (adaptable) model of political control. As for the United States, not only does she still have vast assets of her own – in the realm of public and, above all, private economic assistance to states, most of which cannot afford self-reliance and find the Soviet economic model unattractive – but the cumulative effect of a string of Soviet successes (almost none of which has affected by itself the hard core, or the narrow definition, of American national security) has led to a return to the more expansive definition and to the new militancy mentioned above.

The other trend is both a kind of diffusion and a pulverization of power. Many states, including third-world ones, are becoming important economic actors; they produce and export their own weapons, and in some cases they seem to be moving towards the production of nuclear weapons. Yet they suffer from the internal weaknesses already discussed, and may indeed make them worse through external adventures of their own. The collision of the two trends gives one a major reason for pessimism (in addition to the reason provided by mutual misperceptions and internal developments in the two super-powers): the ability now of clients or proxies to manipulate super-powers or to provoke confrontations. The biggest peril lies in 'grey areas' in which uncertainty exists about the extent of a super-power's commitment to an ally or friend and about the other's likely response. There the diversity of the vital national interests of the local players and the existence of the cold war can combine to produce serious miscalculations and 'misescalations'. The super-powers, concerned with their credibility, have not developed adequate means of avoiding these through consultation and crisis management. Three parts of the world are candidates for such dangers: the Middle East (where the effects of a protracted political crisis in Iran, of a long and costly war between Iraq and Iran and of an indecisive war in Afghanistan have now been added to all the other ferments), Southern Africa and East Asia. The combination of antagonistic nationalisms, rival ideologies, imperatives of 'face' (or alliance preservation, or balance of power) and domestic instabilities is frightening in all three areas.

To be sure, the danger of 'reconnection' is not of the same order all over the world. A more detailed analysis would have to make distinctions between different areas. There will still be a number of sub-systems, each one with its own dynamics – in Europe, the Americas, Africa, the Middle East, East Asia. But all the signs point to greater turbulence in all of them except Europe (which does not mean that there will not be serious instability within each half of the Continent) and to a greater risk of the spread of insecurity from one area to others.

Approaches to the Resolution of Conflict
There is another disturbing element. We have little to learn from past periods of turbulence. I have, at some length, tried to explain elsewhere why previous methods of coping with international insecurity are of little use now, and shall not repeat the arguments here.[5] But it may be worth looking briefly at two specific periods.

1870–1914
The first one was the period of 1870–1914, when the great powers indulged in the scramble for colonies and frequently clashed in what is now called the Third World. Despite Lenin's biased analysis of imperialism, it was not because of those expeditions and conflicts that World War I broke out. France had frequently opposed Britain and Italy, and Britain had opposed Russia, yet they ended up allies. It was not Franco-German conflicts over Morocco that led to the war. It began at the very core of the European state system because of the fatal weakness of Austria-Hungary and of her vulnerability to Slav nationalism. But the precedent of that period does not suggest that third-world turbulence today can be treated lightly. With the exception of a few areas (that were not immediately threatened by the great powers' rivalry in Europe), the economic and strategic importance of the Empires was limited (of course, Tirpitz's naval policy worried Britain, but *that* race was over several years before the war began). Today, several parts of the Third World are very closely tied to the national security (even narrowly defined) of one or the other super-power or of both: obviously, the Middle East and Arabian Gulf regions are areas which, in hostile hands, could threaten the vital interests of the West (and Japan) and which the

Soviet Union has a vital interest in keeping from being entirely controlled by, or friendly to, her chief rivals. There are major American interests in Central America (raw materials, communications and the containment of Cuban influence) and very similar ones in mineral-rich parts of Africa. While South-east Asia may not be intrinsically more important to the superpowers than the Balkans to Germany or Britian in 1914, neither one can afford to see its own regional ally or friend – Vietnam or China – defeated or humiliated. In 1914 each camp's leaders were dissatisfied with the results of past restraints, afraid that new compromise or concessions would undermine their domestic or diplomatic position, convinced that time was working to the other side's advantage, confident that anyhow the other side would find it easier to back down. Whether or not one agrees with those who, rather glibly, equate Soviet policy with Imperial Germany's, the comparison between the pre-1914 period and the present is far more frightening than reassuring, as Miles Kahler has brilliantly shown (particularly when he refers to 'the complications introduced by great-power rivalry superimposed upon local conflicts' and to foreign policy as a means of escape from domestic insecurity).[6] It is absurd to misapply the Munich analogy to recent Western or American behaviour: Soviet advances have not been the result of appeasement; Washington and its Allies have launched counter-moves; no ally of the United States has defected out of fear of Moscow; and the reluctance of various states to align themselves with the United States results from local factors and from the strength of nationalism. But the 1914 analogy cannot be easily dismissed.

The Period After 1945

The other comparison would be with the post-1945 period – a period of great instability in the Third World, since it was the era of decolonization, marked by major wars and the involvement of both super-powers. However, one of the very sources of turbulence in the 1980s is the decline or disappearance of the reasons why the crisis of decolonization, and other crises in the Third World, were handled reasonably well. The first is, of course, the change in Soviet capabilities: we are no longer in 1946, when Truman could force Stalin to give up his claims

on Turkey and his attempt to remain in Northern Iran. The contrast between the Soviet fiasco in the Congo and the operation in Angola too is stark. The second factor is a certain decline in American power – a complex notion, about which one must be careful. In the 1940s and 1950s American military and economic power was greatly superior to anyone else's, and there is no doubt that it provided a stabilizing backdrop to turbulence. There has been a relative decline due to the rise of other nations' power, often helped by American policies. There has also been, since the Vietnam experience, less willingness to use overt or covert force by comparison with the days of Guatemala, Lebanon, the Congo, or Santo Domingo. This, of course, is reversible. But what is not reversible is the inadequacy of military power to counter some of the threats – what Robert Art recently called the inherent limits of military power to achieve economic objectives.[7] And there has been a decline in the ability to use another instrument that had figured prominently in the American arsenal of the post-war era – economic assistance – for reasons that are largely internal to the United States and could be reversed (see below), but not easily.

However, the most important factor is the third: the diffusion of power to third-world countries. Many, as noted above, now produce their own weapons (or can diversify their sources of supply). They are increasingly striving for control over their natural resources and over the operations of foreign enterprises. The oil-producing countries have domesticated the international oil companies.[8] In other words, these countries are both more capable of creating difficulties by their own actions and more capable of depriving of their efficacy the instruments of power that the United States used to police world affairs in the post-war era. Some believe that the effrontery of the 'pygmies' is a direct result of the decline of the power of the United States; they do not understand that the fall is a direct result of the rise of the 'pygmies'. To describe the passing of a (much idealized) *Pax Americana* as the cause of our troubles is myopic. *Pax Americana* emerged not merely because of the will and vision of the United States but also in circumstances that have vanished, and it declined not primarily because of political decadence in Washington but because of changes in world affairs with which Washington finds it hard to cope. The limits on the usability, or usefulness, of the power of the United States are far more serious than the alleged decline of will or the relative decline in the amounts of power. One of the biggest evolutions since 1945 has been a transformation in the nature of power which in part affects its ingredients, in the sense that there is an increase both in offensive and in defensive capabilities, which in turn creates new opportunities for conflict (think of oil, or the spread of nuclear technologies). Mainly, however, it affects the conditions of the use of power. It is increasingly delicate, because in a complex world of multiple and diverse actors it depends so largely on external opportunities which the would-be user of power can try to exploit but may be unable to create – i.e. his own success is at the mercy of chances provided by others – as well as on his own domestic processes and priorities that may be crippling or may, on the contrary, dictate unwise exertions of power. External and internal political preconditions for the successful deployment or uses of force by the United States existed when the areas concerned were Western Europe and Japan. Now that they are in the Third World there is (after Vietnam and Iran) far greater doubt in the United States and a far bumpier or muddier road abroad. Also the uses of power are increasingly asymmetrical; states that are above all military machines (the Soviet Union or Vietnam) are not likely to look at the scene in the same way as states whose deep involvement in the 'economics of interdependence' causes a host of constraints: advanced industrial societies find themselves cosseted and corseted between inflation and recession, trade expansion and protection, and have narrow margins of manoeuvre, while developing countries with limited resources and huge needs are often obliged to accept the drastic dictates of the IMF. From the viewpoint of the United States, it all amounts, in the words of one official, to having both less to offer and less to threaten with.

What is a Vital Interest?
This means that we have to face the future without much comfort from the past. The key question is: in a world of multiple instability and insecurity how can we distinguish between threats and conflicts that are of vital importance and the others? Here we find two extreme positions, both of which I find unacceptable. The first argues that the only way to fill the gap between proliferating Western or American interests and available power is to redefine the former more stringently and to return to a strategy aimed exclusively at containing the expansion of the Soviet Union and of her close Allies.

There are three problems with this proposition. First, it fails to address itself to a multitude of issues which can provoke serious insecurity even in the absence of Soviet intervention (for instance, in international economic affairs) and which, if we ignore them, could provide the Soviet Union with fine opportunities for exploitation. We would have no other resort than to oppose her, too late, with military means, whereas we might otherwise have blocked her efforts or dried up the ponds in which she fishes by earlier and much less dangerous action. In other words, if we neglect such issues as the economic well-being of third-world countries, or the poor treatment of citizens by many of their governments, or festering regional conflicts, we both allow our chief opponent to put himself on the right side of the issues and condemn ourselves to an excessive militarization of our policy (about which more later). Second, the position assumes that any expansion of Soviet (or Cuban, or Vietnamese) influence is necessarily bad for us and should be checked. Despite the intention of narrowing our notion of security, this would end up by extending it to areas or issues of questionable importance and would in fact give to the Soviet Union the ability to determine where and when we shall be engaged – and it is unlikely that she would choose places and times favourable to us. It is the indiscriminateness of what might be called 'reflex containment' and the arbitrary separation between the super-powers' contest and all the issues that form the vortex into which they are drawn, as well as the absence of any ultimate vision of world affairs or world order, which makes this approach unsatisfactory. Third, it is unrewarding because Soviet influence and presence may take so many forms that the somewhat simple-minded imagery of erecting barriers or the goal of excluding Soviet penetration turns out to be far too blunt and inappropriate.

In a sense, containment is a necessary overall objective for the West, but it does not define a strategy.

Universal Linkage

A second approach suffers not from a selective but from an all-inclusive Manichaeism. It is a conception that has gained popularity on the American Right (old and new), the blessings of Richard Nixon and letters of nobility from Henry Kissinger.[9] It amounts to a kind of universal linkage. The world is seen as divided between those who represent international stability and the values of moderation (and who, in Kissinger's latest version, include both traditional regimes and their 'aberration', the authoritarian ones) and the radicals who assault the present international structure and whose rule would spread totalitarianism (described as an 'aberration' of democracy). Our duty is to resist not only Soviet onslaughts but radical attempts as well, since there are objective and subjective convergences between the two kinds of threat. Where the first approach suggests that we ignore the domestic character of countries and watch only for the Soviet Union and her allies, this one tells us to look closely at the nature and methods of domestic forces, since these will shape their external behaviour, and to oppose the bad ones uncompromisingly – by force if there is civil turmoil, or by timely reforms that will keep our friends safely in control either before any turbulence begins or after it has been crushed, or by foreign policies designed to prove that pressure on us does not pay. It is a neo-Metternichian vision, with the advantage of putting us at least verbally into the position of defenders of freedom (since, by contrast with totalitarian ones, traditional regimes are deemed to be restrained, and authoritarian ones are deemed to be capable of leading to democracy).

The strength of this view is that it points quite accurately to the weakness of the opposite one: the latter implies that only Soviet power threatens our core values; this one states that a world dominated by hostile forces, Soviet or not, would strangle our ability to pursue our interests and to promote our values. But there are formidable flaws here too. It turns a distinction that is often one of degree or of opportunity – 'moderates' versus 'radicals' – into a fundamental divide cast in concrete and thus gives up rather too willingly the opportunities to affect positively the views and behaviour of the radicals in favour of fighting them all over. Thus it is a recipe for extraordinary over-extension, since it amounts to underwriting 'friendly' regimes everywhere and would commit our forces not only to the defence of borders against aggression but also to the destabilization of hostile regimes (or regimes assumed to be hostile), as well as to the preservation of governments from revolution. (Had this view been followed, the civil war would go on in Zimbabwe and Somoza, and the Shah would have been kept in place by force – at what cost?) It is also a poor guide for policy whenever the United States finds herself caught between the contradictory demands of conflicting 'moderate' friends – for instance, between those of Israel and Egypt, or of Israel and Jordan or Saudi Arabia, or of Greece and Turkey. It is, finally, a self-destructive view. By judging every internal or regional conflict not on its merits but according to the state of play between moderates and radicals, or between us and the Soviet Union, it would provide splendid opportunities for the latter, could provoke a major crisis in the United States' alliances and could undermine Western influence in much of the Third World. It would, for instance, make us treat South Africa as an ally. Despite the attempt to show that such a policy is compatible with our values, it ignores the fact that many 'moderate' regimes refuse to reform in time and, since it wants us to desist from 'undermining' them by pressuring them, it condones the kind of repression and mismanagement which breed radicalism, Soviet influence and distrust for Western double-talk or double-standards.

Moreover, it is a view based on some ignorance of recent history. Not only should we be careful about embracing all 'moderates' but we should also remember that not all 'moderates' want to be too closely embraced by us, and that nothing is more capable of radicalizing a regime than a clumsy attempt at forcing it to choose sides. In the Middle East in the 1950s

containment failed, not because the remedies used were necessarily inappropriate, but because the diagnosis of the disease was faulty.... Soviet victories were largely achieved, not in spite of Western regional defensive efforts, but because of them.[10]

The Danger of Simplicity

A proper approach must not begin from the top – the super-powers' contest – nor try to fit a complex world into a maddening intellectual straitjacket. (It is fashionable, in the circles that wish for a more 'muscular' United States, to deride the dreary preachers of complexity, but history shows that the real threats are the terrible simplifiers.) We have to start from the bottom. This entails three imperatives. The first is to distinguish between those areas that are not of vital interest – either because they are not of major strategic importance or because they contain no important resources – and the others. It is, of course, a relative distinction: no area is totally without significance, and even from a poor and devastated country (Angola) an enemy can move into 'friendly' territory (Shaba). But the attempt to let the stakes be determined by the simple fact of a foe's presence or influence or escalated by the mere possibility that his victory might have unpleasant side-effects (which might actually be handled or neutralized at low cost anyhow) is a recipe for over-extension.

The second imperative is to distinguish, in the vital areas especially, between different kinds of threat. The key issue is to decide what is unacceptable, what is tolerable and what, in between, is dangerous or unpleasant but bearable under certain conditions. My own list of unacceptables would include outright aggression – a blatant crossing of internationally recognized borders – except in the rare cases where it is a humanitarian intervention (India in Bangladesh, Tanzania in Uganda). It would include too the military occupation of a country following such an intervention (Vietnam in Cambodia) or accompanying or following a coup that put a 'friendly' leader in power (as in Afghanistan in December 1979). It would also include the cutting of vital economic resources by foreign powers or by terrorists. Such acts are unacceptable whether they are undertaken by the Soviet Union and her allies or by others. Dangerous but not unbearable is the coming to power of local radical forces that are not simply the agents or puppets of Moscow, Havana or Hanoi, who have neither received nor called for the support of the Soviet Union or of her allies. We are much too dependent on our own network of clients to be able to apply double standards. And yet Moscow-oriented nationalists are obviously troublesome, especially when the country in question controls resources essential to us. Also dangerous would be the coming to power – through revolution or even mere evolution, such as ordinary succession – of nationalists whose economic policies, based on their assessment of their nations' interests, would mean higher prices and less oil for the rest of the world. Many in the West would regard such decisions as unacceptable.

But this is where the third imperative comes in. While we cannot always align ourselves with forces that have history on their side, to use Peter Jay's formula[11] – many third-world conflicts occur among factions none of which has a safe claim on history – and while we should not 'appease' radicals or condone terror because of some debatable theory of political or economic development or in the vain hope of co-opting our adversary into our own designs, we must start from a clear understanding of the aspirations, ambitions and problems of the local forces, and we ourselves must understand that their main concerns are not the super-powers' contest but their own struggles and objectives, their own survival or their own triumph. We need, in other words, to begin by accepting fully one of the long-term effects of decolonization – the desire of nations to be treated as independent forces, not as tools. On the other hand, we ourselves have our interests, which often transcend a given country or region. This is why we must combine respect for the will-to-autonomy and for the force of nationalism with the need to avoid what I have described as unbearable outcomes and to make those outcomes I have described as dangerous more rather than less bearable (to prevent more Cubas, for instance, or to prevent the radicalization of friends or neutrals which a violent intervention aimed at forcing a sovereign state to meet our estimate of our oil needs would provoke). This requires a willingness both to influence friends whose policies are suicidal and to deal with adversaries whose hostility can still be disarmed.

Soviet policies in the Third World have been successful – and have, for instance, resulted in the granting of military facilities to the Soviet Union – whenever and as long as Moscow appeared to identify its interests with the concerns of local leaders: in Vietnam, in Mengistu's Ethiopia, in South Yemen and currently in Syria. When Moscow failed to serve its clients' interests the Soviet Union lost: in Egypt in 1972 and in Somalia in 1976–77. The United States has been successful when she has been able to meet the needs of a foreign leader (as in the case of Sadat since 1973) and when that leader has avoided undermining his domestic position, as the Shah undermined his own in the 1970s. But in the Middle East, in Black Africa and in Latin America Washington has often failed to avert two dangers: quasi-colonial behaviour (expecting local leaders and peoples to conform to American concerns and priorities) and association with high repressive and reactionary regimes – equating stability with the *status quo*.

A great power must behave in world affairs as a chameleon, not as a vampire. The United States and her Allies are not without assets. There is much they can provide both to the governments and to the peoples in third-world countries. Moreover, for the first time the Soviet Union has indulged in blatantly colonial behaviour in the Third World by invading Afghanistan (Vietnam has done the same in Cambodia). This provides opportunities to the West as long as it addresses itself to the fears and needs of the new nations. This is precisely why the best way to contain the Soviet Union is neither to throw the radicals into her arms nor to neglect the issues of security, economic development or human rights which are the third-world countries' or citizens' daily concerns, but to address these issues directly. And the best way to deal with the dangerous demise of the dissociations of the past is not to try to return to them but to devise the right mix of restrained globalism and careful regionalism.

Coping with International Insecurity

I have neither the space nor the competence to describe here how this mix should look in each area. Instead I will offer some remarks on specific means.

A most important issue is that of the framework for action. The approach I have suggested implicitly rejects two theoretical ones. One is a return to Dullesian pactomania. The experience of the 'Northern Tier', of CENTO and of SEATO should not be repeated. Incidentally, Soviet experiences with comparable treaties have also been mixed: they have been fine when they strengthened or signalled ties with close allies (Cuba, Vietnam); they have not worked when the ally proved too independent (Egypt, Iraq and even Afghanistan's Amin). It is instead in our interest to support existing regional organizations such as ASEAN or the OAU. Military agreements are worth concluding with those who ask for them – unless they also ask for a political price that we have no interest in paying (as with Somalia's war in the Ogaden or Pakistan's request for guarantees against India). In any case, we should not beg others to let themselves be protected by us.

The other unwelcome framework is that which Chinese rhetoric (but not Chinese deeds) often suggests: a holy anti-Soviet alliance of the United States, Western Europe, Japan and China (plus assorted anti-Soviet third-world states). The reasons why a policy of balance is preferable to a 'united front' strategy have been indicated by Robert Scalapino, Allen Whiting, and others.[12] The latter strategy would risk producing unrestrained globalism by feeding Soviet paranoia (and some legitimate fears as well) and making Soviet co-operation with the West more difficult. It would impose heavy military obligations on the United States without commensurate gains in collective strength. Neither Japan nor Western Europe shares the enthusiasm of some Americans for the 'China card', and China's military growth may serve interests that are not those of the West. It may also frighten some of the West's friends in Asia.

The Question of Alliances

The problem of the framework is the problem of the Western Alliances – NATO and the United States–Japan security treaty. It is highly unlikely that Japan, even if she plays a more important role in preserving the military balance in the Western Pacific and in providing economic assistance to third-world countries, will want to formalize this role, unless a kind of Western Directorate is set up, of the sort General de Gaulle proposed to the United States in September 1958 (but with a different membership). The obstacles to such a formula remain large. The United States is reluctant to endorse it, since it would acknowledge the promotion to a world role of powers that Washington has frequently annoyed by describing their interests as merely regional – and to a world role, moreover, as equals, whereas Washington has periodically exhorted them to transcend their parochialism only so that they could play their part in a global enterprise defined by the United States alone. The problem of membership would remain vexing. Another obstacle is the desire of several likely candidates (Paris, Bonn, Tokyo) to preserve a margin of distinction, or at least a nuance, between Washington's Soviet policy and their own and to exploit (not necessarily for selfish purposes) the fact that they are sometimes seen and treated more favourably by third-world countries than is the United States.

Yet at least an informal Directorate is indispensable – a political and strategic equivalent of the economic Summits. (The attempt to pile vital diplomatic and strategic issues on top of the vexing economic ones practically sank the last one, appropriately held in Venice.) A great deal of co-operation can take place through bilateral diplomatic exchanges and within the increasingly more co-ordinated procedures of the Europeans' political co-operation. But the impulse and general directives will have to come from the top if one wants to avoid mutual recriminations and, in the United States, a dangerous (albeit partly unjustified) sense that her allies prefer a division of labour that leaves all the heavy risks and burdens (the military ones) to Washington. NATO suffers from four handicaps: the partial absence of France, the total absence of Japan, more than enough work within its own orbit and the geographical limitation of the Treaty (an attempt at revising it might open a can of worms). This is why an institution other than the NATO Council must be established. The days are gone when the United States could try to provide both the strategy and the means by herself; now she needs the resources of her allies, as well as their own expertise in these matters. Indeed, Western pluralism is one of our main assets. But this is another reason for the approach I have suggested: neither the fixation on the Soviet–American contest nor the global Manichaean view has much of a chance of being adopted outside Washington.

The Role of Military Force

If we turn from the framework to the means, we find at once a heated controversy concerning the role of military force. The first necessity is to discard theological cobwebs. The debate, especially in the United States, has been described by the champions of a greater emphasis on force as the pitting of those who believe that international politics remains what it has always been – a contest of power – against those who believe in the growing irrelevance of force. This is, of course, absurd. Most of those who have stressed the limits of force or the difference between available power and useful power have been very careful to point out, for instance, the enormous importance of nuclear deterrence or of regional balance in Europe. And those who write as if they believe that force is a panacea have been equally careful to keep to themselves their ideas, if any, about the specific (rather than the generalized) uses and benefits of military power or about the precise composition, missions and purposes of the forces that they call for. They have been so busy reminding their intellectual adversaries of something few people ignore – the fact that politics is about power – that they themselves appear to have forgotten that power is about politics. And never more so than when the world is a single, turbulent, strategic stage.

A few points are not in doubt. The presence of American or allied forces in various parts of the world can act as a tripwire against a Soviet invasion in areas that are both close enough to the Soviet Union to make it difficult for the West to achieve a conventional balance, and important enough to the West to suggest to the attacker that such an invasion, if it succeeded in defeating the available Western forces, might trigger nuclear escalation or the geographical extension of the conflict to an area where the West enjoys conventional superiority. It could also deter or defeat an invasion by a Soviet client. Moreover, a military presence can have a generally quieting effect by creating among radicals or revolutionaries a fear of Western intervention, or by giving Western powers the means to help a friendly regime to defend itself against an attempted coup, or by preventing a local war from escalating and from affecting access to Persian Gulf oil (as in the Iraq–Iran war so far). Showing the flag also has the undoubted virtue of affecting the balance of perceptions and thereby possibly the balance of influence.

However, there are serious limitations to force as an instrument of policy. Not only is it of debatable use if the main threat is not a Soviet invasion or an attack by a Soviet proxy but internal instability or a domestic change of policy, but its presence in an unstable area could aggravate internal turbulence, turn the opposition into a shrilly anti-American or anti-Western direction and tempt the Western powers into using the available force to control events, which might be a fatal mistake. When domestic strife is the issue, or when the issue is a regime's threat to deny the West a vital resource, intervention can be both dangerous – if the use of force should, for instance, lead to the destruction of tankers and oil fields – and insufficient because prolonged occupation may become necessary. American or Western bases tend to commit us to the support of the regime that has granted them and thus to deprive us of means of influence. Rather, bases provide the means of blackmail while compromising the regime further in the eyes of its internal or external opposition. As we learned in Vietnam, and as Samuel Huntington once put it, our leverage decreases with our commitment. Ultimately, there is no substitute for sound political, economic and social conditions in the area to be defended; otherwise military bases are built on sand.[13]

This is not a condemnation of the American Rapid Deployment Force. A greater air- and sealift capacity and a greater ability to patrol the seas (without depleting existing fleets) are necessary. But the main threats to Western security in the Gulf area are *not* likely to be direct Soviet or Soviet-sponsored attacks. They will probably result from internal instability, corruption or repression, from traditional interstate conflicts and from the Palestinian issue (all of which may provide opportunities to the Soviet Union). To the reduction of these dangers external military forces can make only a meagre contribution, and they risk aggravating them. It is, of course, true that the West has a vital interest in the free flow of oil, but there are two major differences between, say, the American commitment to Western Europe and the recent commitment to the Arabian Gulf area. In Western Europe it is a pledge to the defence of

people against aggression, and it was given at the request of their governments. In the Middle East it is a commitment to keep oil flowing to the West; it has serious divisive effects in the area; and it does not resolve the issue of how to react, for instance, in Saudi Arabia not to a bungled coup such as that of November 1979, but either to a surgically successful one or to a revolution (or another kind of leadership change), followed, as in Iran, by a decision to reduce oil production, which would make perfect sense from a purely Saudi viewpoint. Also, access to oil is inseparable from the very underlying political conditions in that part of the world – conditions in the oil-producing countries and the Palestinian issue – which no military pledge can cope with. All these considerations plead for a light rather than a heavy force (with respect to composition, numbers and deployment: the emphasis ought to be on facilities, not permanent bases, on air and naval more than ground forces). The purpose is to increase risks for the Soviet Union, not to balance her might. Too heavy a Western force could easily become a distraction (from the most likely threats) and a provocation (for instance, to local terrorism).

Those limits on the usefulness of force suggest, to some, the wisdom of what the French call a *politique de Gribouille*. If conventional defence fails, we must have credible means of nuclear escalation. But, on the one hand, failure in that area risks taking the form not of a fiasco against an advancing army, but of an inability to prevent the coming to power of forces that might, for their own protection, turn to Moscow if they find us hostile, or of an inability to prevent internal turmoil in friendly countries such as Pakistan. To threaten Moscow with nuclear escalation in such cases would not be very credible. And the logic of the argument leads to an increasingly dangerous arms race: the spread of tactical nuclear capabilities and a major effort on the part of the United States to give herself a counter-force ability against Soviet missiles and military targets (many of which are close to cities). Should this lead the Soviet Union to protect and increase her own war-fighting ability, and should the United States react by discarding the ABM Treaty and by providing her own land-based missiles with hard-point defences (if this becomes technically feasible),

71

the posture of the United States (MX plus such defences, plus perhaps a new bomber and a programme to hasten the increase in the accuracy of sea-launched ballistic missiles) could appear dangerously provocative to Moscow. The United States' advantage could be negated by a Soviet ABM effort, as well as by a Soviet effort to build mobile land-based missiles and to multiply launchers and warheads. This is a recipe for spiralling madness.

Preventive Diplomacy

There is no perfect solution, no sure way of closing the gap between military possibilities in the Third World and possible threats. This suggests that such threats must be addressed by different methods, all of which could be called 'preventive diplomacy'. Let us return to the notion of a mix of regionalism and globalism. In so far as the former is concerned, there are three directions to follow. First, there is, of course, the familiar method of security assistance – arms transfers to friendly governments or to governments that request them.[14] It can be most useful to restore a regional balance or to help a country against subversion supported from abroad or internal guerrillas. But it has its own serious dangers. Feeding an escalating arms race in a region may make a diplomatic solution more rather than less difficult, may help a regime to become more repressive or may encourage it to develop excessive ambitions. Those who see in arms transfers a panacea should remember the United States' experience in Iran. Those who believe that arms sales do not increase the probability of war should ponder the case of Iraq and Iran.

Secondly, with respect to inter-state conflicts that can be dangerous sources of international insecurity a variety of diplomatic instruments have to be used, depending on the issue. Wherever possible, the Western powers should encourage regional security arrangements, limited to states in the area and aimed at preserving the members from aggression by external actors, be it the Soviet Union, or Vietnam, or even South Africa, the 'cornered wildcat' described by Robert Jaster.[15] But the initiative should come from within the area. Bilateral links such as those that now exist between France and several of her former African colonies ought to be replaced gradually by such regional schemes. The most dangerous inter-state conflict involving third-world countries remains the Arab–Israeli one. It is, of course, true that even after the Palestinian issue is disposed of there will remain multiple sources of intra-Arab conflict. But the Palestinian issue is both a major factor of anti-Western Arab (and Islamic) solidarity and a factor of internal turbulence within Arab countries as well as in Lebanon. Creeping Israeli annexionism only further strengthens the anti-American bent of the PLO while increasing the pro-PLO fervour of the occupied Palestinians, thus reducing the chances for a 'moderate' Jordanian solution. The Camp David process has gone about as far as it can. The dilemma here is that for a European or a new UN initiative to succeed it needs a green light from Washington. Yet as long as the deadlock is not broken in a way that guarantees, at the end of a transitional period, both Palestinian self-determination and mutual recognition between an eventual Palestinian state and Israel, it is absurd for American politicians to expect that Arab states will place themselves under Washington's protection, that the Palestinian issue will not weigh on the politics of oil or that the Soviet Union can be 'expelled' from the area.

Thirdly, with respect to internal turbulence in third-world countries it is not enough to ask that the West be associated with neither repression nor revolution.[16] Only if we clearly dissociate ourselves from repressive regimes and keep the pressure on them to reform before they explode is there a chance that the forces in opposition, if they come to power, will remain pro-Western or reasonably 'moderate'. It was not American 'harassment' that provoked the Shah's downfall or the overthrow of Somoza, but one of the reasons for the different consequences of the two falls is active American dissociation in Somoza's case. To be sure, the degree of possible dissociation varies from place to place. In Saudi Arabia it may well be very low. But this is where the other imperative comes in – willingness to deal even with a hostile opposition (both before and after its seizure of power), not to take its initial hostility as final. We must take its own goals and priorities seriously. For the United States, which can expect a number of unpleasant changes and challenges in Central and South America, this would entail giving up the attempt to find 'third forces' or moderate progressives (as in Nicaragua before the Sandinista victory) where they do not exist (any more than they did in China in 1946 or in Vietnam) and when the quest only increases polarization and violence. It would also mean formally recognizing the regime in Angola (with which a great deal of co-operation has been possible). For the West as a whole the strategy suggested here entails continuing pressure on South Africa (both for a solution of the conflict over Namibia and for internal change) and contacts with the Black opposition there, even that part of it that has turned East for armed support. It also means that where American relations with a new regime are bad (as in Iran) it is in the interest of the West that other Western nations try their influence.

Restrained Globalism

I mentioned earlier restrained globalism. In this respect, three directions are essential. The first is the consolidation and preservation of a strong international anti-proliferation regime, intended, through the co-operation of the suppliers, to slow down the rate and limit the degree of nuclear proliferation.[17] Accelerated proliferation, especially among 'enemy pairs' of states (India/Pakistan, Israel/Iraq, Argentina/Brazil, etc.), could not fail to increase both local insecurity (given mutual vulnerabilities and underlying political tensions) and to affect adversely the super-powers' contest, since the acquisition of nuclear weapons by the enemy of a great power's client is more likely to incite that great power to shore up the client than to promote mutual dissociation by the super-powers, at least in areas of vital importance to them.[18] It will also be essential to devise the anti-proliferation regime in such a way as to protect the legitimate energy needs of the developing countries and their interest in the peaceful uses of nuclear power. A strengthening of the role of the International Atomic Energy Agency, where both suppliers and clients meet, is likely to result from the need to balance these concerns.

The second direction is that of the international economic system. Not only has the rate of growth slowed down in the advanced countries, but the combination of inflation and unemployment has adversely affected their economic policies towards the developing nations. While accelerated economic growth can produce dangerous upheavals in traditional societies, stagnation or actual impoverishment are both sources of internal tension and of anti-Western resentment. The problems discussed in the recent Brandt Report[19] are urgent. They have been postponed by the West, partly because of its own internal economic difficulties, partly because the measures recommended by practically all the specialists of North–South affairs would require painful internal readjustments. Three kinds of measure are needed. The first would be aimed at transferring resources from Northern to Southern states (especially the poorer ones) so as to promote aggregate growth and industrialization among the latter – for instance, through increased development assistance, mechanisms (such as STABEX and MINEX in the Lomé Conventions) to stabilize export earnings and, above all, greater access of developing countries' exports to the markets of the advanced countries, a requirement both for development and for reducing the burden of debt. A second series would be aimed at dealing with the poverty within developing countries in order to ensure the basic needs of the population, particularly in food production. A third series would enlarge the role of the developing countries in the management of international economic regimes – for instance, in a new global trade organization or through the reform of the IMF and the World Bank. For reasons excellently analysed by Roger Hansen,[20] mere 'co-operation' of a handful of developing countries would not work.

The effect of these measures would be to remove or to reduce one of the chief sources of collective third-world anti-Western acrimony. They would also give developing countries a stake in the operations of a reformed world economy and would link their economic growth – particularly through increased trade – with the open international economy (i.e., with the West). The weakening of official economic ties between the nations of the West and the Third World, at least as much as the occasional high-handedness of private Western enterprises in the developing countries, facilitates Soviet influence there.

The third direction is that of Soviet–American relations. They are an indispensable component of any attempt to improve international security. In the past nuclear deterrence has not prevented Soviet attempts to exploit opportunities in the Third World at levels well below any risk of direct military conflict with the United States. In the future it is likely not only that such Soviet involvements will continue but also that increased Soviet military capabilities will tempt Moscow to export its forces more often – as long, again, as the risk of direct military confrontation with Washington remains low, either because the area is not of vital importance to the West or because Moscow would have carefully avoided putting itself in the position of an aggressor and made it as difficult as possible for Washington to retaliate in kind (a fortiori, to escalate to the nuclear level – a threat that is credible only when the most vital interests of the West are threatened by an aggressive Soviet move). It is futile to expect Moscow to endorse Western notions of stability. The best that can be hoped for is not an end to competition but the acceptance by Moscow of certain restraints in the intensity and means of competition.[21] Ours are often exceedingly static. Moscow expects the 'correlation of forces' to change (at the expense of the West), sees nothing wrong in helping it along and deems destabilizing Western reactions to be against such change. It is equally vain to expect either that the Soviet Union will accept restraints voluntarily or be forced to do so by containment alone. Preventive diplomacy may go a long way towards obliging her to restrict the scope of her endeavours but if it is Soviet intensity and Soviet methods that we may try to affect, we shall have to make efforts to find areas of co-operation.

The Role of Arms Control
One of them must be arms control, even if it should control in more fragmentary or more modest ways than in the past. The relevance of the strategic balance to the contest in the Third World may only be oblique, but it is not unimportant. First, instability, or a perception of instability, in the central balance may tempt the side that believes it has an advantage either to take more risks at a regional level, where it also has an edge, for purposes of intimidation or to try to compensate for a regional disadvantage by threatening to escalate. (To be sure, stability

at the central level risks 'decoupling' a region from it, but coupling would be neither credible nor sensible in case of secondary interests, and remains credible only when the interest at stake is vital, in the sense used in 1980 by McGeorge Bundy à propos Europe: 'no one knows that a major engagement in Europe would escalate to the strategic nuclear level. But the essential point is the opposite: no one can possibly know it would not'[22]). Secondly, the more the superpowers indulge their apparent appetite for warfighting scenarios, the more attractive they make the possession of nuclear weapons to others. Third, the continuing nuclear arms race between them weakens the legitimacy and the authority of their stand against proliferation. In so far as strategic arms control contributes to stability and predictability, it remains important. The scuttling of SALT II was a mistake, even if new discussions should begin soon and in earnest. But to postpone a serious negotiation of strategic arms limitation or reductions until after the United States has restored a 'margin of safety' and given herself some leverage over the Soviet Union would be at best prodigiously wasteful and at worst a dangerous gamble.

Conventional arms control will undoubtedly have to wait until local sources of instability and the opportunities for competitive influence which local requests for arms provide have dried out sufficiently or until enough states produce what they need (by which time such arms control would come too late). However, even the conventional arms races fed by the superpowers could be submitted to restraints resulting from informal understandings aimed at greater super-power control over the purposes for which the arms can be used and at limiting damage and casualties if they are used. Even these understandings presuppose a greater Western willingness either to deal directly (as was finally done in Zimbabwe) with forces or countries that have turned to Moscow for support, so as to give them an incentive to favour moderation, or to accept the Soviet Union as a partner in the search for the solution of regional disputes in which the latter has a vital interest (and not merely an interest in expanding her own influence or in dislodging that of the West). This would obviously not be the case in the Americas or in Southern Africa, but it would be in the areas that lie close to the Soviets' borders.

Containment and Co-operation

One of the weaknesses of the two confrontational approaches described earlier is that they provide only for an interminable series of tests – as in the old Achesonian conception – conducted in the vague hope that the adversary, having been checkmated enough, will throw in the towel and behave according to our wishes. Neither the trends in the world nor her own internal difficulties are likely to force her to do so. The best chance for a gradual change in her behaviour lies in a combination of containment and co-operation. Even the co-operation is likely to be competitive. In a world of states each one, whether through conflict, self-reliance or co-operation, seeks its own advantage. But even the confrontation ought to leave the door open for political solutions, as was achieved in the Cuban missile crisis and as should be the aim of Western policies in Afghanistan and for Cambodia. These may not be popular views today. But nothing is more important for a long-term policy than a sense of perspective, a refusal to accept intellectual fashions uncritically and to yield to sudden bursts of opinion.

The new American Administration, if only in order to react against the strategic incoherence of its predecessor, is likely to seek a comprehensive policy, especially in the Arabian Gulf area, and to want to enlist the support of the United States' allies for it after months of mutual complaints, innuendoes and stalemate. As long as the allies cringe at discussions about the role of force, try to convince themselves that regional fragmentation can still prevail and refuse to hear American complaints about unevenly shared burdens, there will be little progress. But nor will there be any if the United States once more takes refuge in over-simplification, prefers military planning to political analysis or short-term fixes to a long-range integrated strategy, attributes Western European desires to safeguard whatever is left of detente in Europe to crass material interests or to fear alone and generally behaves as if leadership could be exerted exactly as it was in the 1950s. There is little reason for optimism.

The methods sketchily suggested here would encounter not only the resistance of all those whose view of the world is different but also two formidable obstacles within the West. The first one is economic. Unless Western economies in general and the American one in particular take strong domestic measures to reduce their dependence on Middle East oil, to fight inflation and to return to steady economic growth, they will face, in the case of quite probable turbulence in the Arabian peninsula, an unsavoury choice between economic disaster, should the flow of oil be interrupted or production levels be drastically reduced, and the formidable risks and costs of military expedition and occupation. And they will not have the resources needed to provide an economic underpinning for Western policies in the Third World. A willingness not to be outspent in military hardware nor outclassed in military deployments by the Soviet Union is fine as long as the effort required does not become a pretext for neglecting the long-term duty to 'increase the resources needed to support our diplomacy, a diplomacy designed to reduce the chance our military forces may be needed,' in Cyrus Vance's words.[23]

The other obstacle is internal as well. What is necessary is nothing less than a mental revolution – a willingness to discard nostalgia for past golden ages (that seemed not so golden at the time), to stop wavering, in attitudes towards Moscow, between total hostility and excessive hopes and to abandon condescension towards the Third World. It is a particularly difficult reconversion for the American people, impatient with complexity, oscillating between the two equally irrelevant archetypes of the United States – the sheriff at High Noon and world missionary[24] – troubled by mixed strategies, more eager for intervention against a foe than capable of steering towards reform or accommodation with partial or temporary adversaries, more inclined, under the guidance of the familiar but tricky liberal principle of non-intervention, towards endorsing the *status quo* and thus becoming the victims of its clients and the unwilling artisans of its own defeats. But we can neither withdraw from the field, only to re-enter when the Soviet Union and her allies approach, nor turn the whole world into that artificial division between good and evil which produces in crusading spirits such emotional satisfaction, a happy end to all cognitive dissonance and a formidable release of energy. It is a global contest – but it is a complex one and not a war. Coping with international insecurity is not a matter of winning against a single foe or against a deadly brotherhood of evils. It is a Sisyphean task of bringing more restraint more order *and* more justice into a world of turbulence and violence.

NOTES

[1] Richard N. Cooper, *Economics of Interdependence* (New York: McGraw-Hill, 1968).

[2] Robert Gilpin, 'The Politics of Trans-national Economic Relations', in Robert O. Keohane and Joseph S. Nye, 'Trans-national Relations and World Politics', *International Organization*, vol XXV, no. 3, Summer 1971, pp. 398–419.

[3] See Seweryn Bialer, *Stalin's Successors* (Cambridge: Cambridge University Press, 1980).

[4] Arnold Wolfers, *Discord and Collaboration* (Baltimore: Johns Hopkins University Press, 1962).

[5] Stanley Hoffmann, *Primacy and World Order* (New York: McGraw-Hill, 1978), Part 2.

[6] Miles Kahler, 'Rumors of War: The 1914 Analogy', *Foreign Affairs*. vol. 58, no. 2 (Winter 1979), pp. 374–96.

[7] Robert J. Art, 'To What Ends Military Power?', *International Security*, vol. 4, no. 4 (Spring 1980), pp. 3–35.

[8] See Walter J. Levy, 'Oil and the Decline of the West', *Foreign Affairs*, vol. 58, no. 5 (Summer 1980), pp. 999–1015.

[9] Kissinger's view, which can be found in his *White House Years* (London: Weidenfeld and Nicholson, 1979) – see my review, 'The World of Dr Kissinger', *New York Review of Books*, 6 December 1979 – has been laid out even more starkly in his 'statement on the geopolitics of oil' before the Committee on Energy and Natural Resources of the United States Senate, 31 July 1980.

[10] Paul Jabber, 'US Interests and Regional Security in the Middle East,' *Daedalus* (*US Defense Policies in the 1980s*) (Fall 1980), pp. 75–6.

[11] Peter Jay, 'Regionalism as Geopolitics', *Foreign Affairs* (*America and the World in 1979*) (January 1980), p. 487.

[12] See Scalapino's 'Asia at the End of the 1970s', *Foreign Affairs* (*America and the World in 1979*) vol. 58, no. 3, pp. 693–737, and Allan S. Whiting, 'China and the Superpowers: Toward the Year 2000', *Daedalus*, (Fall 1980), pp. 97–113.

[13] See the remarks by Zalmay Khalilzad, 'Afghanistan and the Crisis in American Foreign Policy', *Survival*, vol. XII, no. 4 (July/August 1980), pp. 151–60.

[14] See Richard Betts, 'The Tragicomedy of Arms Trade Control', *International Security*, vol. V, no. 1 (Summer 1980), pp. 80–110.

[15] Robert Jaster, *South Africa's Narrowing Security Options*, Adelphi Paper No. 159 (London: IISS, 1980).

[16] See the Atlantic Council's Policy Paper, *After Afghanistan on the Long Haul* (Washington DC, 1980).

[17] See Joseph S. Nye, 'Maintaining a Non-Proliferation Regime', *International Organization*, forthcoming.

[18] I disagree with Kenneth Waltz's complacent view in a forthcoming Adelphi Paper.

[19] North–South (Boston: MIT Press, 1980).

[20] Roger Hansen, 'North–South Policy – What is the Problem?', *Foreign Affairs*, vol. 58, no. 5 (Summer 1980), pp. 1104–28.

[21] For further elaboration, see my 'Muscle and Brains', *Foreign Policy*, no. 37 (Winter 1979), pp. 3–27.

[22] McGeorge Bundy, 'The Future of Strategic Deterrence', *Survival*, vol. XXI, no. 6 (Nov./Dec. 1979), p. 271.

[23] Harvard Commencement speech, *New York Times*, 6 June 1980.

[24] See my 'États-Unis: le refus de la complexité', *Le Débat*, no. 5 (October 1980), pp. 54–9.

The United States and the Third World: Motives, Objectives, Policies

SHAHRAM CHUBIN

Gone are the days when the United States believed herself to be impervious to developments elsewhere and was convinced of the automatic relevance of her values as a model for other states. Gone, too, is her desire to remake the world in her own image; damage limitation now prevails over universalism. Entangling alliances are now shunned not merely because of the risks inherent in alliances but also because of doubts about whether the United States has in fact anything to contribute in regions which she finds complicated to understand and onerous to deal with. This self-doubt extends to the use of military force, to the widespread, nagging doubt about whether she can wield it at all, particularly in situations of ambiguity in which goals are unclear, victory hard to define and success elusive. It is supremely ironical that the United States when least dependent on the Third World, was endowed in the early post-war period with nuclear superiority (and, putatively, the ability to extend deterrence), with pacts and allies, with bases and access at a time when the USSR had only a primitive deterrent, minimal global reach and few allies in the Third World. In the 1970s, by contrast, when American (Western) vulnerability in the Third World had become substantial, she found her nuclear superiority negated, her base structure shrunk, the Third World restive and conflict-prone and the USSR able to project power globally. Now, at a time of real vulnerability and global interdependence, the environment is both more complex and more threatening.

The Post-War Experience
The first real encounter between the United States and the Third World came at a time when her perspective was shaped by rivalry with the USSR. This influenced the American response to developments in what quickly became both the stake and the arena of the competition. Also influential were ideals and values which the United States cherished and wished to impart to the world community. The continuing interaction between these ideals and the political realities of the cold war forms a skein in American policies towards the Third World which is not easy to define in neat phases. In common with all major declarations of American foreign policy, the Truman Doctrine reflected 'the inherent rationale . . . and the tendency to offer an all-inclusive explanation and justification for a single fixed course of action'.[1] President Truman declared:

It must be the policy of the US to support free peoples who are resisting attempted subjugation by armed minorities or by outside pressures . . . to work out their own destinies in their own way. I believe that our help should be primarily through economic and financial aid which is essential to economic stability and orderly political processes.[2]

The Truman Doctrine came to be viewed as an American commitment to the 'defence of freedom' throughout the world. But, cast in universalistic mould, it 'made flexibility difficult for subsequent crises'.[3] Yet if it was rigid in its rhetoric, it was surely not necessarily so in its practice. There was nothing automatic or inherently militaristic about its application in policy. But in its translation to the Third World it failed. Partly, no doubt, this was due to the inapplicability of the European model (on which it was based) to developing areas which lacked cohesion, identity and often indigenous political traditions. Partly also the concept of

77

'free peoples' was ambiguous in areas where there was no tradition of free expression or assembly. Inevitably, choices had to be made between ideals and interests, between support for free regimes and support for anti-Communist regimes, and inevitably the symbolism of the latter could be manipulated by authoritarian regimes to attract American attention and aid. A further ambiguity lay within the Doctrine itself: did support for 'free peoples to work out *their own destinies in their own way*' (emphasis added) include the right to revolution, the right to adopt radical regimes and even Marxist governments? The preference for regimes that dispersed rather than concentrated power clashed with the needs of those states to accumulate or create centralized power; the outcome was often a choice between authoritarian regimes of the Left or the Right. Again the exigencies of the cold war, of the zero-sum competition, tilted towards the non-Marxist.

This oversimplifies the period, for what is striking about it in retrospect is how multidimensional American policies were in practice. The competition and alternation between the 'cold war' approach to the Third World and the 'explicitly democratic' approach – which sought to foster democratic rather than anti-Communist regimes (and punished military coups in Latin America, for example, in the Kennedy era) – is striking. So, too, in the light of post-Vietnam revisionism, was the non-intervention policy of the United States in the 1960s towards a number of regimes that were Marxist or anti-Western, starting with China, Sekou Touré in Guinea, Nasser's Egypt and Tito's Yugoslavia.[4] There was nothing inevitably indiscriminate about the application of the Truman Doctrine in policy. The limits to American power also were already appreciated: 'there cannot be an American solution to every problem.'[5] The recognition that democracy could not flourish without indigenous roots, that development was a complex process that entailed regression as well as advances and might well accentuate instability and insecurity, and that American preferences for liberal democratic regimes might often have to be subordinated to geopolitical necessities (and that in these circumstances the United States should promote tolerance for diversity) were all ideas far advanced by the mid-1960s.

From Vietnam to Carter

Containment in practice, if not in theory, was expanded into a doctrine of international order which led in turn to imperial and imperialistic intervention.[6] The 'Free World' came to mean those states open to American influence, representing a 'degeneration of the crusading spirit into imperial realism'[7] and tending to promote an uneasy conscience in many Americans. Nevertheless, although it was globalized (by Korea) and militarized (after European rearmament), it was universal more in rhetoric than in application. It remained defensive, accepting spheres of influence, *faits accomplis* and 'grey areas'. Certainly, it did not constitute a military concept – the assurance of physical security – so much as an approach that sought to maintain as wide an area as possible that was susceptible to American influence. But it did require discrimination in application and not the acceptance of custodianship everywhere. Vietnam, as Aron has observed, represented 'the growing tendency to substitute symbol for reality in the discrimination of interests and issues.'[8] Vietnam, of course, fed the uneasy conscience of the American people, and it shattered a consensus on foreign policy which has yet to be rebuilt.

In the aftermath of Vietnam the crisis of conscience was aggravated. Defeat fed doubts about the morality of the intentions of the United States, about the universal applicability of her values and traditions and about the validity of her global role. The trend towards withdrawal, already evident in declining involvement and abstention rather than activism, accelerated. 'Come home, America!' was a neo-isolationist cry which reflected this, but a wide variety of distinguished scholars – for example, Robert Tucker, George Kennan and Arthur Schlesinger, Jr – argued for 'selective involvement' to reduce interests to a central core and for a more detached international posture. A weariness prevailed, stemming from the carrying of the common burdens that had been assumed and the risks that had been accepted, together with a sense of unrequited effort. A determination arose never to repeat this mistake. Not surprisingly, the unattractiveness of many of the regimes being defended looked more stark in this perspective; they appeared hardly worth the effort. Diversity now became an escape from commitment. Only the obvious, natural allies could henceforth expect assistance. Outside Europe these were Israel, Japan and possibly Australia. Henceforth contingencies must be 'pure'.[9] The war in Vietnam also called into question other assumptions. It demonstrated the strength of indigenous nationalisms, the relevance of factors other than raw military power, the dangers of putting 'local' issues into East–West matrices and of incremental involvement. It is small wonder, then, that in the aftermath of Vietnam the attitude of the United States towards the Third World was conditioned by a debate that bore its scars and that generated much fervour but little clarity as to this core of strategic interest and the criteria for and scope of involvement or the appropriate instruments for influence.

The emergence of a new school of influential analysts reinforced the inclination of many who had been transformed by the bitterness of the Vietnam war to interpret the world in new and comforting terms, to deny the centrality of military power in inter-state relations and to argue, for example, that oil was safe because the producers 'can't drink it', or that allies would remain loyal 'because they have nowhere else to go'. These world-order scholars,[10] liberal and internationalist by inclination, were much too sophisticated to deny the continued importance of military power, yet their writings sometimes appeared to do so. They noted that the new international system was characterized by less hierarchy and more complexity and by the prevalence of denials over gains. They questioned the centrality of military power, noting that the traditional agenda of security had narrowed, while issues of global management had expanded other dimensions of security requiring other instruments of influence. They saw power in terms more of bargaining and entanglement than of clear-cut gains. By pointing to the increasing complexity of the global agenda, in which multiple and shifting coalitions formed according to the 'issue area' (e.g. the Law of the Sea and nuclear proliferation), they underscored the blurring of traditional distinctions between ally and foe. Their contribution to policy was their indication of a conception of world order dependent not merely on a balance of power but on a discrete evaluation of events divorced from the centrality of the East–West

rivalry. What they did not do was to indicate in any precise fashion how choices between the longer-run systemic goals could be reconciled with pressing short-term needs, how the two agendas in practice could be divorced, or how manageable such concepts were for policy.[11]

They were extremely influential, nonetheless, because they reinforced a tendency to interpret the international system in a novel way, one that subordinated the requirements of military power and the importance of the rivalry with the USSR to a vision of a world order that called for American strength in ideals, purpose and restraint. Like the world-order theorists, the Carter Administration sought to distinguish itself from its predecessors. Where Kissinger had sought balance of power, the Carter Administration sought world order; where Kissinger emphasized the East–West conflict and loyalty to allies in the Third World, they emphasized diversity, pluralism and human rights. Where Kissinger had used flattery, arms sales and the co-option of regional 'influentials', the Carter Administration eschewed these instruments in favour of a policy more 'responsive' to regional concerns.

In the Nixon–Kissinger era there was no doubt about which came first between immediate security concerns and world-order goals, or between close alignment on security questions and on the type of government an ally represented. The Carter Administration came to office convinced anew of the relevance of the American experience. Confusing moral posturing with policy, it identified a 'tide of freedom' moving in the direction of democracy and human rights. Determined not to be 'irrelevant', it sought to align itself with this benign wave and to adjust to it. Whether such a tide existed is immaterial, for what became clear was that little thought had been given to the possibility that conflicts could emerge not only between American security and world-order interests but also between American interests and those of the Third World. Freedom from 'an inordinate fear of Communism' did not guarantee freedom from clashes of interest. Adjustments between ideals and self-interest might still be necessary. In practice, the Carter Administration turned out to be the mirror image of its predecessor: where the latter had sought substance, the Carter Administration stressed rhetoric (in Africa and in the North–South dialogue); where its predecessor had detected 'linkage' everywhere and saw security threats in the most remote regions (for example, in Chile or Angola), the Carter Administration denied that its 'credibility' was ever affected; where its predecessors had emphasized consistency and nuance, the Carter Administration made a fetish of incoherence and oscillation.

Geopolitics and Regionalism

The differences between the Carter Administration and the Republican Administration preceding it were less basic than often appeared, but, as was the case with parallel polarization in academia between geopolitical and regionalist approaches to the Third World, the emphases were quite different. The debate about the merits of these two approaches is important because it contains what promises to be a continuing divergence in perspective about the sources of third-world instability and the appropriate responses to that instability.[12]

The primary difference between the two schools lies in their assessments of the centrality of the competition with the USSR and the role of force. While the geopoliticians continue to see the world in these terms, the regionalists point to the expanded agenda of world affairs and to multi-polarity, complexity and diversity. The one therefore focuses on Soviet power, the importance of regional balances and allies and immediate American interests. The other, more relaxed about military power, seeks to avoid open-ended involvements while pursuing long-run world-order interests. The geopolitician seeks to cultivate and reward allies, stressing American dependability and credibility; the regionalist emphasizes the compatibility (or incompatibility) of allies with the values of the United States and advocates dissociation.[13] The former fears an eroding balance, divided allies and set-backs that reverberate to the global disadvantage of the United States; the latter fears entanglement, irrelevance and reflexive linkage. The geopolitician sees the risks of war increasing because of uncertainties created by regional retreat; the regionalist, seeking a more limited definition of security, cringes at muscular *machismo* and at loose talk of 'credibility'. The one looks to military security, strong leadership and resilience as the key to world order;

the other believes that world order is nurtured by adjustment, restraint, bargaining and moral example.

These views lead to quite different assessments of the function of military power and of its relationship with the exploitation of third-world conflicts. The geopoliticians assert the continuing and inescapable centrality of military power, and they stress its importance in deterring the USSR. They demand American leadership of the Allies and seek to reassure friendly states in the Third World. It follows that regional military balances are therefore seen as especially critical, both because strategic parity encourages probing[14] and because the United States is reluctant to become directly involved in defending her interests. In short, military power still determines the risk calculus of the opportunistic exploitation of third-world instabilities. The regionalists, on the contrary, are impressed by the limited utility of military power (which they expect that the USSR will also eventually understand), and they see regional successes as determined less by power than by local political conditions. The 'prevailing local winds'[15] are the principal determinants of influence; the trick of diplomacy is to adjust to them and thus inhibit Soviet advances. The regionalists focus on the constraints operating on Soviet power (which, they emphasize, is one-dimensional), on the intractability of many problems to solution by military power, on the strength of indigenous nationalisms and on the costs of alignment with third-world states which face multiple threats and invariably fail to meet minimal standards on human rights.

If the geopoliticians fear disorder arising from American ambivalence towards power, the regionalists are anxious not to seek military solutions to political problems. The willingness of the regionalists to recognize diversity and complexity allows them to be more detached about regional disorder and to argue that one must learn to understand the causes of radical anti-Westernism lest, reflexively, it be equated with pro-Communist or pro-Soviet rhetoric.[16] A corollary of this is the quest for the 'pure' contingency. Since so many issues in the Third World have historical or local causes, only the most massive, blatant, 'purely external' and tangible threats should, according to them, be met by military responses, and then preferably by regional states acting collectively. The regional approach of this school emphasizes the multi-lateral over the bilateral, the longer-term over the immediate. In their view, for example, arms sales should be seen in this perspective rather than as a tool of bilateral relations. Negotiations with the Soviet Union on restricting conventional arms sales or on limiting naval deployments in the Indian Ocean should be judged by their effect not on allies, access, or balances but on atmosphere.

The geopolitical school (with its emphasis on power and on the centrality of rivalry with the USSR) has justly been accused of the excessive simplification of a complicated set of international relationships. Its most indefatigable critic has noted that it 'neglects local circumstance', makes each crisis a test of resolve, sees credibility in the most limited stake, counts on a linkage which cannot work and has no 'substantial conception of world order' other than a military balance.[17] It follows that this school tends to ignore the lengthening agenda of issues on international affairs and 'to see in the West's relations with the South a particular theatre of struggle with the East'.[18] Its strengths, however, are equally clear. By defining security narrowly, it concentrates attention on interests and threats to those interests. It views the relationship with the USSR as central and foresees no early release from a sustained global competition for influence. Without rejecting the new hierarchies, it chooses as its priority the area of political security in which military power is the abiding dominant feature. It is therefore concerned less with the values of its partners in the Third World than with their orientations. It is more sensitive to the limited range of choice in this respect, recognizing that authoritarian regimes are not *always* able to be improved upon. It does not equate change with progress. In a choice between immediate interests and abstract values, the former predominate. In its concept of international relations, this school at least provides the basis for a consistent policy.

The regionalist often finds himself allied with the world-order school. Its important joint contribution has been to sensitize policy-makers to the fact that interdependence has made more difficult the achievement of clear-cut solutions; that bargaining based on a variety of forms of power is the prevalent form of negotiation; that

leadership requires consensus; and that long-term interests and values need to be integrated with today's policies. In noting that traditional distinctions between ally and adversary have been blurred by shifting coalitions (so that today's partner can be tomorrow's competitor), the world-order school has warned against undifferentiated or over-simple responses. By refusing always to view regional disputes in East–West terms, and by espousing a positive political philosophy to combat both Marxism and the stigma of colonialism, the West, with its tolerance for diversity and its multiple sources of power, will be (in this view) in a stronger position in the Third World. Rather than reliance solely on a balance of military power, this argues for a global engagement that is at once tolerant, multi-faceted and humane.

The palpable weakness of this line of thinking is in its consequences, not in its intentions. In seeking to avoid the automatic absorption of issues into the East–West matrix, it provides little illumination of the range of choice or the bargains to be struck. Foreign policy, ideally, always reflects 'values', but the issue is often how far values should dictate policy. The high level of generality of this school, while helpful in describing the system and its constituent parts, furnishes no guide to policy, no criteria for discriminating among interests when they clash or for selecting time-frames in response. For example, when do regional issues become global issues? When Western issues are directly or tangibly affected? Or when outside power involvement reaches a certain level? Not all regional conflicts are tests of super-power credibility and strength but some are – was the Middle East in 1973? Was Angola in 1975? Was Ethiopia in 1977? Few issues are purely regional (witness Afghanistan and the Gulf, the Middle East and the Gulf or the Horn and the Gulf) – how, then, can responses be 'regional'? Which 'prevailing winds' should the West catch in areas where there are several and where no dominant conflict exists (as in Southern Africa and Palestine)? How does 'dissociation' affect a great power's reputation in a region (as in Iran in 1978), and how can influence be furthered *without* involvement? Is the challenge from the Third World primarily one that can be rectified by policy (as some have argued),[19] or is it a traditional claim for a redistribution of power and status in the international system, which should be met as such?[20] There is little allowance in this school for the possibility of a direct clash of interest with the Third World itself.

While so richly evoking the mixed relations of today, this school has systematically underestimated the factor of military power, a basic ingredient of those relations. The residual value of power, of the 'traditional agenda', is starkly evident. The relationship between the Soviet exploitation of regional opportunities, their incidence and the military balance persists and may grow. If outside powers cannot appreciably reduce these opportunities *within* various regions, as seems likely, one response is to increase the risks and costs to the Soviet Union of her exploitation. By understating the importance of military power in the Third World[21] – both for the local state and for its outside partners – this school has contributed to a basic confusion, as a consequence of which issues are put in 'either/or' terms, diplomacy and force are treated as separable and policy is seen as either geopolitical or regional. The result has been to provide the United States with equally reckless choices – abstention (often with the excuse that regional conditions are murky) or threats of massive intervention which are neither credible nor, in most cases, useful.

In the final analysis, however, the differences between the two schools relate to their assessment of the USSR. Divorced from Soviet power and intervention, most of the issues in the Third World would be manageable, and shifts in internal politics, or even alignments, would then be marginal to the real world balance of power – or so argues the geopolitician. The careful balancing of Soviet power, the containment of Soviet influence and the nurturing of Soviet restraint in these areas therefore become critical, lest a shift in a key area like the Gulf should tilt the world balance in a direction adverse to the West. Third-world policy can therefore never lose sight of the East–West competition. The regionalist is less dramatic; he argues that one should look at issues in third-world areas on their own merits. He does not equate 'losses' with 'defeats'.[22] He has more confidence in the West's inherent strengths and pays more attention to Soviet vulnerabilities. Mistaken Western policies rather than Soviet opportunism is the principal danger seen by the regionalist. A more benign and comprehensive view of the West's long-term interests in world order encourages him to advocate benevolent global engagement.

The Carter Administration came to office with a desire to forge a new consensus in American foreign policy and to infuse it with new values for a new era. It failed to do so because it neglected to identify or elaborate any core of security interests. In place of anti-Communism, it emphasized functional issues, but in the process it failed to elucidate any conception of the role of the USSR (and East–West rivalry) in third-world affairs. Thus liberated from power politics ('we have rejected the proposition that [power] ought to be the central dimension of American foreign policy'[23]), it understated the conditions in which military power remained central or even pertinent to the conduct of diplomacy outside of Europe. It also overstated the degree to which a generalized approach to the Third World could yield specific dividends in terms of concrete interests (e.g. access). By seeking to avoid indiscriminate activism, it underestimated the occasional risks of inaction.

The Environment of the 1980s
The tests of the leadership of the United States with respect to its policies towards the Third World in the 1980s will be to reconcile the tendencies towards universal formulae, with the inevitable *ad hoc* responses, and to integrate responses which incorporate both immediate considerations of power politics (where appropriate) with more diffuse (though real) interests in world order. The primary requisites for this are, first, the restoration of consensus on core security interests; next, a sense of realism about what to expect in the Third World; and, finally, an understanding of what can be done to advance American (and Western) interests. No simple formulae are useful here. Some regions are plainly more 'strategic' than others. In some of these the military instrument will remain an extremely important tool of influence (whether to deter, to reassure or to buy time). Doctrinaire regionalism that seeks to disaggregate the world into 'regions' – not because they are, in fact, autonomous but because they would relieve the 'burdens of empire' (i.e. regionalism as a convenience) – is unproductive. Even if theoreti-

cally possible, in practice it would be impossible to pursue a series of divergent or contradictory regional policies. A global policy (or overall strategy) is a prerequisite, both because it would constitute an appeal to certain principles (not simply, as American idealists from Wilson to Carter have recognized, a means of achieving a domestic consensus for American world involvement) and because the security and military infrastructure required in an interdependent world must be global. Military capabilities, including interventionary forces and seapower, are essential. There is thus a need for a global policy which allows for differentiation among regions and between issues. This would take into account both the United States' stake in a world order which she is determined to influence and variations in the intensity of her interests in different regions.

The advent of strategic nuclear parity ended any possibility of extending nuclear deterrence beyond Europe and Japan. It may have made the world safe for conventional wars in third-world areas but it was the combination of lengthened Soviet military reach and instabilities in these regions that made outside intervention feasible. In the next decade it appears likely that some crises between the super-powers in the Third World may, in the final analysis, turn on the perceptions of the state of the central strategic balance obtaining at that time.[24] In areas adjacent to the USSR perceptions of her power will yield political dividends to the Soviet Union. As Defense Secretary Brown has acknowledged, 'Even when Soviet pressure is political, its foundation is Soviet military power.'[25] Proximity, persistence and power tailored to local circumstance (together with fewer domestic constraints) enhance Soviet diplomacy in many parts of Asia and may substitute for its manifest liabilities in other spheres. At a minimum, improved military mobility and greater reach provides the Soviet Union with options that she has increasingly exercised, thus ending a monopoly of two decades of uncontested American intervention. The continuing deterioration of East–West relations will lead to more extensive competition. Greater capabilities for intervention may increase the opportunities for intervention but in an increasingly complex and potentially unrewarding environment.

For a variety of reasons the third-world states[26] are undergoing, and will continue to undergo, a series of pressures and challenges that will test their capabilities both to survive as nation-states and to do so effectively in the face of popular demands. Crises of identity, integration, legitimacy, and the redistribution of wealth (within and among states), sectarian disputes, secessionist movements and regional conflicts will all test fragile state structures and regional stability. Even with its many differences, the Third World has demonstrated great solidarity in its attitude towards the richer states. Partly because of sheer frustration at the intractability of their own problems, partly because of annoyance at the power, the privilege and often what they perceive to be the hypocrisy of the Western states, a degree of basic anti-Westernism exists. Envy tinged with contempt is discernible as these states survey, for example, Western technology and the breakdown of the family. The upshot of this is an unwillingness to choose between the West and East and a rather strict evaluation of both Blocs by reference to their own priorities and values (whether with regard to a settlement of Palestine, to the issue of *apartheid*, to less restrictive tariff barriers or to a desire to be 'taken seriously').

Their foreign policy, too, is dictated by their own concerns; they may be conservative or revisionist with reference to specific regional issues, yet their stance is bound to affect the judgment (and the interests) of the two rival super-powers. With intensified rivalry between the two Blocs, the pressures on these states for alignment may intensify, yet their own prevailing inclination is increasingly to escape alignment. Even where the drift towards non-alignment is genuine, as in the Arabian Gulf, its impact on the two super-powers' interests is unlikely to be the same.

The diffusion of weapons to the Third World has enlarged the scope of regional wars. A myriad of existing tensions, historical rivalries, specific territorial disputes, tribal animosities and resource conflicts have resulted in persistent conflict in Africa and Asia in particular. In the past five years these disputes have become increasingly internationalized (for example, in Cyprus, Angola, Lebanon, Ethiopia, North and South Yemen, Namibia and Cambodia–Vietnam). There is every reason to expect these conflicts to persist in the 1980s, providing pretexts for intervention and opportunities to score marginal unilateral gains. Nor is there any clear evidence that a refusal to sell arms to countries in these regions would substantially affect the incidence of conflict or that suppliers of arms would gain any appreciable leverage.

In the early post-war era it was commonly supposed that the fragile international system could not withstand the shocks of war in the nuclear age. This supposition has been refuted; global security has turned out to be less brittle than was once believed. Yet intensified competition, enhanced capabilities and tempting local circumstances provide opportunities for gain and raise the spectre of a heightened risk of nuclear confrontation that might originate in a crisis in the Third World. To avoid the danger of competitive intervention or the inadvertent involvement of either super-power by regional partners in local crises will require both a careful delineation of core interests and clear communication between the super-powers.

The Super-powers and the Third World

For two decades every President of the United States has sought a dialogue with the USSR to limit the risks of competition in the Third World and to broaden areas of common agreement in this regard. The desire to encourage Soviet co-operation in third-world areas has led to two approaches which are not mutually exclusive. The first, linkage, which sought to induce the acceptance of American rules about what constitutes acceptable behaviour, has largely failed. Whether it was conceptually flawed or impracticable is beside the point. Perhaps it was both. There is some truth in the argument that the approach was proposed as a 'soft' means of covering up the decline in American military power and willingness to take risks.[27] A second approach, favoured by some, has been to invite the restraint of the USSR by acknowledging her interests and by giving her a stake in peace through participation in the co-management of regions. Advocates of this approach in the Arabian Gulf have tended to equate American–Soviet interests in the region and to argue that recognition of her 'legitimate' interests will reduce the Soviet Union's incentives to act as the 'spoiler' from outside.

The difficulty with regional security as a means of managing great-power competition in a sensitive zone like the Gulf is that there exist asymmetrical vulnerabilities and military capabilities in a region which is itself unstable and hence exploitable. As a substitute for a super-power military balance it is seriously flawed. Yet the creation of a military balance requires the rectification of the asymmetries which currently exist. This in turn argues against 'including' the USSR as an equal partner before her demonstrable advantages have been offset. In short, if it is not to ratify Soviet preponderance (as in the Soviet 'Asian Security' formula), regional security on the Asian periphery must be based on military power and must not constitute a 'cost-free' substitute for it.[28]

Another variant of regional security would seek agreement among local states to conform to certain minimal standards of conduct (non-subversion and the denial to outsiders of military bases) or to co-operation in areas of common concern. This approach would aim to address the local pressures that might stimulate invitations to great powers to intervene. It could be useful in areas such as ASEAN, where super-power rivalry is minimal, and could be extended to parts of Africa. In contested areas, however, its value would be limited, for its success would ultimately be dependent on a balance of power between the two Blocs and on the willingness of one of them to check an infringement by the other one.

Regional security as an approach to keep local conflicts local is likely to work best in areas marginal to great-power competition. In areas of intense rivalry its value will be in providing a forum for settlement of minor disputes which do not infringe outside powers' interests.[29] Military co-operation between states with complementary assets (one, perhaps, with money; the other, manpower) can be useful in meeting local security threats directly without involving outside powers. But regional security as an alternative to a military balance of power in order to secure Soviet restraint appears least productive in contested areas precisely because it is based on the view that revisionist states can be made conservative by acknowledging rather than by inhibiting their goals. Particularly in Asia, where Soviet proximity enhances access and claims to 'legitimate' interests, it will be difficult to disentangle regional events from the broader competition or to divorce these from the prevailing balance(s) of power.

Nothing in the record of Soviet foreign policy to date indicates any compatibility with Western notions of orderly change and the non-exploitation of instabilities. The lack of consensus both among the Western Allies and within the United States as to both the core of irreducible interests in the Third World and the nature of the appropriate responses to the murky nature of instabilities there (and to Soviet behaviour towards them) is unlikely to change in the 1980s. American policy must therefore be to intensify dialogue and consultation with the USSR, while making quite clear by her actions the extent to which the United States is prepared to enforce the rules she advocates. The achievement of agreements with her allies, with regard to both goals and the division of responsibilities for their attainment, would greatly reduce the American sense of weariness and provide alternative means of response which would be at once less disruptive and less likely to stimulate escalation.

American Policy in the 1980s
The Differentiation of Regions
This paper has so far argued that the United States has been torn between doctrines of universalist involvement and reliance on narrow security interests served by military power on the one hand and abstention, value judgments and world order on the other.

It will not be easy in the 1980s to bring together these strands, to reconcile values and security interests, to defend without entering open-ended, far-flung commitments, to shape the environment without indiscriminate involvement and to influence without becoming entangled.

What should be the criteria by which the United States should assess developments in the Third World? No particularly original suggestions are put forward here. As noted above, some consensus on a core of vital interests is important. Differentiation of interests among regions may be the simplest approach, bearing in mind that no region will remain unimportant in an interdependent world, that no two regions will be alike and that the question of *degree* will be important. Massive genocide or Soviet inter-

vention in the most peripheral region will dictate interest, while much smaller tremors in more strategic regions will excite similar concern. By delineating those regions in which American (and Allied) security interests are most directly involved, it will be much easier to formulate appropriate responses. In the case of choice between a direct security interest (for example, the strengthening of a partner's defence) and a contribution to a more general interest (the prevention of the proliferation of arms), the latter would have to take second place. In the most sensitive regions the presumption must be that the United States will respond militarily if necessary in the event of a direct threat to its interest. The sensitivity of the region would determine the threshold of American 'tolerance', of instability and external intervention. Yet it has to be admitted that American credibility will continue to matter, for a reputation for loyalty and steadfastness is far cheaper to maintain than to restore. Willingness to commit limited forces early may well postpone or obviate entirely the requirement for larger forces. Symbolic commitment, such as the deployment of seapower or diplomatic decisiveness, may go a long way but only as far as the resolve they are intended to communicate is believed. Responses to developments should be based on the following criteria:

—the degree to which important American interests are directly threatened (this allows for non-Communist threats);
—the impact on American credibility (a derivative interest); this would have to include various factors such as the degree of American commitment to a state or region and the historical relationship;
—the *degree* of Soviet involvement (treaty commitment, financial assistance, arms supplies, airlift, advisers, etc.).

Differentiation by region does not argue for a doctrinaire regionalism that treats regions discretely in an era of increasing interconnections and decreasing autonomy. It does, however, seek to identify those few regions (the Gulf, the Middle East and Korea) where American security is directly affected and those where, whether due to distance, or to lack of interest, or to relative disconnection from the strategic bal-

85

ance (for example, Latin America or Southern Africa), interests are less vital and less immediately subject to threat. This approach facilitates the choice of response to another dilemma – the tension that often arises between security interests which require allies, bases and access (often with regional states that are pariahs such as South Africa or Israel and, now, Somalia and Oman) and America's more general interests in the North–South dialogue. In supporting South Africa as an anti-Soviet force, it has, in fact, facilitated Soviet–Cuban advances in Africa. In cases of tension between these two sets of interests, an approach that recognizes Southern Africa as a theatre of secondary security interest would argue for a more relaxed approach to Soviet military threats and the cultivation of regional states and the OAU. Only in the case of massive Soviet involvement here would an American response be necessary; otherwise treating the issue on its merits rather than in East–West terms would make sense. The policy instruments too would be different. Here there would need to be more emphasis on economic assistance to ease the problems of adjustment. The situation is quite different in the Arabian Gulf. To treat Afghanistan as an East–South dispute and to wait for regional, non-aligned or Islamic states to take the lead would be folly. Direct American interests are potentially at risk, and only concrete responses will communicate the seriousness of the United States on this issue.

In this case the unwillingness to counter the Soviet invasion with substantial military assistance to the Afghan guerrillas suggests a desire to avoid taking risks. There are a number of reasons why arming the guerrillas would be unwise (it would invite their slaughter; Pakistan is too fragile; India matters; this is not the place to draw the line, etc.), but the unwillingness of the United States to act makes some wonder whether she can ever pose as a credible ally in the future and whether any regional context will be so 'pure' that it does not provide an excuse for inaction. Commitment has not in this case been communicated as persuasively as some third-world allies of the United States would have liked.

Clearly, interests in the Gulf are of such sensitivity that all three of the criteria noted above come into play. A threat to American interests does not have to come from the USSR. Regional states are quite capable of creating an atmosphere of turmoil, instability and crisis. The tolerance for the export of revolution or the practice of brinkmanship is necessarily limited in a region where a super-power collision is always possible. In less delicate regions coups, changes in foreign orientations and inter-state conflicts might affect American interests without directly constituting a threat to American security. This may be due to distance, to substantial regional autonomy or to a history of disconnection from the main area of super-power competition. It is, for example, difficult to imagine large-scale Soviet involvement in Latin America or South Africa that would not elicit a *local* response before it affected American interests. To be effective at this distance such interventions would have to be on a scale that would be virtually self-defeating. Here there is a *de facto* decoupling rather than decoupling reached by agreement between the super-powers.

Direct, vital interests need not mean direct involvement. With regard to the Arabian Gulf, Kissinger argued that the risks of selling arms to strengthen regional allies were less than the risks of regional turmoil requiring, but not facilitating, an American presence. He was correct in noting that in this part of the world perceptions of power matter and that military force remains an instrument indispensable to the defence of national interests. In the Gulf and the Middle East, in particular, military interventions may become necessary to maintain or to restore regional balances. Such interventions cannot create political stability, build institutions or enhance the legitimacy of the rulers, but they can deny a 'free ride' to forces opposed to American interests. They can also reassure partners and deter the USSR. Force will buy time but not much else. Preventive diplomacy and involvement will be needed to ensure that the time is well used. Although American interests will require more involvement than many would like, this need not mean unilateralism. There is much to be said for the multi-lateralizing presence of the Western Alliance to demonstrate shared interests. Encouraging regional co-operation between Egypt, Turkey, Pakistan and Saudi Arabia is also important, not only because of its potential contribution to meet local security threats but also because such co-operation could reduce the escalatory risks inherent in interventionary responses from outside the region.

Vital interests cannot be defended by detachment and dissociation, but nor should they be defended by embracing the *status quo* or unattractive regimes. What is required is an enhanced reputation for decisiveness and credibility in defence of the region and a diplomacy that is persistent, selective and modulated. Style is important here. Fluctuations are unhelpful; news leaks are damaging to local partners; and rhetorical doctrines are uninspiring. Against the plethora of potential threats to American interests (invasions, subversion, coups or defence treaties with the USSR), the United States has no tidy prescription, but she should seek to make clear what she will find unacceptable and what she will do when major American interests are seen to be at risk.

The Arabian Gulf has merited the most discussion because it is the most obvious case, even if it is the least typical of American interests in the Third World. In Latin and Central America[30] and in Southern and Central Africa, as argued above, the United States can afford to adopt a much more relaxed approach to developments. In North Africa American and Allied interests are virtually indistinguishable and so seem to require no particular American involvement. Even in the Caribbean an epidemic of internal political transformations, however politically distasteful, does not imply any shift in the immediacy of a threat to American security. The proximity and overwhelming power of the United States in the region should allow for much greater tolerance of uncertainty and fluctuation than in regions where power is more distant, fragile and dependent more on will than on circumstances. In this region (as in others) the United States' inclination to encourage the formation of centre parties may prove to be a chimera.[31] Rather than fanciful idealism, a sense of what is practically possible in the existing political context is required. Ralf Dahrendorf's distinction between the promotion of the rule of law and minimum human rights (which may be realizable) and political democracy (which may not) has much to recommend it as an operational principle. In this connection a more realistic means of differentiating between third-world leaders is essential. There are some who nurse grievances against the West as a result of specific Western policies; there are others who, as Kissinger has remarked, derive their legitimacy from their anti-Westernism. Mugabe should not be confused with Khomeini. Carrots will be needed as well as sticks.

The most difficult cases in the Third World will be those in which American interests are involved only indirectly but in which decoupling is difficult. The Indian Subcontinent, where a regionally preponderant state is in competition with a Communist neighbour (China) that continues its rivalry with the USSR, raises several types of problems. Should the United States, in seeking to take India seriously, welcome her regional hegemony even if that is followed by policies that complicate American access to the Indian Ocean? Should the promotion of India to the UN Security Council or an embargo on nuclear materials be the response to her nuclear status? Should the United States differentiate between her policies towards India and Pakistan on nuclear proliferation and on arms sales? If regionalism is in fact 'good' geopolitics, how should American policies treat the India–China rivalry? The relationship between the international policies of the Subcontinent and the Gulf further complicates the definition of 'good' regionalism.

In South-east Asia the American shift in the 1970s from imperial power to an offshore presence and subdued diplomacy saw a parallel interest in the establishing of ties with the ASEAN states. Yet Vietnam's regional ambitions and her alliance with the USSR have, by bringing in China and raising the possibility of a Sino–Soviet clash, transformed a purely regional issue into one affecting international security. The degree of involvement and the timing of the Soviet commitment to Vietnam bear all the marks of a proxy war, although Vietnam (like Cuba) clearly has her own motives. To what extent the United States can rely on the regional responses of China and the ASEAN states to deter Vietnam and the Soviet Union is unclear. At some point the interests of the United States become involved, due, in this case, not to a question of credibility *vis-à-vis* Thailand or ASEAN but to the consequences of allowing large-scale Soviet-supported military actions to occur unchallenged. There is not much that the United States can do to 'encourage' regional co-operation within ASEAN. The ASEAN states have certain interests in common but retain their individual priorities and even threat definitions which tend to prevent a common military response. Encouragement by the United States will only add credibility to charges by Hanoi and Moscow that ASEAN is an American-sponsored pact. Detachment in this part of the world has been practised; whether it can be maintained depends on the course of relations between the major Communist powers.

The interests of the United States are entangled in South Korea as a consequence, at least in part, of Japanese security perceptions. To a surprising degree, the Carter Administration pursued its commitment to human rights and political liberalization even at a time of political uncertainty in the Korean peninsula. American leverage over Seoul is strong, both because of a large military presence and because of an assessment that South Korea has 'nowhere else to go'. This pressure has yet to yield tangible results, but recent events may bring things to a head. The best that can be expected is the exchange of one more or less authoritarian regime for another, but American leverage in this instance would have been appreciably diminished if the initial inclination to withdraw American troops had been acted upon. Here involvement yields some leverage but with uncertain results. In the future Japan's slow military build-up and increasing influence in the Korean peninsula may come to replace that of the United States, allowing for a scaling-down of the American presence and a more indirect commitment. China's influence on North Korea will be important. Here, too, the possibility of multi-lateralization is worth exploring.

Finally, the case of the Middle East. There are no good reasons for assuming that the inclusion of the USSR in negotiations for a settlement would generate reasonableness or compromise unless it is first demonstrated that an arrangement can be arrived at without Soviet participation. Where the 'hard-nosed' approach is weakest, however, is in assuming that the vicious circle can be broken only by Soviet or Arab-rejectionist compromise. American pres-

sure on Israel will be necessary, as will American inducements, security assistance and guarantees. Greater Soviet involvement *at that juncture* will probably be necessary. Appropriate outside-power guarantees should be no more risky than continued stalemate and occasional wars. Since there exists a substantial domestic consensus on a continued American interest in the issue, guarantees here appear quite feasible. While a 'reasonable' settlement of the issue of Palestine would undoubtedly improve the relations of the United States with the Arab world, it would certainly not be a panacea for stability in the Gulf. Those who advocate it as part of a Gulf policy are correct; those who see in it a substitute or prerequisite for a Gulf policy are deluding themselves. Nevertheless, the interconnections between the two regions are marked and must be taken into account. Kissinger's (initially successful) attempts to separate the issue of Palestine from Gulf security foundered on the Saudi rejection of the Camp David formula put forward by the Carter Administration. This was in part a reaction to the Iranian revolution. By making a virtue out of necessity, some in the West now advocate a positive diplomacy which uses this interconnection.

The Pursuit of an Overarching Policy
The emphasis on key regions derives from an acceptance of their importance to the security of the United States. The containment of Soviet power and anti-Western radicalism and the shoring up of military balances will in these regions assume priority. Yet although the dispersal of power to new states has increased the attractiveness of regional approaches to security, interdependence has at the same time created new links between regions, thus decreasing their autonomy or isolation. An American policy that focuses on only one or two key regions is unlikely to work. Regional security, like the protection of physical security alone, cannot be a sufficient goal for a great power. The development of an environment that is moderate and favourable to diversity will be an essential ingredient of American security policies towards the Third World. The exercise of influence and the allocation of resources will be essential for world order precisely because the international system cannot ultimately

remain unaffected by persistent conflicts, growing radicalism or inequalities, or the recourse to the nuclear option. Whether one foresees 'chaotic fragmentation' in the Third World, or 'transitional crises' bordering on anarchy (combined with a North–South struggle), or a widening agenda of world-order issues of increasing complexity, the United States will remain aloof only at the cost of diminished influence over the kind of milieu in which she has to exist. Those who argue for limited commitments, or for confrontation, or for 'opposition' to the Third World cannot escape the fact that the days of continental, hemispheric or even Atlantic security have passed. The choice is between influencing an interdependent environment or adjusting oneself to it.

Yet there is a strong current of opinion in the United States which, for various reasons, seeks to limit commitments and undertake minimal expenditures abroad. Some urge domestic priorities, seeing little that is useful in what the United States, even with the best of intentions, can actually accomplish abroad. Others see the challenge of the South as political and urge a response in traditional terms where appropriate. Yet others would prefer the United States to affect a studied indifference towards the South as a whole (many of the latter are also sceptical about the optimism of the Pearson and Brandt Commission Reports, which concluded that the interests of the West and the Third World are in fact reconcilable, if not identical). Finally, there are those who argue for an insulation of American–Soviet relations from the turmoil of the Third World. They (like many Europeans) fear that the linkage of instabilities will tend to jeopardize progress in concrete areas of mutual interest (such as detente in Europe or arms control). Yet linkage, whether specifically invoked or not, exists. Unrestrained competition in third-world areas is bound to affect the climate of domestic opinion and, consequently, American–Soviet relations. It is unavoidable that connections will be made between detente and actions taken in regions if those actions are regarded as contrary to American interests.

The mood within the United States is one of frustration, expressed in occasional rhetorical militance, and a reluctance to invest resources in an 'ungrateful' and even competitive Third World. This makes the achievement of a consensus on less tangible goals even harder. Contradictions abound. The Carter Administration self-consciously both promoted the idea of the basic reform of the international economic order and followed its predecessors' attempts at co-opting the potentially influential through a 'graduation' strategy.[32] Neither succeeded, and a concrete policy towards the South failed to emerge from a government that was ostensibly sympathetic to fundamental rather than to cosmetic changes. The declining contribution of official American foreign aid (0.19 per cent of GNP compared with 0.52 per cent for Britain) is indicative, as is the concentration of 85 per cent of the total security assistance of the United States in the states of the Eastern Mediterranean. This reflects not just a diminishing concern for the South and the pressure of competing domestic demands;[33] it also reflects pessimism about the scope of influence and a belief that if there are problems, they stem not from an unequal international economy but from the domestic structure of states unwilling to make the necessary reforms. This in turn has led to a 'basic human needs' approach. There is little widespread enthusiasm for trade liberalization or commodity agreements and considerable resentment that past American contributions have been construed by some *dependencia* theorists as selfish attempts by the United States to perpetuate her hegemony and to distort the economies of the recipient countries. But there is a continuing and deep hostility towards intervention to secure access to resources, with one notable exception – oil. Only to secure oil could intervention realistically be contemplated, and then not to affect price but to prevent complete, irreversible, denial – presumed to be through Soviet control.

Torn between the facts of growing interdependence (and the costs and frustrations of involvement) on the one hand and the desire to attend to domestic priorities on the other, the United States is unable either to opt out or to fashion an effective policy for participation. The passing of an international order based on American military and political primacy[34] has been paralleled in the economic arena. Economically, third-world states can now assert their independence, and they can bargain for capital, technology and expertise elsewhere (from Japan or from Europe and from within the Third World itself). The potential disequilibrium between the global political commitments of the United States and her economic resource base, which was obscured in the 1960s by the growth of multi-national corporations and the position of the dollar as the world's reserve currency,[35] became all too evident by the 1970s. In different ways both the USSR and OPEC raised the price of maintaining the commitments, while competition from Japan and Europe decreased the capacity of the United States to pay.[36]

In the Third World development has brought neither stability nor order. It may, on the contrary, have brought the United States more assertive neighbours, commercial competitors and states which in time will directly affect American security interests through the acquisition of nuclear weapons. Far from allowing a decrease in American responsibilities and a respite from a troublesome world, development has made the world a more complex one, in which the simple verities no longer hold, the lines of partner and adversary relationships are ill-defined and the demands for involvement have grown more imperative. While the costs of involvement have increased, the costs of non-involvement have increased by even more.

Conclusion

The policy of the United States towards the Third World will have to accept both limits on her ability to determine or impose outcomes and the necessity of seeking to influence them. The extraordinary diversity of the countries in the Third World (a label which itself reflects an East–West bias) will ensure that any policies which assume any great uniformity among its members will fail. The one exception to this is the reform of the international economic order, a context in which even limited gestures far outweigh rhetoric. The United States will not find any convenient universal doctrine to replace that of anti-Communism. Policy towards the Third World will inevitably differ from region to region. But the principles on which it should be based – respect for diversity, compassion for suffering and a reputation for steadfastness – should inform policy everywhere. Once it is recognized that the aim of policy is the securing of interests and that respect rather than popularity will be conducive to this, it may become clear that there is no need for a particularly positive doctrine. The reduction of security interests to an irreducible core should facilitate the creation of a consensus ranged behind them. But without a sustained commitment to issues that do not yet constitute direct threats, that core will tend to increase.

NOTES

[1] Kenneth Thompson, 'The Ethics of Major American Foreign Policies', *British Journal of International Studies*, Vol. 6, No. 2 (July 1980), p.122.
[2] Truman Doctrine, 12 March 1947.
[3] Thompson, *op. cit.*, in n.l, pp. 121–2.
[4] Even in the case of Castro, President Kennedy was ambivalent, seeing him at times in the Bolivar tradition.
[5] John F. Kennedy, speech in Seattle, November 1961.
[6] Raymond Aron, *The Imperial Republic* (London: Weidenfeld & Nicolson, 1975), p. 302 (on which I rely in this section).
[7] *ibid.*, p. 306
[8] *ibid.*, p. 312.
[9] Though not isolationist, the mood had much in common with detachment. But, unlike the old isolationism, which held that the United States was too good for international affairs, the new feeling was that Americans were not good enough. See Norman Podhoretz, *The Present Danger* (New York: Simon & Schuster, 1980).

[10] Particularly Stanley Hoffman, Joseph Nye and Robert Keohane.
[11] Stanley Hoffman's criticism of the Carter Administration, on the first points, in *New York Review of Books*, 30 January 1980, p. 24, and of Kissinger, on the complexity of his foreign policy, in *Primacy or World Order* (New York: McGraw Hill, 1978), p. 79, therefore seems curious.
[12] The 'schools' being discussed subsume a wide variety of views, but they seem to fall essentially into two groups – those that emphasize the competition with the USSR and the role of military power and those that argue that regional politics condition the local environment and stress the existence of factors other than military power and rivalry with the USSR. Note especially that these two approaches are not a purely academic matter. The differences between the Republican and Democratic party platforms on foreign policy in 1980 almost exactly correspond to the globalist–regionalist divisions noted here. For a good discussion, see William Schneider, 'US Foreign Policy in the

Eighties: A Consensus Restored?' (unpublished paper).

[13] For example, see Peter Jay, 'Regionalism as Geopolitics', *Foreign Affairs* (*America and the World 1979*), January 1980, p. 488.

[14] See Henry Kissinger's Dallas speech, 22 March 1976.

[15] Jay, *op. cit.*, p. 511.

[16] Curiously, this sensible attitude sometimes becomes transformed into a masochism that sees a correlation between the 'authentic nationalism' of a group and the degree to which it is anti-Western. This lack of faith in Western values has often been evinced by liberals who prefer not to support 'moderates' in the Third World because they are 'unrepresentative'.

[17] Stanley Hoffmann, *Primacy or World Order, op. cit.* in n. 11, pp. 14–28.

[18] Hedley Bull, 'Kissinger: The Primacy of Geopolitics', *International Affairs*, vol. 56, no. 3, (Summer 1980), p. 486.

[19] See, for example, Tom Farer, 'The US and the Third World: A Basis for Accommodation', *Foreign Affairs*, (October 1975).

[20] See Robert Tucker, 'America in Decline: The Foreign Policy of "Maturity", *Foreign Affairs* (*America and the World 1979*), January 1980, and *The Inequality of Nations* (New York: Basic Books, 1977).

[21] For example, by supporting restrictions on the sales of arms, by arguing against Western involvement and against interventionary forces, by denying the need for proximate bases and by urging regional arms control agreements that, in the case of the Indian Ocean, inhibit the seapower of the distant state – the United States – while preserving Soviet land-based air superiority.

[22] Tom Farer, 'Searching for Defeat', *Foreign Policy*, no. 40 (Fall 1980), pp. 155–74.

[23] Z. Brzezinski Address to the Baltimore Council on Foreign Relations, 9 May 1980. This represents the views of Cyrus Vance more than Brzezinski, who in practice was more of a realist.

[24] For some reflections on this theme, see Philip Windsor, 'The Future of Strategic Studies' (unpublished paper).

[25] Secretary Brown's remarks at the West Point Graduation Ceremony, 28 May 1980.

[26] Of course, this discussion homogenizes a highly variegated group of states. Some are new, others are old. Some are city-states, others of continental dimension. Some were colonized, others remained independent; some are well integrated, others heterogeneous. They vary in levels of economic development and differ in foreign orientation and strategic significance. What they have in common are economies that are weak and not yet well diversified and, usually, non-democratic political systems. They also share an antipathy to colonialism and a desire for the reform of the international economic order.

[27] See Robert Tucker, 'America in Decline', *op. cit.* in n. 20.

[28] For a thoughtful discussion of 'cost-free' policies, see Thomas Hughes, 'The Crack-Up', *Foreign Policy*, no. 40 (Fall 1980), pp. 33–60.

[29] Such as the minor rectification of a border dispute in the Arabian Gulf.

[30] In Latin America the United States can accept a Brazilian–Argentinian preponderance and the continued insulation of the continent from the strategic balance (despite growing political and economic ties with Africa and Europe). Due to the region's autonomy, the longer period of independent statehood and mutual interaction and the relative paucity of contemporary inter-state conflicts, South America appears somewhat detached from the forces affecting other parts of the Third World.

[31] On the difficulties in El Salvador, see William Leo Grande and Carla Anne Robbins, 'Oligarchs and Officers', *Foreign Affairs* (Summer 1980).

[32] For various approaches, see Roger D. Hansen, *Beyond the North–South Stalemate* (New York: McGraw-Hill/Council on Foreign Relations, 1979). See also his 'North–South Policy – What's the Problem?', *Foreign Affairs* (Summer 1980).

[33] Of 17 major industrial states, American aid contribution as a percentage of GNP ranks 13th. Note that the revival of American interest in 'internationalism' has been 'defence-oriented' rather than non-military. See Schneider, *op. cit.* in n. 12.

[34] For a discussion of the interrelationship between the political supremacy of the United States and her economic position, see Robert Gilpin, *US Power and the Multinational Corporation* (London: Macmillan, 1976).

[35] *ibid.*, p. 150.

[36] *ibid.*, p. 218.

Super-Power Security Guarantees in the 1980s

SHAI FELDMAN

This paper will begin with a theoretical discussion of the likely effects of super-power guarantees, based on the rather extreme assumption that they are perfectly credible. This proposition will be qualified by a consideration of why, and of the extent to which, in the real world such guarantees are likely to deviate from the perfect model. The effects of such deviations on the super-powers' ability to attain regional stability through external guarantees will then be discussed.

Security guarantees are a sub-set of politico-military alliances. The former are distinct primarily in two respects. First, whereas an alliance can be formed between two or more states, irrespective of the distribution of power between them, a guarantee implies an asymmetry in the capabilities of the parties. The guarantor will invariably be more powerful than his clients and will often bear a disproportionate part of the costs of the alliance. This truth led Robert Rothstein to note that 'in substance, multi-lateral alliances like the South-east Asia Treaty Organization (SEATO) and the Central Treaty Organization (CENTO) really constitute unilateral great-power guarantees'.[1] Second, whereas alliances may be both defensive and offensive in goals and character, a guarantee clearly implies a defensive alliance. The guarantor promises to come to his client's rescue only in the event that the latter is attacked. Often, however, the object of the guarantee is not the territorial integrity or sovereignty of a client state, but rather the fulfilment of a peace treaty, international agreement or some other form of regional accommodation.[2] In this latter case the guarantee retains an equally defensive character: the guarantor appears as the guardian of the *status quo* by promising to utilize his capabilities against whomever is found to be in violation of the terms of the treaty, agreement or regional accommodation.

Guarantees and War: The Theory

Super-power security guarantees to regional clients should increase regional stability and should reduce the likelihood of regional wars by deterring potential violators of the peace and by mitigating the various causes of regional wars. The deterrent role of guarantees requires little elaboration. From the standpoint of the client state, the main purpose of the exercise is to combine its power with that of the guarantor 'in order to deter actual or potential enemies, or to defeat actual attacks'.[3] If the guarantees are credible, regional rivals will have to think hard before attacking a client state. Fear that the attack will force the guarantor to intervene on his client's behalf is likely to deter the potential offender from embarking upon such an enterprise. The guarantees are likely to have a dampening effect on regional violence: many a war which could not otherwise be deterred is averted because of the deterrent effect of external guarantees.

External guarantees may reduce the likelihood of war not only by deterring potential violators directly but also by mitigating various causes of war. The latter connection requires greater elaboration. Kenneth Waltz found war to be caused primarily by the anarchic nature of the international system. Anarchy causes war both because of its permissive aspect and because it breeds insecurity. Waltz stressed its permissive aspect: since the international system is composed of many sovereign states and lacks a superior agent capable of enforcing laws among them, war is always possible. Because the condition of anarchy allows each state to judge its 'grievances and ambitions' according to the dictates of its own objective and subjective interests, 'conflict, sometimes leading to war, is bound to occur.' A state may use force to attain its goals 'if, after assessing the prospects of success, it values these goals more than it values the pleasures of peace'.[4] Since in conditions of anarchy each state is the final judge of its own cause, any state may at any time use force to implement its policies.

The injection of super-power security guarantees into third-world regions can be expected to mitigate the effects of this cause of war. With the introduction of such guarantees and the capabilities needed to make them credible, various regional sub-systems are transformed into less anarchic and more hierarchical structures. Before initiating a war, a local state is forced to go beyond judging its own 'grievances and ambitions'. It must also take into account the desires of its protectors. Thus Egypt in the early 1970s and Syria today must take into account the Soviet Union's reluctance to endorse a military solution to the Arab–Israeli conflict. Not surprisingly, the present regime in Somalia calculates that a strong American military presence in Berbera may limit Somalia's ability to pursue a military solution in the Ogaden. Super-power presence leaves local rivals less room to initiate war. Thus, from the standpoint of regional stability, super-power guarantees can be expected to have a war-limiting effect.

The second consequence of international anarchy is that states are in a constant state of insecurity because they fear that war may be waged against them at any time. Fear of war confronts states with what John Herz calls a 'security dilemma'.[5] Since in the anarchic realm any state may at any time use force, 'all states must constantly be ready either to counter force with force or to pay the costs of weakness'.[6]

Once granted security guarantees, states can be expected to feel more secure. Knowledge that a super-power would come to their aid if attacked provides them with an assurance that they will be better able to defeat attackers. Assessing the deterrent effect of guarantees upon potential challengers has the further effect of persuading client states that they are less likely to be attacked. As security is less threatened, states feel less compelled to fight wars with the aim of improving their security, and international conflict diminishes dramatically.[7]

Another cause of war has been the periodic advantages of pre-emption, prevention and offence over the defence. In the absence of a single authority with a monopoly of force and capable of providing and guaranteeing security, each state is moved to take self-help measures to enhance its security. The launching of pre-emptive and preventive wars is among such measures. In turn, whether or not states will either fear pre-emption or decide to embark upon such a strategy themselves is largely a function of the relative attractiveness of offence over defence. The greater the advantages of offence over defence, the more likely states are to feel insecure and to initiate offensive action. When defence has the advantage, the opposite is the case. If defence has enough of an advantage, 'not only will the security dilemma cease to inhibit *status quo* states from co-operating, but aggression will be next to impossible, thus rendering international anarchy relatively unimportant'.[8]

Local rivals are expected to be less inclined to pre-empt each other once they are protected by external guarantees. Under such conditions, pre-emption will not make much sense because even if a temporary advantage over a local rival is gained, a state remains vulnerable to intervention by the latter's external guarantor. In a similar fashion, super-power security guarantees reduce the incentives for preventive war. Since the likelihood of both is a function of the advantage of offence over defence, and since super-power security guarantees essentially constitute the advantage of 'defence through diplomacy',[9] the odds that either type of war would be initiated in a region tied by a network of effective external guarantees are much reduced.

Another frequent cause of war has been the fact that many of the means by which one state tries to increase its security decrease the security of others.[10] Since this is true for each state from its own perspective, and since all states resist efforts to undermine their security, the general quest for security often leads to war. Thus war becomes more likely to the extent that different forms of security are mutually exclusive.[11]

Indeed, war often takes place not over security itself but rather over those assets that add to security. As Brodie has pointed out, states often interpret 'their requirements for security expansively, and the objects sought in its name often become in themselves the causes of conflict'.[12] For example:

In order to protect themselves, states often seek to control, or at least to neutralize, areas on their borders. But attempts to establish buffer zones can alarm others who have stakes there, who fear that undesirable precedents will be set, or who believe that their own vulnerability will be increased. When buffers are sought in areas empty of great powers, expansion tends to feed on itself in order to protect what is acquired, as was often noted by those who opposed colonial expansion.[13]

Expanding one's buffer zones necessarily places one's forces in greater proximity to other states' centres, thus threatening them. Threatened states take preventive actions, and this may lead to war.

External security guarantees may decrease the odds of war by making different forms of regional security less mutually exclusive. When a state's security is based on indigenous military capabilities that can assume both defensive and offensive roles, it often threatens the security of others. However, when security is based instead on external guarantees, it does not pose such a threat to others. When states are less dependent for their security on their own deeds, and, similarly, are less affected by the deeds of their regional rivals, they become less inclined to adopt self-help measures to improve their security. The odds that wars will be fought over resources that may add to security are consequently lower. War caused by attempts to escape the 'security dilemma' are thus less likely to occur.

A final cause of war that is mitigated by external security guarantees is the effect of optimistic misperceptions. Within the realm of systemic pessimism injected by the anarchic nature of the international system, states are often driven to momentary optimistic misperceptions of the distribution of power. They may perceive what seems to be an opportunity to increase their security by expansion or by defeat of the enemy and may rush to exploit it before the distribution alters to their disadvantage. Thus many pre-emptive or preventive wars are the outcomes of momentary miscalculations of the distribution of power.

Geoffrey Blainey, in *The Causes of War*, examines various conditions that favour such optimistic misperceptions. Prominent among such misperceptions are mistaken assessments of the likely behaviour of third parties in the event of war.[14] Erroneous expectations that third parties will join them if they initiate war have often driven states to take precisely such a step. Unjustified assessments that third parties will not come to the rescue of their rivals have likewise propelled states to imagine non-existent opportunities for a victorious war.[15]

Formal and perfectly credible external guarantees lower the odds of war by reducing the likelihood that the behaviour of third parties will be optimistically misperceived. As the obligations of the external powers are stipulated in the terms of the guarantees, there is less room for imaginative speculation about what they are likely to do, or to avoid doing, if war erupted. The likelihood that one regional rival will attack the other, basing his expectations of victory on the judgment that his victim's allies will not become involved, is far lower when the defensive alliance is formalized and well publicized.

The stabilizing effect of reduced uncertainty through the formalization of external obligations is felt far beyond the regions and states to which these obligations apply. Reduced odds that external powers' behaviour in different regions will be misperceived are beneficial also from the standpoint of great-power relations and hence from that of the entire international system. An external power may move to affect outcomes in a region on the assumption that other external powers will not be significantly affected and will therefore refrain from intervening. The assumption may turn out to be mistaken, leading to a direct clash between the great powers over regional outcomes. Indeed, this may occur even if the power conducting the initial intervention has only limited interests in the region and would have avoided intervening if it had calculated beforehand that its own intervention would lead others to intervene as well. Thus an unintended confrontation between the powers, with possible adverse consequences throughout the international system, may occur. In our own era, when such a feud may escalate to the unleashing of arsenals of unlimited destructive capabilities, it becomes imperative that miscalculations of this type be avoided. When external obligations are formalized, thus delineating clearly the regional responsibilities and interests of the external powers, the odds of such miscalculations occurring are significantly reduced.

The discussion so far has revolved around the theoretical role of external guarantees in maintaining regional peace. However, just as important is their role in achieving peace, i.e., as bargaining chips in the negotiations leading to regional accommodations. As external guarantees make states more secure and hence less in need of initiating war to improve their security, they also make states more forthcoming in the establishment of the initial state of peace. By providing states with alternative modes of security, external guarantees may allow for greater flexibility on issues that require compromise for regional accommodation to be reached. For example, since 1967 external guarantees of Israel's security have often been proposed as an alternative to the security provided by the occupied territories as buffers.[16] Indeed, it was in the process of negotiating the Israeli–Egyptian Peace Treaty, and in order to encourage Israel's withdrawal from her southern buffer (Sinai), that the United States agreed to provide her client with a quasi-guarantee in the form of the American–Israeli Memorandum of Agreement of March 1979. The Memorandum may serve as a possible model for super-power guarantees in the 1980s.

Security Guarantees and Credibility

The preceding analysis may lead one to conclude that super-power security guarantees in third-world regions are highly desirable. Such a conclusion, however, would be premature. Very rarely do external guarantees conform to theoretical assumptions of perfect reliability and credibility. 'There is only one chance in three that the protector will come to the aid of its ally in wartime, and then only at the discretion of the protector.'[17] More often than not, outside guarantees fall short of expectations, thus leaving both guarantor and clients extremely discontent. The shortcomings of external guarantees in the real world will be examined with special emphasis on those that may plague super-power guarantees in the 1980s.

The deterrent effect of super-power guarantees is a function of their credibility. The threat to intervene in the event that the client is attacked must be perceived as credible if a client's local rival or another external power is to be deterred from attacking. The credibility of a guarantee, in turn, is a function of the guarantor's capability and will. If the guarantee is to provide effective deterrence by either denial or punishment, the guarantor must be able to muster the forces required to punish the violator or to deny him his objectives. In other words, the guarantor must either station sufficient forces in whatever regions or states are placed under his security umbrella, or he must have impressive force projection capabilities. Intentions are no less important. The guarantor must demonstrate not only that he is capable of effective denial and punishment, but also that he is willing to bear the costs and consequences of fulfilling his obligations. Of course, intentions and the availability of appropriate instruments interact. The acquisition of tools for effective action signals intentions; the two reinforce each other to produce credibility.

Why has the reality of external guarantees so often fallen short of expectations? Why have they turned out so frequently to lack credibility? There are a number of reasons for such periodic disappointments. First, external guarantees are not always backed up with the capabilities required to make them credible. Alan Dowty stresses that in many cases of guarantees that failed to meet expectations 'the weakness of the guarantor as against the threatening state was the cause of failure'.[18] Whereas this problem has often plagued the credibility of big powers' guarantees against possible aggressive action by other big powers, the super-powers now face unprecedented problems in trying to meet threats presented by their clients' local rivals as well. Only a century ago some regions of the world were armed so inadequately that the mere appearance of a foreign gunboat could tip the local balance decisively. This is no longer the case. Many states in various regions are now well armed. Therefore a guarantor's attempt to intervene against a client's local rival, let alone an attempt to halt an attack by another power, requires that the guarantor be able to project forces over great distances. For example, any American effort to intervene against an Iraqi attack on Saudi Arabia would now require that the sizeable armed forces of Iraq be countered. An American guarantee to Somalia would require that American forces be capable of confronting the large and well equipped armed forces of Ethiopia. Far more than a gunboat would now be needed in order to tip a local balance in either case. Moreover, the high attrition rates involved in current weapon technology will often impose a particular strain on the long logistics tail of the intervening guarantor. The credibility of the guarantor is significantly affected if he is unable to meet the demands of a modern battle conducted in distant lands. The ability to stabilize various regions with credible external guarantees is thus reduced.

The prognosis in this sphere for credible American guarantees in the early 1980s is not encouraging. After many delays the United States seems to have finally launched the construction of a 200,000-man Rapid Deployment Force, but this plan will take time to materialize. A study conducted by the Congressional Budget Office concluded: 'assuming full availability of existing airlift resources . . . as many as five weeks would be required to deploy a two-division force to the Persian Gulf region.'[19] The pace of deployment is severely affected by the United States' limited sealift capability. The United States Navy, neglected for many years, now finds itself unable to sustain a large-scale transport operation of the kind required for intervention in distant regions. It lacks overall tonnage and is short of manpower.[20] Clearly, until the force-projection capabilities of the United States correspond more closely to expected threats, the credibility of her guarantees is likely to suffer.

A second problem that has often plagued the credibility of guarantees is that of will. Guarantors have not always demonstrated the necessary willingness to bear the costs involved in fulfilling their obligations under various treaties of guarantee. Consequently, their threats have not been believed and the guarantees have failed either to deter or to deny.

The problem of establishing credibility through the demonstration of will has two facets. The first is related to capabilities. The development of capabilities that closely correspond to the requirements of a guarantee signals an intention to meet obligations. Thus an American base in Oman will clearly signal an intention to fulfil a possible guarantee of free navigation through the Straits of Hormuz. The connection between capabilities and will may also take on a more general character. The overall willingness to invest in developing capabilities is an indicator of will. Thus, for example, current unwillingness in the United States to support anything beyond registration for possible conscription may very well be read by potential challengers as indicating a general lack of will to bear the costs of obligations abroad. Its effects on the capabilities of the United States notwithstanding, the lack of enthusiasm for the reinstitution of the draft is likely to have an adverse affect on the credibility of American guarantees.

Will should be communicated through diplomacy. The guarantor must tell potential challengers what he considers important and what he does not. The United States was apparently willing to tolerate direct or indirect Soviet advance in Angola, Ethiopia and South Yemen and to observe passively the downfall of the Shah of Iran. She was not willing to tolerate a direct and overt Soviet invasion of Afghanistan. However, if the Soviet Union were to be deterred from this invasion, the United States should have clearly communicated that she considered an overt invasion fundamentally different from less direct Soviet involvement. Guarantees require constant cultivation. The continued commitment to carry out obligations must be constantly communicated to potential challengers if the latter are to be deterred.

A third problem that often plagues the credibility of guarantees is over-commitment. No power is likely to have either the capability or the will to meet obligations everywhere. By declaring all regions vital, even a super-power faces the problem of spreading its capabilities and will too thin. The ability to fulful obligations suffers and so does the credibility of guarantees. Many Europeans objected to the involvement of the United States in Vietnam for fear that it might weaken her ability to react to threats in Europe. Indeed, when Egypt's President Nasser blockaded the Straits of Tiran (Sharm el-Sheikh) in May 1967, the United States' involvement in South-east Asia played some role in weakening her ability and will to fulful her pledge to Israel, given in February 1957, 'to exercise the right of free and innocent passage' in Sharm el-Sheikh.[21] The American pledge turned out to lack credibility, and Israel was forced to fall back on her own resources. Every power must determine its priorities and act in accordance with them. In some regions guarantees will not be credible because others will judge that the region is of insufficient importance to the guarantor and will expect him to ignore the obligations he has assumed. Consequently, it should not be expected that super-power guarantees could stabilize all regions but rather – if at all – only those regions that are of importance to the super-powers. Only in the latter instance are the powers likely to support their guarantees with sufficient will.

A fourth problem that may affect the credibility of guarantees is the nature of the challenges to regional stability. External guarantees often fail to secure regional stability when the threats to that stability derive from a regional rival or domestic unpheavals among the region's states. A super-power is less likely to be concerned about regional outcomes if they do not affect the global balance. Conversely, if a rival super-power attacks a guarantor's local client in an attempt to affect the regional balance to its advantage, the guarantor is likely to fulfil his obligations. Indeed, most big-power guarantees have been extended in anticipation of precisely such a contingency. Fully 87 of the 104 great-power guarantees since 1815 examined by Alan Dowty have been directed at great powers; in only 17 cases has the guarantee been aimed at a *local* rival.[22] A super-power may also fulfil guarantees aimed at a local rival, but this will occur only if the latter is perceived to be closely associated with the rival super-power or as posing a direct threat to the guarantor's interests. An example of the former occurred in 1950, when the United States identified North Korea with the Soviet Union and China. The ineffectiveness of super-power guarantees when the local violator is neither associated with the rival super-power nor perceived as a direct threat to the guarantor's interests results from a presumed lack of will. The odds are that in such circumstances the guarantor will be unwilling to bear the costs involved in meeting his obligations. Yet greater reluctance can be expected where both the local client and the local violator are closely associated with the guarantor, who will do his best to avoid difficult choices.

Some challenges may render security guarantees ineffective regardless of the nature of the attacker. For example, guarantees can be eroded by incremental challenges that lead to a slow deterioration of the *status quo*. Each incremental step may appear to provide insufficient grounds for the implementation of the guarantee. The guarantor may thus be gradually lured towards paralysis. This was clearly reflected in SEATO's inability to cope with the slowly deteriorating situation in South Vietnam in the late 1950s and early 1960s.[23]

The ineffectiveness of external guarantees against domestic sources of instability is likely to result from lack of capabilities, not of will. For example, the United States probably does not lack the will to prevent the realization of domestic threats to the present regime in Saudi Arabia. However, her capacity to act efficiently to meet such threats is probably quite limited. In such cases the question of timing is crucial. If the guarantor waits too long, intervention becomes either impractical or too expensive. The behaviour of the United States in the case of Iran is a case in point. Once domestic rivals establish themselves firmly in command, external intervention involves prohibitive costs. However, a proper understanding of when external intervention may be effective requires accurate and timely intelligence about the domestic context in distant regions. Neither the Soviet Union (in the case of Egypt) nor the United States (in the case of Iran) has demonstrated particularly impressive capabilities in this sphere.

The implementation of external guarantees against domestic sources of instability is extremely difficult even when good intelligence is available. External intervention – even when conducted in a timely fashion – is either ineffective or too costly once significant domestic social forces have begun to undermine the stability of the guaranteed regime. The American experience in Vietnam and the Soviet experience in Afghanistan demonstrate this difficulty. In the case of Iran, an accurate intelligence analysis could have led the Carter Administration to refrain from further eroding the Shah's position by pressuring him on the issue of human rights and to increase the Shah's boldness by reinforcing its commitment to him instead of weakening it. Later, an accurate reading of the Iranian domestic scene might have led the Carter Administration – particularly during the visit of General Huyser – to prompt the Iranian General Staff to place itself in power. However, it is doubtful that any of these possible avenues of action could have saved the Shah.

The preceding comments do not imply that there have not been cases of successful external intervention against domestic threats. British intervention in Malaya and Singapore in the 1950s and the United States' intervention in Lebanon in 1958 are cases in point. The guarantor can act effectively against a variety of low-level threats to the client's regime. For example, by transferring intelligence about a prospective coup, the guarantor can enhance the client's ability to help himself. However, once the regime loses the support of significant social, political and military forces, it will be constrained from taking such measures, even if excellent intelligence is made available. Thus external powers have only limited ability to guarantee specific regimes against domestic upheavals.

The United States is therefore unlikely to provide effective guarantees against domestic instabilities in client states. However, once formally extended, American guarantees against direct Soviet attacks are likely to stabilize regions in which there is a possibility of such attacks. This is particularly the case if vital American interests are involved in those regions. (The Arabian Gulf is a case in point.) Conversely, external guarantees are unlikely to stabilize regions in which the interests of the super-powers are more limited, such as Central Africa. At the same time, even in regions that are of considerable importance American guarantees are unlikely to be credible if the local offenders are sufficiently dissociated from the Soviet Union. As relations between Egypt and the United States improve, the credibility of American guarantees to Israel against Egyptian violations of the 1979 Peace Treaty will diminish. Should Iraq dissociate herself from the Soviet Union, the United States may become somewhat less likely to respond to Iraqi activities in the Gulf. Similarly, American guarantees to Pakistan are likely to be effective against the Soviet Union, but not against India.[24]

A fifth problem that is likely to interfere with the effectiveness of guarantees involves the possible existence of competing super-power interests. Guarantees are designed to make local clients secure. Thus various activities designed to enhance clients' power are consistent with the purpose of guarantees. However, some of the super-powers' other foreign policy goals may require quite the opposite. One such competing interest involves the control of nuclear proliferation. Efforts to halt proliferation may propel a guarantor to punish local clients who attempt to develop indigenous nuclear capabilities. Punishment may take the form of a ban on military or economic aid. However, such bans contradict the purposes of security guarantees and make clients less secure; in addition, they may be dangerously misread by potential challengers. A guarantor's willingness to permit the deterioration of his relations with a client may be regarded by others as indicating a loss of interest in the region. They may conclude that the guarantor will not react to aggression. Thus it would not be unreasonable to suggest that the Soviet invasion of Afghanistan may have had something to do with the United States' decision to ban all military and economic aid to Pakistan. That ban was imposed in April 1979, when Pakistan was discovered to have acquired a uranium-enrichment plant. The United States willingness to permit her relationship with Pakistan to deteriorate over the nuclear issue may have been read by Soviet analysts as indicating that she had lost interest in that region and consequently was unlikely to respond vigorously to aggressive Soviet acts there. Thus the goals embodied in super-power guarantees may collide with other foreign-policy goals to the extent that the latter may seriously damage the effectiveness of guarantees.

Bilateral and Multilateral Guarantees

The odds are that guarantees provided jointly by the United States and the Soviet Union, as well as multi-national guarantees, would not be effective. Guarantees provided by the two super-powers in concert would lack credibility for two reasons. First, their functioning would depend not only on an enduring super-power consensus on the fact that co-operation between them on regional affairs is preferable to confrontation, but also on an enduring common perception and interpretation of regional events. If the former condition were not met, co-operation between the super-powers would not survive in the face of their conflicting interests; if the latter condition were not met, the guarantees would be meaningless because the guarantors would never be able to agree that a situation warranted the activation of the guarantee. Furthermore, the co-ordination and consultation mechanisms that bilateral guarantees require would make their fulfilment a slow and inefficient process. Each guarantor would be able to veto the other's decision to meet its obligations. Such a system could neither be effective in time of need nor inspire credibility in times of tranquillity.

A second reason why joint bilateral guarantees would be unreliable is that great powers demonstrate the requisite will for the fulfilment of guarantees only when they confront one another. Big powers' interests in various regions are likely to be a function of the extent to which developments there threaten to affect the global distribution of power. Regions that are important enough for events there to affect the global balance are likely to be arenas of big-power competition and conflict, not co-operation. The stakes in such regions would be very high, and each power would fear that co-operation could result in a relatively greater gain for the other power.

Only in regions that are of secondary importance are the super-powers likely to co-operate to the point of awarding joint guarantees. However, in such regions the reliability of such guarantees would be regarded as suspect because the super-powers are less likely to bear the costs of meeting obligations in regions that are relatively unimportant.

Multi-lateral guarantees such as those that could be provided by the United Nations would be even less reliable. As Aharon Klieman has pointed out:

a broad international framework of guarantees is objectionable on two counts. It would be too unwieldy an instrument; and it fails to take into account the shortcomings of the UN organization. The UN, like its League of Nations predecessor, is too cumbersome to offer aid rapidly. It lacks coercive machinery; its process of decision-making is decentralized and is also subject to great power rivalry.[25]

The collective will of a body as diffuse as the United Nations can hardly provide reliable guarantees. A body both lacking in capabilities and unstable in its collective intentions cannot serve as an effective guarantor. Thus only unilateral guarantees may hold out the hope of providing credible security.

In order to secure Western interests worldwide in the future, security guarantees would have to be provided principally by the United States. Guarantees provided by Europe are unlikely to be credible. If they were provided jointly by a number of Western European powers, they would be likely to be plagued by the problems normally affecting multi-lateral guarantees. In addition, such guarantees would probably require that NATO be involved somehow in assuming responsibilities beyond the European theatre – an unlikely prospect. Individual European nations are unlikely to provide effective guarantees because they are increasingly vulnerable to Soviet pressure as well as to pressure exerted by oil-producing countries. Therefore client states that are threatened either by the Soviet Union (directly or by proxy) or by the armed forces of a major oil-producer would not be able to rely on European guarantees.

The preceding comments are not meant to imply that European nations should play no role in providing security guarantees. On the contrary, it is difficult to believe that the United States will be willing to shoulder all of the costs of securing Western interests in the Third World for ever, through guarantees or otherwise. Although the guarantor (obviously, the United States) should continue to be the least vulnerable unitary actor, the European nations will have to contribute both funds and labour. Otherwise the American people will increasingly come to believe that Europe is getting a free ride, a perception that may lead the United States to abandon her responsibilities abroad and to retreat to Fortress America.

The Third-World Context
The deficient credibility of external guarantees also affects their capacity to mitigate various causes of war. Because of this deficiency, guarantees will not diminish third-world conflict to the extent that this theoretical analysis would lead one to expect.

First, with respect to mitigating the effects of regional anarchy, the increased limitations on the ability of the great powers to tip local balances rapidly will affect their political influence. Being increasingly armed themselves, clients more frequently feel that they can ignore the expressed desires of their guarantors. In 1973 Syria ignored Soviet distaste for a military solution to the Arab–Israeli conflict, and in 1976 she ignored an explicit Soviet request – in this case a plea by Gromyko, who made a special trip to Damascus for that purpose – that Syria should avoid intervention in the Lebanon. For some time now Israel has ignored clearly communicated American preferences on the questions of the Lebanon, the Palestinians, Jerusalem and Jewish settlements in the West Bank and the Gaza Strip. Although neither Syria nor Israel enjoys formal super-power guarantees, the basic dynamics of client–patron relations would endure even if the respective Soviet and American commitments were formalized. The guarantor's ability to control his clients is more limited today, as is his ability to prevent his clients from waging war against one another. As a result, the peaceful effects of external guarantees are limited.

Similarly, the guarantees have only a moderate impact on that aspect of international anarchy that breeds insecurity. Since, in a variety of circumstances, external guarantees are likely not to be credible, they will not provide a solution to local clients' 'security dilemmas'. Consequently, these clients will need to help themselves (measures may include the initiation of war) to increase their chances of survival.

The incentive to wage pre-emptive war will be lower for local rivals tied by a network of external guarantees but higher for the guarantors themselves. Consider, for example, possible American guarantees to the Gulf States. The United States' deficient force-projection capabilities could well lead her to develop a pre-emptive or 'tripwire' strategy. Should the initiation of a Soviet move towards the oilfields be detected, token American forces would be flown in. Their purpose would be to force the Soviet Union to decide whether her goals were worth the risks involved in a direct armed clash with the United States.[26] Irrespective of whether or not the strategy could succeed, it would be bound to introduce a considerable

degree of instability. The temptation on both sides to pre-empt each other would be considerable. Both sides are likely to lean towards worst-case analysis: ambiguous changes in the disposition of the Soviet Union's forces along her southern border could well be misinterpreted by the CIA as indicating an imminent invasion. This in turn could lead to a pre-emptive launching of the Rapid Deployment Force, and the Soviet Union would then be forced to counter American intervention by moving southwards. Both parties' capacities to avoid a direct clash would be stretched to the limits. Thus instead of enhancing regional stability by reducing local rivals' incentives to pre-empt, the guarantor's weak force-projection capabilities might lead both super-powers to employ pre-emptive strategies of their own, causing possibly fatal regional instability.

Deficiencies in the credibility of external guarantees are also likely to affect the odds that regional wars will occur through misunderstanding. Credible guarantees reduce the odds of such wars by making it less likely that third-party behaviour will be wrongly assessed. However, guarantees that lack credibility become insufficient indicators of what guarantors are likely to do in the event that clients are attacked. Under such conditions local rivals – as well as the opposing super-power – may calculate that the guarantor will avoid implementing the guarantee. The calculation may well turn out to be in error, but meanwhile war will already have been initiated.

A further limitation on the ability of the super-powers to stabilize third-world regions by external guarantees is the willingness of various states to accept such guarantees. Small states may be reluctant to become recipients of such guarantees for a variety of reasons. They may calculate for example that guarantees lacking in credibility are not worth the risks entailed, or they may assess that by accepting a guarantee from one super-power they may antagonize the rival power to the extent of compelling it to take aggressive counter-measures. The acceptance of a security guarantee may thus increase a client's 'security dilemma' instead of alleviating it. This calculation may be seen in Pakistan's current reluctance to accept American protection unless it is accompanied by massive economic and military aid.

A second cause of small states' reluctance to accept super-power guarantees is their fear that acceptance may result in a further loss of their freedom of manoeuvre. Security guarantees invariably place some obligations on the client. As a guarantor will wish to avoid being dragged into military conflict unwillingly, a recipient may be required to obtain the guarantor's prior agreement before initiating external activities. This would clearly constitute a loss of sovereignty. Fear of such constraint may lead potential recipients to reject offers of external guarantees.

Third, there is the problem of loss of prestige. Small states may regard external guarantees as confirming their inferior position. The unwillingness to acknowledge what they feel to be dependent status may therefore lead them to forgo such guarantees.

A fourth cause for the rejection of guarantees is their possible impact on the recipient's domestic structure. Guarantees may exacerbate domestic instability by driving to greater militancy those internal forces that oppose close relations with the guarantor. This is particularly the case in states where important segments of the population reject on either social or religious grounds, relations with white or 'Christian' powers. If a guarantee is to be accompanied by the stationing of the guarantor's troops, it may be more forcefully rejected for fear that the recipient's social fabric will be affected. Saudi Arabia, for example, is extremely sensitive to the effects of foreigners on her religious and social structure. The predictable effects of foreign troops on social morality influence the judgment even of relatively progressive Western-oriented states.

Fifth, a potential recipient may reject offers of external guarantees for fear that his society may be less inclined to help itself. As stressed above, dependence is likely to increase regional stability, but even in individual client states concern may arise that reliance on external guarantees will cause decadence, that it will encourage citizens to imagine that they need not do anything themselves (let alone make significant sacrifices) to improve their country's lot. It may also be feared that if all this were to happen, and if the guarantee were to be exposed later as inadequate to match a particular external challenge, the recipient would then no longer be capable of meeting the threat on its own. The guarantee would thus have weakened, rather than strengthened, the recipient.

Finally, recipients may reject security guarantees for fear that the formalization of the commitment may actually diminish the guarantor's capacity to come to their aid. For example, Israel may consider that, in past and present circumstances, the President of the United States has enjoyed sufficient flexibility and will to provide support should the need arise without any formal guarantee, whereas the formalization of the American commitment by treaty would mean an agonizing ratification process by the United States Senate. Although ratification is probable, the odds are that numerous amendments would be offered to limit the application of the guarantee. The rationale for such amendments would be to ensure that the United States was not made a hostage of her client. The effect of the process might be a lesser American commitment to Israel than the one she enjoys at present.

Thus for a variety of reasons states may judge that super-power guarantees would either diminish their security or not be worth the cost.

Guarantees and Conflict Management

The preceding analysis should not induce despair with respect to the efficacy of super-power guarantees, however. Despite their somewhat dubious credibility, such guarantees do have a significant deterrent effect upon potential violators of the peace. Nor is their effect in mitigating various causes of war inconsequential. Finally, external guarantees can play a significant role in negotiating regional accommodations. When offered as alternative sources of security, guarantees may allow local rivals to be more flexible on other issues involving their national defence.

Beyond these justifications, there is an additional and compelling reason to support the extension of super-power guarantees in the early 1980s. For some time now the super-powers have demonstrated an increasing inability to read correctly each other's foreign and defence policy. The fault lies less with Moscow than with Washington. The Carter Administration appeared to establish a record for inconsistent conduct in foreign affairs. It demonstrated this in its treatment of various issues, such as the United States Defense Budget, the affair of the neutron warhead, the pursuit of human rights abroad, nuclear proliferation, the Soviet brigade in Cuba, the downfall of the Shah of Iran, the hostage crisis and, finally, the Soviet invasion of Afghanistan. When one super-power continuously demonstrates its inability to establish its own priorities, the other is bound to find it difficult to read rapidly altering policies correctly. The result has been that the Soviet Union has become increasingly incapable of predicting the United States' next move.

In the nuclear era the super-powers' inability to interpret each other's foreign and defence policy accurately may have detrimental consequences, not only for the powers themselves but for third-world bystanders as well. A direct, premeditated clash between the nuclear powers does not look likely. However, a nuclear confrontation may well develop through an unintended escalation of conflicts in 'grey areas'. If the super-powers are increasingly unable to predict each other's moves, there is a real chance that one of them will base its regional activities on the mistaken assessment that the other will not react. The opposing super-power may in turn react forcefully, thereby throwing both of them into a spiral of action, reaction and counter-action.

A decision on the part of either super-power to grant security guarantees in various parts of the Third World may seem an anachronism. It would imply the establishment of fairly static spheres of influence and would therefore be reminiscent of the cold war. On the other hand, a major decision to extend such guarantees would force both to establish their priorities and, once established, to communicate those priorities to each other. In effect, they would be compelled to conduct a full-scale strategic dialogue. This would increase their ability to read each other's intentions and preferences and would reduce the odds that they would clash unintentionally. Since, for the moment, the subject of SALT cannot provide a focus for a super-power dialogue, it becomes particularly important that an alternative focus for such a dialogue be provided. An effort by both super-powers to redefine their responsibilities in the Third World, for themselves and for each other, may provide a useful alternative focus for this much-needed dialogue.

NOTES

[1] Robert L. Rothstein, 'Alignment, Nonalignment and Small Powers, 1945–1965', in Julian R. Friedman et al., eds., *Alliance in International Politics* (Boston: Allyn & Bacon, 1970), p. 354.

[2] Alan Dowty, *The Role of Great-Power Guarantees in International Peace Agreements*, Jerusalem Papers on Peace Problems No. 3 (Jerusalem, 1974), p. 19.

[3] Yair Evron, 'An American–Israeli Defense Treaty', unpublished draft, August 1979, p. 3.

[4] Kenneth N. Waltz, *Man, the State and War* (New York: Columbia University Press, 1954), p. 159.

[5] John H. Herz, 'Idealist Internationalism and the Security Dilemma', *World Politics*, vol. 2 (January 1950), pp. 157–80.

[6] Waltz, *op. cit.*, pp. 159–60.

[7] Stephen W. Van Evera, 'Offense, Defense, Nuclear Weapons and the Causes of War', unpublished paper, p. 4.

[8] Robert Jervis, 'Cooperation under the Security Dilemma', *World Politics*, vol. 30 (January 1978), pp. 187–8.

[9] Van Evera, *op. cit.*, p. 2.

[10] Jervis, *op. cit*., pp. 169–70.

[11] Henry Kissinger, *A World Restored* (Boston: Houghton Mifflin, 1973), p. 2; Raymond Aron, *The Great Debate: Theories of Nuclear Strategy* (New York: Doubleday, 1973), p. 212.

[12] Bernard Brodie, *Strategy in the Missile Age* (Princeton: Princeton University Press, 1959), p. 224.

[13] Jervis, *op. cit.*, in n. 8, p. 169.

[14] Geoffrey Blainey, *The Causes of War* (New York: Free Press, 1973), p. 57.

[15] *ibid.*, p. 58.

[16] Evron, *op. cit.*, in n. 3, p. 18.

[17] N. A. Pelcovits, *Security Guarantees in a Middle East Settlement*, Foreign Policy Papers No. 5 (Beverly Hills/London: FPRI/Sage Publications, 1976), p. 21.

[18] Dowty, *op. cit.* in n. 2, p. 18.

[19] *U.S. Airlift Forces*, Congressional Budget Office, April 1979, pp. xiv–xv.

[20] *Shaping the General Purpose Navy of the Eighties*, Congressional Budget Office, January 1980, p. 208.

[21] Pelcovits, *op. cit.*, p. 14.

[22] Dowty, *op. cit.* in n. 2, p. 17.

[23] George Modelski, *SEATO: Six Studies* (Melbourne: F. W. Cheshire, 1962). p. xvi.

[24] W. M. Hale and Julian Bharier, 'CENTO, R. C. D. and the Northern Tier: A Political and Economic Appraisal', *Middle East Studies*, vol. 8, no. 2 (May 1972), p. 220.

[25] Aharon Klieman, 'International Guarantees and Secure Borders', PhD Thesis, Tel Aviv University, 1976, p. 11.

[26] 'A big US buildup in the Gulf', *Newsweek*, 14 July 1980.

greater would be the impact of another Khomeini-type insurrection or another war in the Middle East between producers – not to mention their simultaneous occurrence.

One aspect of supply which is central to our concerns is the possibility that through the use of the 'oil weapon', or through the less aggressive decision simply to restrain production for another reason, imports to a country or group of countries would be reduced below that minimum level essential to the functioning of their societies. What this level is for a particular country is always difficult to define, but in terms of general international supply, a reasonable guess is that 26 MMB/D represents the point of peril. Below that level some countries could be grievously short. Unless there were compelling reasons to believe that reduced supply was a short-term phenomenon, importing governments might conclude they had no alternative but to use force to restore supply.

What do we mean by that? Who in the Western Alliance would have the requisite political will to act and the military means to accomplish the purpose? Would not damage to oil facilities be so extensive as to negate the effort? What if the USSR were to react with a move of her own, confronting the West with an ultimatum? The Allies have no convincing answers to these questions – but some of them, notably the United States or France, might conclude that such an emergency was of compelling proportions. The point is that producers ought not to believe that their actions would, in the end, be unopposed militarily because they imagine that no importer would have sufficient confidence in military success to warrant the use of force. An importer might indeed conclude it had no alternative but to attempt the near impossible.

While we can probably avoid these worst-case scenarios, the observation holds that continuing competition for available oil is certain to be the most likely condition. The competition is far more than merely a commercial one, for governments of both exporting and importing countries are now fully involved and are engaging the instruments and powers available to them to secure supply. As noted above, the very involvement of governments ensures the politicization of oil, but their intervention is a consequence of the inability of most industrial states

and many LDCs to pay for oil through the ordinary processes of trade. Special deals are struck and special arrangements concluded. Ten years ago the bulk of international oil moved as a result of commercial decisions; today scarcely one barrel of oil goes abroad without government approval.

The uneasiness in world oil today stems in large part from this politicization of oil, but it is also the product, in large measure, of the fact that the observance of contracts is no longer believed by producers to be a necessary condition for the sale of oil. The importing nations, singly and collectively, are to blame for not having insisted all along that the peaceful transfer of power from the oil companies to the producing governments – itself an extraordinary circumstance – implied the assurance of performance under agreements freely concluded. We are paying the price for that lapse of rectitude. It corrodes relationships and is likely to lead to confrontation.

The Implications of Conflict: The Middle East
The question of levels of supply, the problem of how oil is to be paid for and the issue of respect for agreements are some of the causes of the tension found in international oil. There are others, but those which might involve conflict and might affect supply are usually found in the Middle East, although confrontation between Malaysia and Indonesia, or eventually between Japan and China for access to South-east Asian oil, are other possible causes of conflict. (Another example is the possibility of a Norwegian–USSR confrontation over petroleum resources off the Norwegian northern coast.) These tensions can be seen in the actions of regional states whose difficulties with each other may have very little to do with oil *per se* but come to involve it, or in the actions of external powers in a region in which access to oil could be a prime cause for conflict. What might be the causes of such conflict? How might it come to a head, and to what effect?

Foremost among the causes is the unresolved question of a Palestinian entity. While Arab hostility towards Israel seems unremitting and general, we think we can sometimes distinguish between the rhetoric of Arab states and their commitments and willingness to act. But we can take little comfort from these distinctions because there is probably no issue as likely to inflame the region as this one. Yet we need not assume that each producer would use its oil weapons uniformly; the record suggests this would not be the case. What makes the current situation difficult to deal with – as compared with 1967 and 1973–74 – is Israeli and Arab possession of a medium-range missile capability which permits either side to launch a pre-emptive attack. In the case of Israel the question always arises of whether her targets would now include the truly vital gathering facilities and terminals through which the Gulf oil supply passes. However desultory some producers' use of the 'oil weapon' might be, an Israeli attack on these crucial installations could precipitate a significant crisis in oil supply.

The Iraqi–Iranian war and the damage done to facilities has been a timely reminder of the vulnerability of all installations to attack; the possibility of additional conflicts is now, or ought to be, a constant concern. Oil facilities are, of course, liable to terrorist attack from almost any direction (such attacks could even be made to appear to be Israeli initiatives) and are vulnerable to action by local dissidents. Terrorists could also sow confusion and uncertainty by mining a few very large crude carriers. We know now something about the dimensions of the loss in international supply that could occur as a result of such conflict. There is still the possibility of another cause of lost supply – a revolutionary coup, or an attempt at one, followed by intervention by the armed forces of a neighbour or of an external power. One can only guess at the damage that might be wreaked upon oil facilities either because a new government chose to reduce exports drastically and an external power intervened, or as a result of a military response to a revolt; the damage could be deliberate or accidental. Saudi Arabia is one such potential case. Iran is another. Either the USSR or the United States, or both, may yet become militarily involved there. In any case, the distinction which used to be made between conflicts which did not originate in an oil issue, so facilities were unlikely to be attacked, and one in which installations were an object of war is no longer useful. Whether damage is deliberate or accidental may not be even of academic interest. Any conflict must now be considered dangerous to international supply.

Soviet Energy Needs

There are actors other than the states of the Middle East; most particularly, there are the Soviet Union and the United States. If the Soviet Union were to need imported oil (either on her own account or for Eastern Europe), how would this affect Soviet policies and actions in the Middle East? Will her needs increase the probability of conflict? We know much less about the extent and timing of the Soviet need for imported oil than those who argue for one assessment or another are likely to admit. Nevertheless, we have to consider several eventualities, as a matter of prudence. First, any Soviet leadership would be greatly disturbed by its loss of energy autarchy; the implications for strategic vulnerability would be assessed with great care. Second, the Soviet Union has time within which to make her moves. Imported oil may not be a crucial need for many years to come. Precipitate action to secure supply would seem to be an unnecessary option now, and anticipated oil needs in the future would not preclude the Soviet Union's taking advantage of the confusion in Iran for other reasons. The fact that the importing industrial world has managed so far to live through the supply shortages caused by the Iran–Iraq war (thanks, in part, to Saudi Arabia) may persuade the Kremlin that it could move in Iran with less risk than before. One must always consider the extraordinary strategic leverage over the OECD oil supply which Soviet presence on the Gulf would provide. But in terms of access to someone else's oil (as distinct from improving the Soviet Union's ability to influence international supply), the USSR may not believe that she must act in a confrontational manner for some time yet.

There are three main options open to the Soviet Union, each with its particular advantages and disadvantages: first, to intensify efforts to develop domestic energy resources and to limit the internal consumption of oil; second, to obtain her needs from the international market despite the foreign exchange costs involved; third, to forge a special relationship with a producer state, comparable with what she may have hoped to arrange with Iraq and Libya, which would give the USSR preferential access to oil (there are possibilities outside the Middle East for additional supply, such as Mexico or Norway). The USSR could employ political and economic tactics, military aid or even the pressure of military power to secure such arrangements.

Only the third option would raise the possibility of conflict. But unless there were strong armed opposition to a Soviet move, damage to facilities would seem not to be a primary concern. The effect of the first two options on international supply might be the same – in either case, present importers would have to adjust and producers, in setting their preferred production rates, would have to reckon on accommodating a Soviet claim for a share of foreign oil. There may, therefore, be less likelihood of conflict as a result of new Soviet oil requirements, unless the search for oil were to be associated with a great strategic objective (such as establishing a Soviet presence in the Gulf or keeping the United States out of Iran). The chances that Soviet import needs will in themselves be a cause for war are probably slim.

As for the United States, she remains the only Western power capable of making a major military response in the region and the only power able to challenge the USSR by applying pressure in other parts of the world if that were considered necessary. American plans to build a Rapid Development Force (RDF) reflect a real military strategy and should in time be an effective force in being. But it needs to be backed by an effective strategic petroleum reserve and rationing programme, both of which are lacking. Moreover, the RDF will require a political strategy for the region that will enlist the support of key Arab states and the NATO allies.

Relations among Allies
Access to oil will profoundly affect relationships among the Allies as each importer seeks to obtain its needs. The United States was slow to recognize the extraordinary importance to the Allies of adequate and continuous oil supply, but the centrality of this matter ought now to be evident. Neither Japan nor any European state, save Britain and Norway, can accept a major, sustained loss in supply whatever the cause. However unlikely it may seem that supply could be cut for more than a few months through concerted action by the producers, the appalling consequences, if it should last longer, are bound to cause importing states to look to their energy defences, especially as they must also anticipate

generally tight supply resulting from low production levels. A knife-edge balance between demand and supply will be a continuous concern.

The International Energy Agency (IEA), created to help member nations to cope with emergency shortfalls, is a distinct improvement over its predecessor, the OECD Oil Committee. But the lack of political will and discipline that enervated the Oil Committee may haunt the IEA if a crisis were to occur. Too many of its key members already speak as if this were the case and could thus rob the IEA of its potential. Additionally, however, the loss in flexibility of the great international oil companies to manage supply in an emergency is a new and troubling factor for which there is no remedy. Nor has the IEA as yet developed mechanisms to allocate oil if supply became short for some reason other than a producer's embargo on supply. The IEA cannot deal with the propensity of importing states to try to arrange for preferential access to the producing states' oil (although in a sense it was created to help avoid the need for importers to follow the example of the United States with Saudi Arabia and Iran). It is the unrelenting search for assured supply that characterizes so much of the oil strategies of France, Germany, Italy and Japan. We have no apparent means for coping with this phenomenon and are greatly in need of them.

Given these tendencies, is there something too facile about the assumption of the European nations that they can become more involved with Arab producers – without the United States – and that something can be agreed between them to improve upon Europe's supply? Could a European initiative proceed without regard for the oil needs of the United States or Japan and without impairing relationships with the United States? Both questions imply a divergence in energy policies and strategies which the Reagan Administration will be likely to address in its assessment of Allied relationships and in an insistence on mutual support, which means a fuller appreciation of American interests. In response, Allies ought to press harder for an American political strategy in the Middle East which takes into fuller account their own greater stakes in the region's oil. Such a strategy has to include a modification of the present imbalance in the relationships of the

United States with Israel and with Arab states; otherwise Allied support for American actions in the region will remain problematic. Europe and Japan will also have to make clear their own attitudes towards the question of aiding the Soviet effort to exploit domestic energy options. They may want to do so for commercial reasons, or in order to diversify their own imported supply (gas), or to offer witness to their own commitment to detente, but this is likely to exacerbate differences with the United States. It does not seem likely that the Regan Administration will conclude that it is in the US interest to help the USSR retain the strategic advantage which energy autarchy has given her.

In short, the specific contingencies that are likely to affect oil resources and supply would seem to demand three different sorts of response. First, if supply is restricted by producers, importers will endeavour, through economic and financial incentives, plus political measures, to elicit higher volumes. Second, the risk of the loss of major sources of supply as a result of revolution or damage to installations through sabotage or wars between producers will cause importers to build up adequate strategic oil reserves, to try to make the IEA credible and to establish in or near the Gulf sufficient military credibility to allow for the use of force if necessary. Finally, if the USSR seeks to purchase from the Middle East, the response by producers and importers should be to accommodate those needs as long as she obtains them without undermining Western strategic interests. However, if the USSR were to seek to exercise effective leverage over OECD supply from the Gulf, there can be very little doubt that this would be regarded as a threat to the West's vital interests. War, in those circumstances, would be a strong possibility.

Resources and Conflict:
Requirements and Vulnerabilities of the Industrialized World

ROBERT PERLMAN and ANTHONY MURRAY

Since the early 1970s there has been a great deal of discussion, as well as a great deal of anxiety in the industrialized countries, about the security of supply of the most important industrial raw materials. It is interesting to note that there is less worry in the rich countries about supplies of foodstuffs, which, after all, are ultimately the most important commodities of all. The developed countries have devised incentive systems and farm-support measures which not only rule out the prospect of any serious shortages but actually generate regular and embarrassing surpluses. There are political explanations for this, with some implications for minerals policy, which will be touched on later in this paper.

These worries about raw material supplies are not new but have recurred in the industrialized countries over the years. There was general anxiety in the face of the sharp rises in prices set off by the Korean war in the 1950s. This generated a spate of reports on the dangers of shortages and measures for dealing with them. One consequence was a greatly expanded acquisition programme by the General Services Administration in the United States, whose stockpile of minerals and metals continues to be a major factor in a number of markets.

Most major industrialized countries have gone through at least one period when the security of future supplies has been a source of worry. The worry has generally been incited by the running down of the commercially exploitable domestic reserves of some important non-renewable resource. Indeed, the present level of concern around the world is at least partly a consequence of the fact that the last major boom, and the oil price rises which marked its end, coincided with a marked decline in the self-sufficiency of the United States, the biggest consumer of almost everything, whose praiseworthy habit of discussing her national worries in public has helped to focus attention on raw materials questions.

Other countries less well endowed with minerals than the United States have faced similar crises in the past. In the case of Britain, overseas sources had to be resorted to in the first half of the nineteenth century. We are so used to this expedient now that it comes as a surprise to learn that until then Britain was not only self-sufficient in most of the minerals she needed but she was also a significant exporter and remained the largest producer of primary copper until the middle of the nineteenth century. It is scarcely less startling to recall that until 1955 Japan met 100 per cent of her copper and zinc consumption and 80 per cent of her lead consumption from her own domestic mines and from scrap sources.

Most of the older established metal-smelting and refining industries were set up to work local ores but have developed and survived on overseas materials. A supply of metal concentrates is clearly a necessity if a metal-smelting and refining industry is to stay in business, but we must distinguish between the importance of the income earned from particular industrial processes and the final consumption needs of a population. To get a clear picture of dependence and vulnerability, we must discuss how far such supplies – and supplies of other raw materials – are a national necessity because national income depends heavily on them or because the materials are needed for consumption, and how far nations will behave *as if they were* national necessities; then we must look at levels of self-sufficiency and finally at general availability.

Consideration of strategic materials is not usually conducted in this order. Most of the attention in these discussions has been concentrated on assessments of reserves, locations of economic sources and measures for securing supplies. Rather less attention seems to have been given to the primary questions of what makes particular materials important and whether consuming countries must necessarily remain dependent on supplies from particular sources or in need of direct supplies of particular raw materials at all.

Furthermore, the very important distinction to be made between the immediate position and the longer term is not always drawn. It may be possible to reduce vulnerability by developing substitute sources or substitute materials, for instance, but this could take many years, and even when many sources already exist, finding immediate supplies is often difficult in a sudden crisis.

Dependence

If we start by considering ordinary necessities, we can easily identify the supplies that we need to sustain life and, going one stage further, those that we need to maintain our living standards. There are also easily identified necessities of industrial processes – particular materials necessary for their normal functioning. Thus raw materials needs fall into two classes:

—those needed to satisfy final demand (providing what consumers want): food, fuel, clothes, furniture, shelter or services (which may depend on machinery, hence indirectly on metals, chemicals, fuel, etc.);
—those needed to enable economic activity to be sustained – to enable industries to earn a return by adding value through processing, fabricating and distributing raw materials and their products or consuming them in the process of providing services; this includes selling goods and services abroad to pay for more industrial supplies and for consumer goods and services.

The list of materials which may give rise to anxiety varies from country to country, as the list reflects industrial structures as well as final consumer needs. For example, the Japanese economy was built up after World War II by a huge expansion of basic industries, followed by a gradual move downstream to more advanced manufacturing. It remains heavily dependent on its basic industries, and this is reflected in its consumption of raw materials per unit of national output, higher in almost every case than any other country. There are some difficulties in making comparisons between countries, and these difficulties are associated mainly with the consistency of definitions of materials and forms of consumption, the accuracy of statistics and the selection of an appropriate measure of dollar values. Nonetheless, a number of studies have produced comparisons and, in spite of difficulties of detail, have provided a good general guide to national differences.

A few years ago a team under Professor Malenbaum (of Wharton School, Pennsylvania) undertook a detailed study for the United States government which contained both historical data and forecasts. A unit of gross domestic product of US$1,000 in constant terms was used. Japan was shown to have the highest requirements for materials in almost every case – 180,000 tons of iron, compared with 95,000 on average for Western Europe, 60,000 in the United States and 150,000 for the USSR; in the cases of nickel and chrome, double the average Western European requirement, five times the United States' requirement; in the cases of copper and zinc, Japanese needs were shown to be closer to those of Western Europe but still double or more the United States' unit requirement; Japanese unit aluminium needs were also estimated to be above those of the United States, despite the strong position of aluminium in the American economy.

Of course, none of this means that final consumption levels of these materials are higher per unit of national income in Japan than in other developed countries. Much of the metal is incorporated into the exported products of Japanese metal-engineering companies. The differences reflect the ways in which Japan makes her living – she is heavily dependent on basic metalworking.

The list of requirements for a particular country varies over time as well, because industrial structures, industrial processes and consumer tastes and disposable income all change.

Dependence on a particular material is really dependence on the special properties it contains – energy, electrical conductivity, ductility, strength or the supply of protein or whatever. Since these properties are often shared by many raw materials, but in different combinations, demand for one or other raw material will vary according to technical suitability, cost competitiveness, availability and even taste. A country's industrial structure changes in accordance with general economic development, its trading opportunities and prowess and in response to the availability or relative cost of major raw materials, which help to determine the profitability of particular industrial processes, and demand changes as a result. Changes in structure are usually slow but under certain conditions can be surprisingly fast. The availability of cheap oil supplies from the late 1950s, during a period of generally expansionist economic policies and the relaxation of trade barriers, stimulated energy-dependent and petrochemical-dependent industrial growth and structural changes. These very quickly resulted in heavy dependence on oil, exploited so effectively by oil suppliers since 1973. This comparatively recent development can be reversed but, since the dependence is a result of 20 years of high levels of oil-biased capital and consumer investment, the cost of rapid change away from oil is likely to be similar in scale.

Energy supplies, and hence oil, present a special case. Applications of oil are much more generally diffused through all economies than even such common materials as steel and copper, and oil is, moreover, fully consumed by final users and by manufacturing industry in daily uses rather than being embodied in equipment which subsequently has a long useful life. As a result, there is an urgency about immediate supplies of energy that is not felt in the case of many other raw materials. The dependence is on energy, however, rather than on oil. Oil is convenient, and it used to be cheap, so it became the preferred energy source, replacing coal, the previous dominant source, just as coal and steam had earlier replaced human and animal muscle power. Change away from oil is already taking place (although perhaps at too slow a rate) in response to higher prices and the prospect of ever higher prices and uncertain supplies.

Change away from more specific raw materials is also possible, although it may impose special difficulties and high costs in the short term. This change can take the form of pure substitution (aluminium instead of copper wire for electric power transmission and telephone cables) and technically based product change (satellite communications eliminating some cable links altogether) or changes in industry structure (the purchase of wire rod from integrated overseas producers of copper and aluminium instead of the purchase of concentrates from mines, the operation of smelters and the casting of lines). Manufacturers may become dependent on metal or wire-rod supplies and only indirectly dependent on primary materials.

Ordinary market developments can improve the security of supply by changes on the production side of the raw materials equation. High prices call into production ore bodies hitherto commercially unattractive, or justify increased exploration efforts, or stimulate research and development which makes more potential sources commercially attractive even without resort to substitute materials. In this way the very price rises with which an active market anticipates impending chronic shortage help to correct the market. However, there are often imperfections in markets, in market signals and in industry perceptions. The time taken to bring new sources into production makes it difficult to match supply capacity precisely to demand and results in cycles of surplus and shortage rather than in continuous balance. This is so even when a large range of near-economic sources are known. When there are wide differences in production costs between existing and potential sources of supply, adjustments are particularly difficult. One of the difficulties facing oil consumers is that there is a wide difference between costs at OPEC sources and sources elsewhere. OPEC members can maintain their prices well above production costs, yet many alternative oil sources remain barely profitable.

Directly or indirectly, the industrialized countries depend on primary exporters of materials other than oil. But then they have chosen to be dependent on these suppliers – 'chosen' in the sense that they have built income-generating industries around a range of imported supplies and a particular cost structure. In the short run their industries, their income and hence their living standards are vulnerable to cost rises and supply interruptions, although in the long run there may be a prospect of reducing vulnerability through changes in sources, in the materials required or in the industries which they rely upon for their international income.

Vulnerability

Dependence on foreign sources of supply, which may mean no more than a preference for imported materials that are somewhat cheaper or of better quality, need not amount to *vulnerability*, which implies a dangerous exposure and a lack of choice. We must consider more closely the nature of vulnerability in the context of raw materials to see what dangers there may be. Import-dependent industrialized countries have to consider the answers to five questions:

—Is there going to be a scramble for world resources?
—Will important materials supplies be controlled by producer cartels?
—Will primary exporters reduce supplies of raw materials and establish their own processing industries?
—Will there be political interference in supplies?
—Will war, or disorder, or simply technical inadequacies cut off supplies or subject them to frequent interruptions?

A Scramble for World Resources?

The question raises memories of nineteenth-century resources wars and has undertones of the fear of the exhaustion of resources. It has been asked increasingly in the face of the Soviet Union's rising import requirements in recent years.

We should certainly abandon the alarmist idea of a world scraping the bottom of its barrel of resources and the prospect of increasingly violent conflicts between nations over what remains. Mineral resources do not occur in discrete bodies but in various forms of concentration and diffusion in the Earth's crust. Deposits of minerals become usable sources under certain conditions of demand and with particular assortments of technology. Companies and governments are anxious about their

security of supplies and would, no doubt, like complete control of rich and low-cost sources. However, they no longer assume that they have to fight wars and extend empires to guarantee access. Japan's reaction to declining self-sufficiency in materials in the 1950s was to stimulate and encourage exploration and investment in new areas. As a result, known world reserves and supply sources have been added to. Governments elsewhere have since framed policies on similar lines, although on a more modest scale, and some new projects are now beginning under these schemes. The EEC Commission has, for a year or so, been working along similar lines by trying to co-ordinate and extend the programmes of member governments to improve the security of overseas mineral investments and hence the security of supplies.

The case of cobalt illustrates how a market threatened by insecurity can subsequently be transformed by new development. The world has for years been dependent on Zaire for about a third of its supplies of this metal; Australia, Zambia, New Caledonia and the Council of Mutual Economic Assistance (CMEA) countries provide much smaller quantities. It is an important alloying element in certain special steels and is virtually indispensable to the manufacture of small high-powered magnets used in weapons-guidance systems, microphones, loudspeakers and similar applications. Designers have optimized the use of cobalt alloy magnets and are unable to change designs at short notice. Users in Western Europe, Japan and the United States have been vulnerable to supply interruptions in Zaire; hence during shortages users have certainly scrambled for the small amounts of cobalt they needed and will continue to do so. Disturbances in the cobalt-producing Shaba province highlighted this dependence. However, high prices and the prospects of continued reliance on cobalt have transformed sub-economic deposits into commercial prospects. Production has now expanded in Zambia, and a new mine in Canada will shortly add large quantities to supplies. In the longer run, although not before the end of the century, cobalt by-product recovery from ocean nodules could dwarf the output of all present mines taken together. Indeed, this pinpoints one of the important developments in the pattern of raw material availability since World War II: sources of supply have been increasing as more and more countries have become first-time producers of minerals and metals. The exhaustion of existing ore bodies has resulted in a wider spread of sources and has, in some respects, improved security of supply rather than stimulating a scramble for diminishing reserves.

Although there is a possibility of finding and developing new supply sources, these will still have to be realized, and if efforts are pitched at too low a level, there will be insufficient additions to reserves to guarantee supplies to meet projected demand. For a time this could produce shortages through lack of exploration and investment rather than through lack of materials in the ground. The current anxiety is that shortages in the mid 1980s, resulting from depressed prices for most non-fuel raw materials and consequent under-investment in new capacity in the second half of the 1970s, will be exacerbated by the growing needs of the CMEA countries. Once mainly sellers of raw materials, especially minerals, they have recently become net buyers.

Too little is known about the main producer, the USSR, to indicate whether or not this will be a permanent position. Certainly, it can be expected that the countries of the CMEA will continue to develop industry on lines similar to those of industries in the West, away from dependence on basic extractive and transformation industries, towards more emphasis on downstream industries. This will result first in a fall in their primary materials and basic metals exports and later in an import requirement for these. Will they be content to compete with Western countries on purely commercial terms? Will they want to remain dependent on outside sources in the long run?

On the supply side there has already been some quasi-commercial involvement by CMEA countries in minerals developments abroad. Hungary is giving technical assistance in alumina production to Jamaica and India and to a new development in Greece (where the bauxite has characteristics similar to the Hungarian deposits). East Germany has in the past co-operated in the planning and development of African potash deposits, and there are also CMEA technical assistance schemes in Africa.

But in the short run Soviet purchases of lead and copper, and a decline in Soviet and in other CMEA exports of aluminium ingot and other primary metals, have helped to keep prices up when they would otherwise be languishing during the present recession. The changed position may be purely temporary, reflecting slow development of new mines and production difficulties in mines and smelters. The USSR in particular seems always to be short of ordinary production technology, design capacity and skilled labour. Exports of Western technology and equipment may be one way to correct production shortfalls, which would be a double advantage to the West under present conditions.

But to return to the main point, if there is no danger of terminal shortages of raw materials through the exhaustion of resources such as to set off a wild scramble and price rises, are there other causes for concern? More specifically, is there a danger of OPEC-type producer cartels being established, able to restrict supplies and manipulate prices and hence to exert international leverage?

Producer Cartels
Cartels do not become effective simply because producers set up a club and call out a price. A number of conditions must be met by members of a successful cartel, and they are rarely found together:

—They must control a large proportion of supplies;
—these should include lower-cost supplies and any large sources which can be increased at short notice;
—there should be no easily used substitute, at least in the short to medium term;
—they should have interests similar enough for them to accept the disciplined control of output.

OPEC has met these conditions, although even it has protracted arguments about policy, partly because some members (such as Saudi Arabia and Kuwait) have an interest in long-term revenue maximization, whereas (in the past at least) others have had an interest in maximizing short-term earnings. OPEC has many imitators, but none has equalled its success. Morocco, holder of the largest reserves of phosphate rock

113

in the world, tried single-handedly to transform the phosphate rock market in 1974. She was able to raise prices by exploiting an inelastic market in the short run, but the rise provoked an expansion of production elsewhere, and the price soon slumped and remained low for some years.

Unlike either OPEC or Morocco, the metals producers have to contend with scrap-based supplies, which are necessarily prevalent in established consuming countries and as near perfect a substitute as can be imagined. Few producers enjoy the same obvious cost advantage as OPEC against alternative sources. This is a necessary condition if demand is to prove as inelastic as oil demand. Whereas a scramble for resources ends with winners and losers among the consumers, *all* consumers are losers when a cartel forces prices up. The effect is to transfer income to the cartel members. If this transfer is very large, it acts as a deflationary tax on the consumers' economies and, in the absence of sufficient compensating expenditure by the cartel members, the consumers' economies wind down and require low levels of raw materials supplies. When price rises coincide with recessionary pressures a supply surplus soon builds up. This happened with oil as the world economy went into recession in 1974–75 and is happening again.

Although there may be some satisfaction in seeing that economic forces do set limits to the level to which even oil prices can rise, the oil surpluses we have seen in two recessions are a source of danger because they have led to false conclusions about the supply position. Oil is as nearly indispensable as any industrial material can be. Its former cheapness and continuing convenience has resulted in its wide diffusion through all economies, and our lives and industrial processes have been adapted to, and have become dependent on, its availability. Hence demand for oil is virtually price-inelastic in the short term – a price rise does not result in reduced consumption. However, for much the same reasons it is highly income-elastic – consumption rises and falls almost exactly in proportion to changes in national income levels.

The industrial nations can reduce dependence on oil, particularly dependence on OPEC supplies, by developing alternative fuels and alternative oil sources and by using different fuel-consuming processes and equipment which either dispense with oil or reduce unit consumption. However, this is an expensive and time-consuming exercise. A start has been made, but the oil surpluses of the mid-1970s and of 1980 and weakening prices have reduced the immediate incentives for pressing on with oil-replacement programmes. Yet as soon as economies revive demand will rise again and will restore a sellers' market.

There are no prospects for other raw material cartels with the strength of OPEC because no other commodity or producer group fits the requirements so perfectly. For example, the International Bauxite Association (IBA) can co-ordinate members' pricing policies and negotiating terms and thereby improve revenues, but the most significant move in bauxite markets was made by a single producer, Jamaica, which did no more than exploit her special position as local supplier to the American market. Her first bauxite export tax almost precisely matched the difference between the costs of production and transport and the potential c.i.f. price, at American bauxite ports, of supplies from other sources. In economic terms, Jamaica took (and is taking) the 'producer rent' on her exports.

Other IBA members can exploit special positions equally, and the exchange of ideas among IBA members helps them to recognize the market possibilities, but these fall far short of oil's possibilities, mainly because of the scope for substitution. This is possible at two stages: the raw material stage – the technology of alumina production from non-bauxite sources is known and tried (the USSR up to the present, Germany in Norway during World War II, etc.) but it is expensive by comparison and it would, of course, take time; and the finished metal stage – aluminium sales have expanded faster than economies as a whole through gaining market shares, often on cost grounds, but they could equally well be lost on cost grounds. The aluminium example could be multiplied by reference to most other materials. However, the absence of conditions necessary for a successful and long-lived cartel through the control of supplies does not mean that producers will not be in a strong position from time to time during the business cycle as a result of demand rising faster than supply.

Such demand-induced shortages give producers temporary power which may seem similar to the power of a strong cartel. This power may be used only to raise prices or it may be used for longer-lasting effects, such as the establishment of local processing. This general move to more processing could have the effect of reducing the availability of raw materials supplies to dependent processors, irrespective of the total materials output. How serious a threat will this be?

Local Processing by Exporters

This is declared policy and one which is already in evidence in the rich primary producers, in less developed primary producers and in the USSR. In the short to medium run it will cause difficulties for industrialized countries committed to a large primary processing sector. These will face rising supply costs and, ultimately, can expect to reduce their scale of operations unless they have some special skill to offer which is not easily acquired – such as the treatment of difficult metal concentrates or high rates of recovery of saleable by-products and elements present in small concentrations.

In the long run these basic industries could be expected to decline in the industrialized countries anyway, and the switch to processing at origin will only speed these changes. Dependence on raw materials will be replaced by dependence on refined metals, refined petroleum and so on. If processing at origin is efficient and can be done at low cost and if deliveries are reliable, the consumer countries may be no more vulnerable in future than, say, European companies currently importing steel from Japan are now. The conclusion is obvious: technically experienced companies from the advanced countries should bid to design, install and, if possible, operate the new processing plants rather than seek to discourage them.

Political Interference

The more serious problem for companies and industrial importing countries to deal with is interference in trade from political motives. Consumers are vulnerable to two kinds of political interference: the effects of government ownership or control in primary producing countries and the deliberate disruption of supplies by enemies.

Since the 1960s there has been an increasing tendency for governments to take control of national mineral resources. This has disturbed supplies quite accidentally in some cases. New proprietors require time to learn their business and in the process make some mistakes – miscalculate the effect of changes in tax and equity ownership rules, fail to appreciate the nature of prospecting and exploration and so on. There is also an inevitable decline in total flexibility when a business formerly operated on a world-wide basis is changed into a series of separate national operations. The prospects of profitable new finds are mathematically diminished when exploration work is confined to a single country. There are also short-term effects, summed up with respect to the oil industry in a recent Shell publication:

One of the strengths of the integrated oil companies was their ability to accommodate the very substantial fluctuations in demand levels in the consuming countries. This flexibility enabled them to fill supply deficits resulting from technical or political problems as well as matching the more predictable seasonal demand variations – worldwide, up to 8 million [barrels per day] between summer and winter levels – and the corresponding change in the balance of demand for different oil products.

Aside from the more accidental repercussions, however, the involvement of governments can also lead to more deliberate interference in supply, or the threat of it, for purely political motives. But, again, for permanent political pressure of this sort to be effective, the same conditions have to be met as for a long-lived cartel. So, except for oil, it is only the possible short-term dislocations that governments dependent on foreign sources of supply have to worry about. If these are considered serious enough one obvious solution is a stockpile. But, as with any insurance policy, the benefits have to be traded off against the costs of building up and maintaining such a stockpile, though the very existence of the stockpile will reduce the chances of politically motivated disruption occurring in the first place.

This leads on to the sort of supply disturbances which are essentially unpremeditated in origin but can nevertheless be fairly disruptive in their effects.

Supply Interruptions

The accidental disruptions to supply which result from transport breakdowns, technical failures at mines and oil wells, civil disorders, industrial disputes and local wars are as damaging as deliberate interruptions. They are not new to mining, but they may have become more frequent as a result of the resort to remote and underdeveloped mining areas and the localization of ownership and management and a consequent lack of access to experienced staff. Production and deliveries from the Central African copper mines have been the most frequently disturbed over the last ten years. Indeed, fears for copper supplies at the time of the illegal declaration of independence by Rhodesia prompted the British Post Office to embark on ambitious and successful pioneering work in the development of aluminium telecommunications cables. The disturbances were neither as serious nor as long-lived as the Post Office engineers had feared, but they now depend on a more reliable material, with more predictable prices, and can count this as a benefit.

In many countries these disturbances to supplies are regarded both as the most likely and as the most damaging prospect for the 1980s. Reports on national exposure have usually concentrated on vulnerability to disruptions resulting from war and civil disturbances. This can fairly be referred to as the 'Southern Africa effect' in view of the unanimity with which stockpile reports recommend holding tonnages of minerals, supplies of which are dominated by South Africa – chromite, vanadium, platinum, manganese and so on. Since disruptions to supply are nothing new to the raw materials industry, the market and the users have learnt to absorb these shocks by maintaining stocks. As long as disturbances are no more frequent or more severe than in the past (or than expected), industry and merchants between them could be expected to deal with them, whether the causes of the disturbances are purely technical or political, but not if they are worse than expected.

It is this risk, that the market will not take precautions for very speculative possible disruptions or will exploit a strong sellers' market, which prompts governments to investigate the prospects and scale of disruptions and to devise ways of adding to stock levels so as to iron out price peaks and to avoid shortages. However, there is a danger that simply setting up a government stockpile will actually be counter-productive. Companies and stockholders who would otherwise raise their level of precautionary stocks might actually reduce them and might rely on the availability of government stocks in a crisis. Fears of this effect have led to the proposal in West Germany for a special financing scheme. This requires stocks to be held as an addition to normal stocks by traders and consumers, with loans at preferential interest rates for the additional stocks.

In a free market economy it is difficult to recover the extra costs which would be imposed on users by the resort to sub-economic sources of minerals while supplies from cheaper sources are available. However, old-established industries with political influence (and importance within the economy) may be able to convince their governments of the need to support a domestic minerals procurement programme. With the obvious exceptions of the United States, Brazil, the USSR and China, the industrial consuming countries are mostly too small to hold a wide range of potential mineral sources, but if they operate in larger economic groupings they may have scope for collective self-sufficiency in a number of minerals. It will be interesting to see how attitudes will develop in the enlarged EEC. There the great political influence of the agricultural sector has enabled it to achieve a degree of protection and support for sub-economic farms that generate regular gluts which are difficult to dispose of for a number of reasons.

There are many differences between minerals and food production, of course. Even sub-economic resources are far less evenly distributed around the world than good farm land, and no mining and metals sector in the advanced countries could expect to match the political influence of the agricultural sector. However, the difference between market prices and estimated costs for some sub-economic deposits is no greater than the difference between some of the EEC support prices and world market prices. For general consumers the restricted occurrences of ore bodies would at least have the advantage of setting a natural limit to an EEC Minerals Support budget which is lacking in the case of the Common Agricultural Policy (CAP).

Although nothing as extravagant as the CAP is likely to develop, the mood of protectionism in advanced country industries, opposing the drive for industrialization based on local processing among the primary exporters, could extend into mineral production. In closing, we should consider whether the ultimate result of fears of dependence and vulnerability in the developed countries will be not a growth of independence through the international division of labour but a more protectionist world, dedicating an excessive proportion of labour and income to raw materials and suffering more frequently from surpluses than from shortages.

Conclusion

In assessing the dependence and vulnerability of the industrial countries and the conflicts in the Third World which could affect these, the following main points should be borne in mind. First, dependence on imports for raw material supplies does not amount to vulnerability unless major supply sources are limited and alternative sources or substitute materials are very expensive or difficult to develop. Second, the major industrial countries have become increasingly dependent on foreign sources for their raw ma-

terial supplies but, other than in oil, this development has not made these countries dramatically more vulnerable than they were a decade or two ago. Third oil is a special case because it is of such generalized importance in all economies; dependence on OPEC oil supplies has persisted because industrial structures were built up on cheap oil in the 1950s and 1960s, and oil surpluses in recessions have deterred the single-minded development of alternatives. Fourth, as for non-fuel raw materials, short-term disruption to supplies is more likely and more damaging than long-lived squeezes on supplies but can be insured against by stockpile investment. Fifth, reducing vulnerability in the long term requires financial and resource-using programmes now. Supplies of some important raw materials are effectively secure because of past development programmes. The development of synthetic materials or changes to the industrial base are usually expensive in the short term but effective in the long term. Finally, if policies for reducing dependence are pursued too vigorously, we may see a future disturbed more often by raw materials surpluses and the waste of productive resources in less developed countries than by shortages. Fears that this could happen are already detectable in discussions on ocean-nodule exploitation in sessions on the law of the sea.

Index

Afghanistan, Soviet invasion of, 7, 20, 21, 31; difficulties in assisting guerrillas, 86; seen as part of expansionist policy, 27

Africa: non-alignment, 11; relaxed approach to political developments in, 87

Air forces: availability for 'Saudi Core' mission, 46, 50, 51 (air cover and support, 47; air defence forces, 47–8; logistic air-lift, 48)

Anarchy, as cause of war, 92–3; moderate impact of guarantees, 100

Angola, 12; Cuban expeditionary forces, 11, 29; great-power rivalry, 26; Soviet involvement, 29 (positive and negative effects, 29–30)

Arab-Israeli conflict, 72; great-power rivalry, 26; Soviet involvement, 32

Arabian Gulf, 19; benefits of military presence, 31, 86; likely military threats, 41–2; managing great-power competition, 84; possible US pre-emptive strategy, 100; pre-Iranian Revolution oil production, 104; settlement of outstanding disputes, 3; strategic vulnerability, 8–9; US military presence, 31, 49 (divisive effect, 71); US search for coherent policy, 75; see also Oil supplies: military action to protect

Armed forces: increasing expenditure in Third World, 25; involvement in coups, 24; see also Military power

Arms control, 74

Arms sales: drawbacks for diplomacy, 72; regionalists' approach, 81; to Third World, 19 (effect of weapon diffusion, 83)

Army, see Land forces

Association of South-East Asian Nations (ASEAN), 3, 14, 69; US ties with, 87–8

Australia, co-operation to maintain Indian Ocean presence, 50

Authoritarian states, characteristics of, 53; political revolution and coups d'états, 53

Balance of power: complications after Vietnam war, 79; military, 19; need to maintain, 38; post-war shifts, 77; regional differentiation, 10; unaffected by Third World shifts of allegiance, 9

Bauxite supplies, 114

Brandt Report, 18, 73

Buffer zones, expansion leading to conflict, 94

Caribbean region: US military involvement, 31; US tolerance of uncertainty, 87; see also Cuba

Central America, relaxed approach to political developments in, 87

China: alignment, 5; suggestions of anti-Soviet alliance, 69

Cobalt production, 112

Colonialism: great-power conflict (1870–1914), 64; see also Third World: decolonization period

Common Agricultural Policy (CAP), 117

Conflict resolution inter-country mechanisms, 16; use of security guarantees, 101–2; see also Third World: conflict

Conscription, 96

Copper supplies, 116

Corruption, not important cause of revolution, 57

Coups d'état, 53

Cuba, 53, 61; ideology of opposition, 56; increasing military involvement, 32; US sufferance, 10–11

Culture change, 63; as source of conflict, 22; effects in South-East Asia, 14–15; Westernization resisted, 24

Democracy: transfer of power, 16; see also Political participation

Development, see Economic development

Diplomacy, 33

Economic development: dissociated from strategic policies, 61, 63; not matching political modernisation in Iran, 52; of ASEAN countries, 14; problems as source of conflict, 22; problems leading to unrest, 23–4; under US military security, 5–6; see also Foreign aid

Economic policies: avoidance of oil dependence, 75; political aspects, 63

Energy sources, 111; alternatives to oil, 104; effect of price on ASEAN countries, 14; threat from Arabian Gulf instability, 9; see also Oil supplies

Ethiopia, 53; Soviet involvement, 32

Ethnic conflict, 57

European states, western: alignments, 5, 12–13; importance of oil supplies, 41; involvement in Korean war, 31; military involvement in Third World, 31; raw material requirements, 110; US pressure for decolonization, 6

Food supplies, 116–17
Foreign aid: as means of achieving stability, 28; at too low a level, 25; principally western, 11; problems created by recession, 73
Foreign policies: linked with domestic politics, 60–1, 62; of third world countries, 83; weaknesses of regionalism, 81
France: military involvement in Third World, 31; naval forces in Indian Ocean, 49; see also European states, western
Frontier violation, 68; less fear of retaliation, 8; US opposition to, 7; see also Territorial disputes

Geopolitics, 80–2; strengths and weaknesses, 81
Guarantees, see Security guarantees

Horn of Africa, 12; ethnic separatism, 23; pattern of military intervention, 37–8; reversal of allegiances, 11

India, problems of US attitudes to, 87
International Bauxite Association (IBA), 114
Internation Energy Agency (IEA), 107
Iran: disparate interpretations of Shah's downfall, 52; ideology of opposition, 56; problems for US guarantees, 97–8; Revolution, 7, 22, 24, 31 (influence on Moslems in South-East Asia, 15; reaction of US allies, 8); Shah's power aspirations, 52; US response to Soviet warning, 8
Israel: complications of conflict with Arabs, 25 (see also Arab-Israeli conflict); external security guarantees, 95; ignoring US preferences, 100; limits of power, 11; not supported by US in Sharm el-Sheikh, 96; unique situation, 6

Japan, 19; importance of oil supplies, 41; mineral resources, 109; possibly replacing US in Korea, 88; raw material requirements, 110; role in Western Pacific, 69

Korea: US involvement, 7, 30–1; US policies in, 88

Land forces, availability for 'Saudi Core' mission, 45, 50–1
Latin America: acceptance of US dominance, 10; development programmes, 6; frequency of coups d'états, 53; in US sphere of influence, 26; interaction of causes of conflict, 23; relaxed approach to political developments in, 87
Liberation movements, 22–3; anti-colonial, 24; cause of internationalizing internal conflict, 24
Libya, possible source of US oil supplies, 42

Maracaibo, possible source of US oil supplies, 42
Marines, see Land forces
Middle East: Carter Administration involvement, 7; complications of Arab-Israeli conflict, 25; failure of containment (1950s), 67–8; great-power rivalry, 26; implications of conflict for oil supplies, 105–6; Moslems and Arabs split into many nation states, 22; need for Soviet participation in settlement, 88; potential for US Soviet clashes, 10; principal oil suppliers, 103; Soviet military involvement, 32; US land-based aircraft, 35
Military aid, influencing course of revolutions, 58
Military bases, to give credibility to guarantees, 95

Military power: achieving reduction in use, 39; adherence to 'rules of the game', 36; aims, 32; central to geopolitics, 80; changing attitudes to, 79; consequences of direct intervention, 33–4; credible responses to developments, 85 (historical precedent influencing, 34); debate on role, 2–3, 70–2; determinants of success, 33–8; factors affecting super-power attitudes, 36–7; in global policy, 83; in regions of strategic importance, 82; increasing in Third World states, 100; indirect application, 32; involvement in South-East Asia and Caribbean, 31; limited use for policy objectives, 39; little great-power confrontation, 33; preventing Soviet invasion, 70; rapid deployment force, 44, 50, 71, 96; resources available for 'Saudi Core' mission, 45–6; simultaneous great-power intervention, 35–8; types of force used, 32–3; underestimated by regionalists, 82; utility affected by political leaders, 34; utility assessment, 29; utility related to aim of intervention, 35

National unity: in ASEAN countries, 15; sources of threats to, 21–2
Nationalism, as root of conflict, 17, 23
Nationalization of mineral resources, 115
Naval forces: availability for 'Saudi Core' mission, 46, 50, 51 (assault sealift, 47; cargo requirements, 48; logistic sealift, 48, 96; protection of sea lines of communication, 48); deployment, 32–3; French, in Indian Ocean, 49; intervention less credible than land-based forces, 35; US merchant fleet strength, 49
New international economic order, 18; unlikely to occur, 12, 25
Nicaragua, 10, 52; ideology of opposition, 56
Nigeria, possible source of US oil supplies, 42
North Atlantic Treaty Organization (NATO), 70
Nuclear strategy, 71–2; anti-proliferation regime, 73; deterrence, 60; possibility of mistaken assessments, 102; production of weapons in Third World, 64; question of balance, 83; readiness to employ, 35, 39; see also Arms control

Oil supplies, 2, 71, 111; access affecting allies' relationship, 107–8; conventional and unconventional sources, 104; future prospects, 103–5; implications of conflict, 105–6; importance to West and Japan, 41; maintenance of flow during military operations, 44; military action to protect, 2, 41, 89, 105 (choice of area, 42–3; need for bases close at hand, 49; object, 43; phases, 44–5; problem of distance, 50; rapid deployment ability, 44, 50; 'Saudi Core' study, 45–9; time factor, 46); necessary imports, 103; need to reduce dependence on Middle East, 75; politicization, 103; of rate of production, 104; reducing uncertainties, 41; reduction adversely affecting importing nations' economies, 105; remaining important, 103, 114; uncertainties affecting international security, 63; varying degrees of dependence on, 103; vulnerability of Gulf facilities, 43, 106
Organization of African Unity (OAU), 69
Organization of Petroleum Exporting Countries (OPEC): self-interest, 25; success as cartel, 113–14

Political instability, search for pattern in, 52–3
Political participation: denied to ethnic minorities, 23; in South-East Asia, 15–16; not keeping pace with